DISINHERITED:

The Lost Birthright
of the
American Indian

DISINHERITED:
THE LOST
BIRTHRIGHT OF THE
AMERICAN INDIAN

Dale Van Every

William Morrow & Company
New York, 1966

CONTENTS

MAPS

DISINHERITED:

The Lost Birthright
of the
American Indian

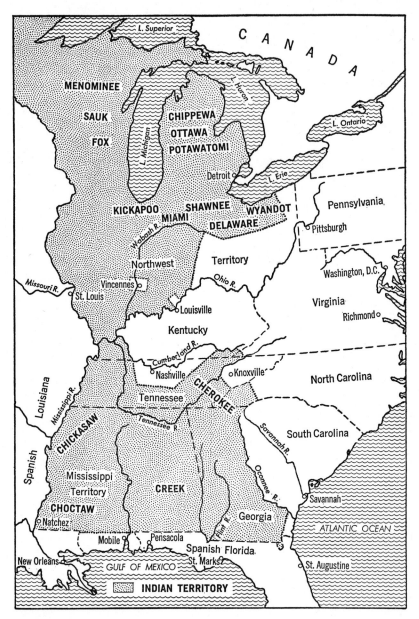

Shaded areas represent major Indian holdings east of the Mississippi not yet ceded to the United States, January 1, 1800. Until the 1797 Treaty of San Lorenzo, Spain was still in possession of Florida, the Gulf coast and the whole of the continent west of the Mississippi, and continued to claim all territory west of the Flint River and south of the Tennessee River.

1

About 100 yards from the town-house we were received by a body of between three and four hundred Indians, ten or twelve of which were entirely naked, except for a piece of cloth about their middle, and painted all over in a hideous manner, six of them with eagle tails in their hands, which they shook and flourished as they advanced, danced in a very uncommon figure, singing in concert with some drums of their own make, and those of the late unfortunate Capt. Damere; with several other instruments, uncouth beyond description. Cheulah, the headman of the town, led the procession, painted blood-red, except his face, which was half-black, holding an old rusty broadsword in his right hand, and an eagle's tail in his left. As they approached, Cheulah, singling himself out from the rest, cut two or three capers, as a signal to the other eagle-tails, who instantly followed his example. This violent exercise, accompanied by the band of music, and a loud yell from the mob, lasted about a minute, when the headman waving his sword over my head, struck it into the ground, about two inches from my left foot; then directing himself to me, made a short discourse (which my interpreter told me was only to bid me a hearty welcome) and presented me with a string of beads.

The narrator was Ensign Henry Timberlake, lately with George Washington at the fall of Fort Duquesne. He was engaged in a lonely peace mission 240 miles beyond the outermost settlements of his native Virginia. The Indians were Cherokee of the Carolina-Tennessee mountains who for the last three years had been resisting the successive invasions of three English armies. The captured drums had been taken at the 1760 surrender of Fort Loudon, first English military post to be established west of the Appalachians. And "Capt. Damere" had been the fort's commander, Captain Paul Demere, who at the culmination of that disaster had been dismembered and his mouth stuffed with the Cherokee earth he had been supposed to covet.

Timberlake's encounter with his unpredictable hosts had come at the end of a desperate canoe journey down the Holston, accompanied only by an interpreter and Sergeant Thomas Sumter, destined to become the last surviving general officer of the Revolution and to provide a name for the opening engagement of the Civil War. They had been impeded by the midwinter freezing of the river, had suffered terribly from exposure and hunger and had been constantly subjected to the risk of attack by prowling packs of Indians, whether unreconciled Cherokee or raiding Shawnee from the far Ohio. It had been a mission so apparently foredoomed that Timberlake's commanding officer, Lieutenant Colonel Adam Stephen, had declined to order it and had only with difficulty been persuaded to permit him to volunteer for it. Yet these extraordinary trials and dangers had not seemed to the youthful adventurer too great a price to pay for the opportunity to observe genuine savages in their native haunts. To pay a personal visit to the fearsome Cherokee appealed to Timberlake as an experience to be savored, an achievement that set him apart from his countrymen. In the dry minutes of Virginia's Council there was direct testimony to the urgency of his impulse. Though his peace mission proved a success of immense benefit to the Colony, Virginia refused even to reimburse him for the expenses of his perilous journey on the grounds that in the judgment of the members of the Council he made it "for his own profit or pleasure."

Timberlake's remarkable adventures were recorded in his no less remarkable 1765 book, *Memoirs,* but he was not alone in harboring an insatiable curiosity about Indians. Most of his contemporaries shared his interest if not his temerity. Beyond the forbidding and so nearly impenetrable wall of the wilderness bordering the narrow coastal strip of colonial America were the remote towns, enlivened by weird rites and festivals, of strange, wild denizens of another world and another age. They offered the beckoning promise of sights, sounds, impressions, surprises and novelties altogether outside the range of any civilized man's experience. The only glimpses of authentic wild Indians available to Timberlake's generation were occasioned by the attendance of their chiefs at conferences with white officials or the devastating descent of bands of their warriors on an outlying settlement. To see how different Indians might really be, at home, with their women, at leisure and at play, offered a prospect of unlimited appeal. Young Englishmen hired themselves to traders not so much for gain as for the sake of making visits to distant hostile nations which under no other circumstances could have been approached. Young Frenchmen roamed the most remote forests, lakes and rivers so widely and so long that many became in all outward aspects Indians. White captives having become inured by compulsion to the Indian way of life often became so attached to it that they refused every opportunity of deliverance.

This acute interest in Indians, often coupled with a secret, instinctive identification with Indians, was not confined to whites in North America who lived in the shadow of the wilderness. It was as prevalent in Europe. When, after enjoying some months of Cherokee hospitality, Timberlake returned to Virginia, he was accompanied by a large delegation of his former hosts, three of whom he took with him to England as unofficial good will ambassadors. In London the visit of the totally bemused Cherokee became an immediate sensation. They could not stir from their lodging without being inundated by a press of curious and friendly humanity. The proprietors of such recreation areas as Vauxhall importuned their attendance with a view to the increased ticket sales to the throngs that followed them everywhere. Their innkeeper's conduct became a scandal with the disclosure that he had been charging admission, even to cabinet ministers, to devotees eager to observe them at table or toilet. Meanwhile, the government had officially welcomed them and they had been presented at court, entertained by society, painted by eminent artists and endlessly interviewed by journalists.

The popular reception accorded the 1762 visit of the Cherokee to London was not an isolated phenomenon. Earlier and later visits of Indian delegations were as warmly received. The appearance of Indian ambassadors on the streets of Paris invariably precipitated parallel scenes. This public predilection for the Indian persisted and spread through later generations and all countries. A whole literature developed to satisfy people's appetite for more revealing reflections of the Indian world or, at any rate, for more guidance, however distorted, denatured and romanticized, for the public's flights of fancy concerning the nature of that world.

In later times, after the grim realities of inter-racial frictions along an advancing frontier had drifted into the past, the world's curiosity about Indians had degenerated into a form of escapism, an easy search for vicarious adventure. The wild Indian had long since ceased to exist. But in the street crowds of 18th century London and Paris there were deeper stirrings. The Indian was then still unconquered, still free, still master of his own domain. He was envisaged not as a bloodthirsty savage nor as a drunken beggar but as a happier and patently superior being. To the ordinary inhabitant of a European city, immersed in filth and squalor, harassed by class distinctions, condemned to unremitting toil, the Indian enjoyed a far more fortunate and rewarding existence. He roamed at will in a land of forest and stream in which his every want was supplied by nature and he was free to cultivate his most passing fancy. His life was marked by an Arcadian simplicity and innocence which other men had lost as they had become enmeshed in the restraints and drudgeries of civilization. He still dwelt in the Isles of the Blest, the Golden Age, the lost Eden, the better time that once was, celebrated in every folk lore. He was not to be despised or feared. He was to be envied.

There had been an original basis for this lost paradise conception in the reactions of the first English colonists when they had first encountered Indians on the Carolina coast in 1584. Captain Arthur Barlowe had reported to his patron, Sir Walter Raleigh:

We remained by the side of this island two whole days before we saw any people of the country; the third day we espied one small boat rowing toward us, having in it three persons: this boat came to the island side, four harquebuz-shot from our ships, and there two of the people remaining, the third came along the shore side toward us, and we being then all within board, he walked up and down upon the point of land next unto us; then the master and the pilot of the admiral, Simon Ferdinando, and the Captain Philip Amadas, myself, and others, rowed to the land, whose coming this fellow attended, never making any shew of fear or doubt. And after he had spoken of many things not understood by us, we brought him, with his own good liking, aboard the ships, and gave him a shirt, a hat, and some other things, and made him taste of our wine, and our meat, which he liked very well; and after having viewed both barks, he departed and went to his own boat again, which he had left in a little cove or creek adjoining; as soon as he was two bow-shots into the water, he fell to fishing, and in less than half an hour he had laden his boat as deep as it would swim, with which he came again to the point of land, and there he divided his fish into two parts, pointing one part to the ship, and the other to the pinnace; which, after he had (as much as he might) requited the former benefits received, departed out of our sight. The next day there came unto us divers boats, and in one of them the king's brother, accompanied with 40 or 50 men, very hand-some and goodly people, and in their behavior as mannerly and civil as any in Europe. His name was Granganimeo, and the king is called Wingina, the country Wingandacoa, and now by her Majesty Vir-ginia. The manner of his coming was in this sort: he left his boats altogether, as the first man did, a little from the ships, by the shore, and came along to the place over against the ships, followed by 40 men. When he came to the place, his servants spread a long mat upon the ground, on which he sat down, and at the other end of the mat four others of his company did the like; the rest of his men stood round about him, somewhat afar off. When we came to the shore to him with our weapons, he never moved from his place, nor any of the other four, nor ever mistrusted any harm to be offered from us; but sitting still, he beckoned us to come and sit by him, which we performed; and being set, he made all signs of joy and welcome, striking on his head and his breast, and afterwards on ours, to shew we were all one, smiling and making shew, the best he could, of all love and familiarity. . . . The king's brother . . . was very just of his promise; for many times we delivered him merchandise upon his word, but ever he came within the day and performed his promise. He sent us every day a brace or two of fat bucks, conies, hares, fish the best of the world. He sent us divers kinds of fruits, melons, walnuts, cucum-bers, gourds, peas, and divers roots, and fruits very excellent good, and of their country corn, which is very white, fair and well tasted. . . . After they had been divers times on board our ships, myself with seven more went twenty miles into the river that runneth towards the city of

Skicoak, which river they call Occam; and on the evening following we came to an island, which they call Raonoak, distant from the harbour by which we entered seven leagues; and at the north end thereof was a village of nine houses, built of cedar. . . . When we came towards it, standing near unto the water side, the wife of Granganimeo, the king's brother, came running out to meet us very cheerfully and friendly; her husband was not then in the village; some of her people she commanded to draw our boat on shore for the beating of the billow; others she appointed to carry us on their backs to the dry ground. . . . When we were come into the outer room, having five rooms in her house, she caused us to sit down by a great fire, and after took off our clothes and washed them, and dried them again; some of the women plucked off our stockings and washed them; some washed our feet in warm water; and she herself took great pains to see all things ordered in the best manner she could, making great haste to dress some meat for us to eat. . . . We were entertained with all love and kindness, and with as much bounty as they could possibly devise. We found the people most gentle, loving, and faithful, void of all guile and treason, and such as live after the manner of the golden age.

The sentiments of the first white men as they regarded their first Indians, however, could not compare in poignancy to the surge of conflicting emotions with which the Indians contemplated the occasion. Their astonishment mixed with awe amounted to stupefaction. Every aspect of the incredible occurrence added to the magnitude of the phenomenon. The newcomers were an inconceivable apparition taking shape out of the mists of that vast ocean which to Indians had marked the limits of the known world. They came in enormous winged craft miraculously propelled by the wind. In appearance and behavior they varied so widely from any former Indian experience that they seemed not another race of men but another order of beings. They possessed huge animals upon which, once ashore, they could move about at an unnatural speed. Their warriors were clad in a strange, bright metal so hard it was proof against arrows, their swords and lances were of the same mysterious substance and they wielded yet more terrible weapons which vomited fire and thunder to kill at a distance. By every outward indication they seemed endowed with powers raising them above the status of mortal men. But when, at first by signs and then by halting words, the beginnings of communication were established the visitors proved incongruously mean, irrational and avaricious. Their first demand was for pearls, gold and slaves. Their second was that Indians forthwith accept their religion, a principal tenet of which pronounced that any who did not, along with all preceding Indian generations who had had no opportunity to accept, were condemned to burn throughout eternity. Their third was that Indians make haste to deliver up their native land.

The moment it became apparent that the alien intruders had come not to visit but to stay the awful dimensions of the Indian predicament became unmistakable. White strongholds, supplied by ships from inexhaustible European bases, sprouted on every strategic estuary. Initial requisitions of food were followed by seizures of land then more land. Faced not only with dispossession but with the total obliteration of every value they had inherited as a people, the sea coast Indians undertook a desperate resistance. They fought with the frenzy of men defending their homes. At times Indian counterattacks threatened the very existence of white colonies in Quebec, Massachusetts, Virginia and South Carolina.

But it was an unequal contest. However conscious he might be of the justice of his cause, the Indian was fighting against impossible odds. It was essentially a conflict not so much between men or nations or even races as between ages. The white man was armed with social, economic, military and technological disciplines developed through 50 centuries of progressive experimentation. The Indian was still in the more primitive stage of a hunting culture. The white man's ability to make productive use of land enabled the white population to increase at a prodigious rate. The Indian's need of immense expanses in which to hunt forced him to keep withdrawing into the wilderness. Most destructive of all to any Indian hope was the operation of the white man's greatest ally—his diseases. Many day's march ahead of every white advance epidemics reduced whole nations to insignificance. Nothing could prevent the alien invaders' occupation of the Atlantic tidewater and the establishment on the continent of a lodgment that was forever unassailable.

Meanwhile the only white man who had experienced prolonged actual contact with Indians, the isolated settler struggling for a foothold on the border between the races, had from the outset abandoned all romantic or idyllic notions about the pristine innocence and simplicity of Indians. Necessarily these contacts had been with nearer Indians who had already been contaminated by white proximity. Instead of seeing them as nature-favored occupants of a wild Utopia, the white borderer had learned to regard them as fools, drunkards, demoniac enemies, wretches of sub-human depravity, whose existence constituted an intolerable nuisance which could only be abated by extermination.

Of all the virtues presumed by fancy or theory to be inherent in the Indian way of life, only one, but that the greatest, was apparent to the white borderer. For him this one glittered with an irresistible appeal. It was the priceless boon for which all men of all times have yearned the most profoundly. Whatever his other circumstances, the Indian enjoyed total freedom as an individual. However cruelly buffeted otherwise by fortune, he lived out his life wholly untroubled by the restraints and dictates that make the individual the creature of government and commerce in every more developed society. Having become familiar with the edge of the wilderness, the borderer plunged into it in pursuit of an equal freedom for himself. In so doing he made himself the decisive enemy of the Indian he was imitating. He was also accelerating by generations the rate of white advance westward across the continent. For, emboldened by his example, thousands of more ordinary families seeking land and economic opportunity were soon surging westward over the trails the fore-running freedom-seeker had opened.

The proportions of the acceleration soon became apparent. The advance of the white settlement line, supported by trans-Atlantic bases and parent governments, had required a century and a half to edge from the seacoast to the foot of the Appalachians. But in the next half century in one tremendous surge it crossed the mountains and then the Mississippi. An immense region of which Indians had been masters for thousands of years had been occupied in so short a term by white commonwealths numbering millions. No aggression in the annals of mankind had ever proved so swift, so successful, so irresistible or so catastrophic to the dispossessed. No alteration in man's adaptation to life on this earth had ever been more abrupt or achieved on so vast a scale. The half of a continent had in the span of a lifetime been jerked through 5,000 years of man's history. To the white men invading the wilderness the sudden, tremendous metamorphosis was in essence a continuation of their former way of life. To the Indians, so recently its sole human occupants, it was more than a change or a defeat. It was the end of the Indian world. That world had been inundated by a cataclysmic wave of overwhelmingly superior force and numbers.

Since the dawn of his ability to reason man has been troubled by the spectacle of his own aggressions. The most primitive societies have without exception been moved to censure and discourage the aggressions of an individual upon the person or property of another individual. But the aggressions of men acting as groups have not been so consistently deplored. When groups have attained the stature of nations their aggressions have through the ages been regarded as praiseworthy expressions of patriotism and the highest manifestations of public spirit. There is an even wider ground upon which to base a theoretical justification of Indian dispossession. It was more than a war between nations or between races. It was another inevitable step in the apparently pre-destined progress of the human race in wringing a greater productivity from its environment. This has been a natural law as immutable as gravitation. In the area east of the Mississippi where a hundred thousand Indians once roamed, as many millions of people now flourish. That was not a development that could have been averted or stemmed by whatever appeal to morality or ethics. A second theoretical justification appears in the long run as acute. The astounding rapidity with which American settlers overran the eastern Mississippi Valley, however painful to the Indian victims, was the sole factor raising the young United States to the status of a continental power at a pace that denied rival powers the opportunity to counter the sudden augmentation. The nation's worldwide influence today, with all its attendant significance, becomes a direct consequence of the headlong rate of Indian dispossession in the last quarter of the 18th century.

However, a little later the rising republic did commit an altogether unprovoked aggression against Indians not nearly so easy to justify. In 1830 the government of the United States after long and deliberate consideration decreed the exile of all surviving eastern Indians to the plains of the far west. The inexorable mandate came at the end of a period in which the Indians had made the most earnest efforts to conform to the wishes of their

white conquerors. They had submissively accepted federal jurisdiction as their sole remaining defense against injustice. They had
long since ceased to exercise any military power whatever. They
represented no physical threat to the weakest frontier community.
They were confined to continually shrinking reservations where
most were making laborious efforts to learn to plant and reap.
Nevertheless more than 20 nations were suddenly required to
abandon an environment to which they had been attached for
unnumbered generations.

In the long record of man's inhumanity exile has wrung moans
of anguish from many different peoples. Upon no people could it
ever have fallen with a more shattering impact than upon the
eastern Indians. The Indian was peculiarly susceptible to every
sensory attribute of every natural feature of his surroundings. He
lived in the open, as responsive to sun, wind, rain, snow as any
wild animal. He knew every marsh, glade, hill top, rock, spring,
creek as only the hunter can know them. He had never fully
grasped the principle establishing private ownership of land as any
more rational than private ownership of air but he loved the land
with a deeper emotion than could any proprietor. He felt himself
as much a part of it as the rocks and trees, the animals and birds.
His homeland was holy ground, sanctified for him as the resting
place of the bones of his ancestors and the natural shrine of his
religion. He conceived its waterfalls and ridges, its clouds and
mists, its glens and meadows, to be inhabited by the myriad of
spirits with whom he held daily communion. It was from this rain-
washed land of forests, streams and lakes, to which he was held by
the traditions of his forebears and his own spiritual aspirations
that he was to be driven to the arid, treeless plains of the far west,
a desolate region then universally known as the Great American
Desert.

The northern Indians in their dispersed locations scattered
across the Great Lakes region into which they had been forced by
the advance of white settlement accepted their fate with dismay
but without serious protest. Seneca, Shawnee, Wyandot, Delaware,
Miami, Ottawa, names at which the white frontier once had
shuddered, were now but names attached to the vestiges of nations
whose numbers had been reduced to impotence by war and disease
and whose once proud spirit had been broken by long continued

adversity. Since physical resistance was hopeless they submitted to the removal decree with sullen resignation. Some even saw a glimmer of new hope in the wider room to hunt expected on the western plains. Others found some consolation in the mere prospect of getting farther away from their white tormentors.

It was a different story in the south. There the more numerous and less primitive southern Indians occupied a relatively homogeneous block of territory in Mississippi, Alabama, Georgia, Tennessee and Florida. The Cherokee, Creek, Chickasaw, Choctaw and Seminole had made such progress in the adoption of white manners and skills that they were already being termed the "five civilized tribes." Many had become proficient artisans and with the exhaustion of hunting resources all were supporting their families by dependence on farming. Some had developed large plantations, owned scores of slaves and herds of cattle, sent their children to school and were more prosperous than most of their white neighbors. The southern Indians were adapting to the white man's world at such a rate that there was every prospect that they might soon merge into the mainstream of American life as fully acceptable citizens. This dawning hope was crushed by the removal decree requiring them to abandon all that they had accomplished to start over again among the discouraging handicaps of the barren far west.

After desperate protests the Choctaw, Chickasaw and Creek yielded to the inevitable posed by overwhelmingly superior force. In their migration shepherded by bayonets they lost most of their property and a third of their numbers. The Seminole elected a resort to arms. They were only routed from their sanctuary in the Florida swamps by an eight-year-long war costing $20,000,000 and 1500 American lives. The Cherokee elected to resist by claiming the protection of the laws of the United States through an appeal to its courts. This also became an eight-year-long struggle but one which in the end gained them no safer refuge than the everglades had afforded the Seminole.

The Cherokee were probably the most talented and certainly the most interesting of all Indians with whom the United States has had to deal. Once they had been the most warlike. In 1830 they were unquestionably the most progressive. They had recently invented their own written language and in three years had learned to make general use of it. They had adopted a constitution under which they governed themselves by elective democratic processes. Most of their leaders were well educated. A large segment of the nation had been converted to Christianity. In a single generation they had made an advance most other peoples have only made by centuries of effort. In their ancient homeland in northern Georgia, northeastern Alabama and southeastern Tennessee they tilled their fields, tended their flocks, schooled their children, attended their churches and asserted their rights to be considered citizens of the republic.

The Cherokee appeal to American conscience divided the American people along the same line the slavery question was beginning to divide them. Northerners tended to sympathize with the Cherokee as an oppressed minority being victimized by the callous greed of their racially prejudiced white neighbors. This disposition to regard the dispute as a moral question infuriated the southerners, already incensed by Cherokee obstinacy. Georgia responded to northern castigation by confiscating Cherokee property, dividing their lands among white claimants by means of a land lottery, depriving the Cherokee of the right to appear in state courts even in their own defense, forbidding their meeting whether for political, social or religious purposes, and imprisoning their white missionaries, most of whom were northern clergymen.

The controversy had by now gripped the nation's attention. It had become a principal topic for discussion in press and pulpit in both north and south. Throughout the thirties it remained the subject of more disputatious speeches in Congress than was the slavery question. It became a prominent issue in the presidential election of 1832. Among historic champions of the Cherokee cause were Henry Clay, Daniel Webster, Edward Everett, Theodore Frelinghuysen, John Howard Payne, Sam Houston and Davy Crockett.

When the Cherokee appeal reached the Supreme Court of the United States, Chief Justice John Marshall read a sweeping decision which ruled state laws discriminating against the Cherokee to be unconstitutional. The south furiously rejected the decision. The legislatures of Georgia and Alabama voted to resist, by arms if necessary, any federal effort to enforce the Supreme Court's decision. The nation was convulsed by storms of sectional passion and prejudice reaching a pitch of intensity not again to be reached until 1860.

The Cherokee case could not have been more aptly stated than in the last Cherokee memorial to the United States:

The title of the Cherokee people to their lands is the most ancient, pure, and absolute known to man; its date is beyond the reach of human record; its validity confirmed by possession and enjoyment antecedent to all pretense of claim by any portion of the human race. . . . The Cherokee people have existed as a distinct national community . . . for a period extending into antiquity beyond the dates and records and memory of man. . . . These attributes have never been relinquished by the Cherokee people . . . and cannot . . . be dissolved by the expulsion of the Nation from its own territory by the power of the United States Government.

The north's view of the moral issue was given voice by Ralph Waldo Emerson in a letter to President Van Buren:

The soul of man, the justice, the mercy that is the heart's heart in all men, from Maine to Georgia, does abhor this business . . . a crime is projected that confounds our understandings by its magnitude, a crime that really deprives us as well as the Cherokee of a country for how could we call a conspiracy that should crush these poor Indians our government, or the land that was cursed by their parting and dying imprecations our country, any more? You, sir, will bring down that renowned chair in which you sit into infamy if your seal is set to this instrument of perfidy; and the name of this nation, hitherto the sweet omen of religion and liberty, will stink to the world.

The south's answer was given in a speech in Congress by Wilson Lumpkin on the eve of his election as Governor of Georgia:

Pages may be filled with a sublimated cant of the day, and in wailing over the departure of the Cherokee from the bones of their forefathers. But if the heads of these pretended mourners were waters, and their eyes were a fountain of tears, and they were to spend days and years in weeping over the departure of the Cherokees from Georgia, yet they will go.

2

So complete a disaster as befell the Indian occupants of what had become the eastern half of the United States leads to speculation upon the degree of their responsibility for their own misfortunes. There can be but one answer. Guiltless as they may have been when overwhelmed by the culminating disaster of the 1830's, they had during the preceding two centuries, while there was still scope for Indian action which might at least have postponed their decline, taken every action calculated to accelerate their downfall. They had made every mistake that an endangered people can make. Judged by the harsh law governing survival of any species, their total failure to adapt to new circumstances had amounted to an embrace of extinction. They had persisted in this suicidal course until in 1830 their sole remaining hope was reliance on the magnanimity of their white conquerors. This proved a hope as vain as had been their former illusions.

The basic Indian weakness in coping with the ever-growing threat to their existence as a people was from the outset their failure to recognize the community of their interests as a people. They were confronted by an appalling and unmistakable clear and present danger. Their homeland was being overrun by alien invaders bent upon their extermination. Yet, from the days of the first white appearance on the continent to the days when the last flickers of Indian resistance were being extinguished, Indians exhibited no urgent impulse to combine in their common defense.

14

Occasional inspired leaders of the stature of Pontiac, Brant and Tecumseh, preaching the doctrine of Indian union with compelling eloquence, succeeded only in contriving temporary, regional confederations which dissolved at the first strain. No Indian nation was too insignificant in numbers or power to consider its interests as distinct from those of its Indian neighbors. Throughout the period of progressively accelerating white conquest Indians continued to devote much more energy to their wars upon each other than to efforts to resist the invaders. In the last frontier wars fought east of the Mississippi Indians were still fighting Indians.

The preoccupation of Indians with making war on each other was among the first and strongest impressions of the new world gained by the first white men to set foot on its shores. Everywhere, from the St. Lawrence to the Gulf of Mexico, the natives were discovered to be engaged in obscure but persistent wars with their neighbors. No sooner did nearer Indians begin to appreciate the superiority of white weapons than they sought the assistance of the newly arrived aliens in attacks on their more distant rivals. No sooner did proximity permit them to be first to trade for possession of those weapons than invariably and relentlessly they employed their new arms against other Indians who had not yet gained that advantage. This eccentricity in Indian diplomatic and military policy immensely gratified the early colonists. Had tidewater Indians instead combined to set up a united resistance most colonies must have been short-lived. The economic returns from newly founded colonies were at first so scant that their parent governments must soon have tired of their support and the colonization of the eastern seaboard been indefinitely delayed, perhaps until the Indians through commercial contacts had developed defense capabilities enabling them to negotiate as equals.

Intertribal Indian hostility had not been a consequence of the white man's approach. Since long before the white era war-making had been as inherent a feature of the Indian way of life as hunting. The young Indian male was expected to demonstrate his skill as hunter by taking game. Community opinion committed him as completely to the demonstration of his courage as a man by the taking of scalps or captives. Wars were fought not for territory or trade advantage but to prove the private valor of the participants. They tended to be desultory and intermittent and to consist largely of raids, surprises and feats of individual daring, as each new generation of young warriors strove to attain personal status.

The advent of white men did, however, introduce a new element into Indian warfare almost as destructive to the prospects of Indian survival as was the devastating exposure to new diseases. The moment that Indians became aware of the superiority of white tools, utensils and weapons they were consumed by a desire to possess them. This compulsion was accompanied by a collateral compulsion to deny trade goods to their Indian neighbors in order to augment their own relative power or to gain for themselves the profits of middlemen. Intertribal war had ceased to be a hazardous sport dedicated to the education of young men to become instead a struggle for material advantage, for trade monopoly, for control of trade routes or for the exaction of tribute. With these more sophisticated incentives, it was waged with a formerly unknown ardor and persistence.

These Indian trade wars produced a portentous train of consequences with a decisive influence not only upon Indian survival but upon the rate of white expansion into the center of the continent. They became so merciless that whole nations which otherwise might have assisted Indian resistance to the spread of white settlement were obliterated or their remnants driven into helpless wanderings among distant refuges. In the north the Iroquois by their remarkable 17th century conquests sought to establish a trade empire covering the entire region of the Hudson, the St. Lawrence, the Susquehanna and the Great Lakes and in the course of their tireless aggressions all but exterminated their nearer rivals, the Huron, the Erie, the Mohican and the Susquehannock. In the warmer south where furs had less value in payment for the coveted white man's goods the Indian nations of the region fell upon one another to gain war captives who might be sold as slaves to white buyers on the seacoast for shipment to the West Indies or New England. In the process the powerful Yamassee nation was destroyed, the Catawba reduced to insignificance, the Shawnee and Tuscarora driven into northern exile, and the energies of the Cherokee, Creek, Choctaw and Chickasaw dissipated.

The Indian trade wars had been an unalloyed blessing to early colonists struggling to develop their scattered beachheads along the Atlantic coast. From Maine to Georgia they had denied the Indian occupants of the coastal lowlands every opportunity to repel the intrusion while the intruders were still weak. Their aftermath was so destructive to any later Indian hope that a line of resistance might somewhere be found that it became a controlling factor in the continuing westward thrust of white settlement.

In the north the Iroquois grasp at trade empire had succeeded in barring French advance into the upper Ohio Valley for more than a century. No development could have had a more serious long term effect on the Indian cause. The French penetration of the interior was a type of exploitation which permitted the maintenance of Indian culture and Indian independence. The penetration of France's English rival, on the other hand, was one committed to the seizure of land and total Indian dispossession. As a result of the Iroquois attempt at trade monopoly the French had not reached the headwaters of the Ohio until the English colonies had gained an importance that prompted England to make the successful effort to drive France altogether from the North American mainland. The Indians were left to cope with the victors without the support of their former patrons.

In the south the aftermath of persistent Indian trade wars had been as fatal. The flight of Shawnee and Tuscarora to northern sanctuaries had precipitated a half century of conflict between northern and southern Indians. During the critical period of the white frontier's approach to the mountain barrier the two most militarily potent Indian nations, the Iroquois in the north and the Cherokee in the south, absorbed in this endless, long range war with each other, ignored the white threat. Under the stresses of this war the entire area between the Ohio and the Tennessee became an unpopulated no-man's land inviting eventual white occupation. In the ensuing French and Indian war both Iroquois and Cherokee took the English side in opposition to their fellow Indians of the interior who were allied with the French, thus helping to insure that what remained of the Indian world would thereafter be dominated not by indulgent French missionaries and traders but by land-seeking English settlers.

Even greater policy mistakes were to follow. A cluster of Indian opportunities to stem white expansion at the Appalachian mountain barrier was squandered in rapid succession. Pontiac's rebellion against English rule ravaged the frontier, captured every English position in the west except Pittsburgh and Detroit and cost 3,000 English lives. Yet these dramatic victories roused no general Indian response. Instead, his striking effort to promote Indian union was throttled by a general Indian demand for a resumption of normal trade relations. Meanwhile a frantic British cabinet had by imperial dictate established the Proclamation Line along the crest of the mountains, prohibiting the extension of settlement west of it and reserving the interior to undisturbed Indian occupancy. The Line was designed not so much to protect Indians as to render the increasingly restive colonies more manageable but in any event the Indians themselves struck aside the proffered advantage. The Iroquois and Cherokee, each with some dim idea that all that they were sacrificing was the other's interests, by formal treaties promoted the isolation of the Shawnee and breached the mountain barrier by opening Kentucky and Tennessee to white settlement.

This monumental fallacy in Indian calculations marked the supreme crisis in Indian affairs. Their last opportunity was fading. In the immediately ensuing Revolution Indians for the first time mustered at least the semblance of united action. In sporadic concert both northern and southern Indians threw themselves upon the white frontier. For the next 20 years they were able to hold the line of the Tennessee and the Ohio and to inflict untold miseries on the intruding settlers. But Indian awakening had come too late. Through the gap in the mountain barrier that they themselves had breached poured more settlers by the thousand, and then by the hundreds of thousands. The Battle of Fallen Timbers in 1794 crushed the last significant hope that the tide of white settlement might ever be stemmed.

The Indians who in 1830 were appalled by the dread specter of removal were guided by few memories and less comprehension of these mistakes of their ancestors. They could not evade, however, the sharpest recollection and the most remorseful understanding of their own generation's mistakes which had been as grievous. They were falling into a pit which they themselves had dug.

In the north there was still a certain latitude for continued maneuver. Indians could yield to the inexorable pressure of the advancing white frontier by continuing to withdraw north westward into regions that were still wilderness. It had been therefore made to seem no worse than a reasonable gamble to enter into an alliance with the British during the War of 1812. War, however, is a game in which the stakes can be very high indeed. The result of the Indian resort to arms was to harden the American government's determination to solve the frontier problem once and for all by insisting upon total Indian removal.

In the south there was no such available escape route from an advancing frontier into an adjacent wilderness. The Indians controlled a large and solid block of territory but it was an island already encircled by white settlement. There was no room for retreat or maneuver. They were obliged to stand their ground by whatever means they could muster or submit to immediate exile. Their response to this crisis provides an illuminating case history of the range of expedients to which a minority may resort when threatened by mortal danger.

The southern Indians were being afforded one last opportunity to realize that their interests were inseparable and that those interests might only be protected were this realized. The great Shawnee, Tecumseh, had been striving for years to reactivate the confederation of northern Indians that Brant had briefly assembled in the years of Indian militancy after the Revolution. In August of 1811, foreseeing the imminent outbreak of war between the United States and Great Britain, he embarked upon a tour of the southern nations to preach the absolute necessity of Indian union in the approaching crisis. With the prospective support of British military power, he maintained, there had appeared a last chance to require the Americans to recognize Indian right to what remained of their homeland.[1]

Tecumseh was a legitimate spokesman for any all-Indian policy. He was neither a northern nor a southern Indian. His mother was a Cherokee living with the Creek, he had been born in the south and in his youth he had fought as often on the southern frontier as the northern. He represented in experience, viewpoint and heritage as near an approach to a universal Indian leader as the race was ever to produce.

---

[1] Among the preliminary terms offered by Great Britain in the negotiation of the peace treaty ending the War of 1812 was the peremptory demand that the United States join Great Britain in guaranteeing against further settler encroachment all lands then occupied by Indians.

He was accompanied on his embassy by an entourage of northern Indians as devoted as he to the extension of Indian confederation to all Indians exposed to American aggressiveness. Every care was taken to impress the multitudes who gathered to hear him with the dramatic immediacy of his doctrine. His every entrance and exit was theatrically contrived to satisfy Indian appreciation of ceremony and pageantry. His disciples performed nightlong rituals and dances. The beating of drums and the chanting of ancient songs never ceased. To drive home his major premise, he himself always wore as his sole regalia of leadership two crane feathers, one white and one red. The white symbolized the imperative need that all Indians keep the peace with one another, the red that they must remember that the white man was their only enemy. In his progress across Mississippi, Alabama, Florida and Georgia he preached his crusade to rapt assemblages of many thousands. But nowhere could he linger to press his point or deal with doubt. He had no time. The imminence of the British-American war compelled him continually to hasten on, for he had still to deliver his message to the Indians west of the Mississippi.

In his wake the southern Indians grappled with their problem. It was a moment for the most excruciating soul-searching. If any failed to realize the gravity of the hour they were reminded by terrifying natural portents. Unprecedented storms swept the region. A comet blazed in the sky. The Great Earthquake shook the very hills. In countless and endless council meetings every town and every nation debated the issue. Witch doctors, conjurors and prophets vied with chiefs, elders and warriors in beseeching a frantic public's attention. Then, July 18, 1812, the United States declared war on Great Britain and there was no more time for debate.

The months spent in discussion without decision had sealed the failure of Tecumseh's crusade. Everywhere his appearance and his message had stirred the enthusiasm of the multitude but everywhere also the more prominent and influential figures in the community had held aloof, each still as reluctant as in the past to risk the interests of his town or nation for the sake of the general Indian cause. The great debate generated by Tecumseh's plea for unity had degenerated into an aggravation of disunity, particularly among the Creek, the most populous of Indian nations. They were torn by a long-standing and increasingly embittered cleavage between a progressive faction which believed the Creek future could only be assured by an accelerated adoption of the white man's ways and a conservative faction which believed that only by clinging to primitive customs and traditions could the integrity of the Creek people be preserved. With the outbreak of the British-American war, the conservatives, better known as Red Sticks, could no longer contain their impatience. Accepting British arms, they attempted to force their still pacific progressive neighbors to share their belligerence. The dissension erupted into a Creek civil war. In the course of a hot pursuit of a party of their rivals, Red Sticks overwhelmed a white stockade, Fort Mims, in which the fugitives had sought sanctuary along with some hundreds of white settlers. In the ensuing massacre more than 400 died. Revolted by the outrage, the United States and adjacent states launched three invading armies into the Creek country, from Mississippi, from Georgia and from Tennessee.

The other southern nations, subjected to the combined pressures of the British-American and Creek-American wars, were compelled to take positions with reference to both. To their agitated councils two supportable courses were open. They could move to defend the Creek, by this defiance of the United States accepting an alliance with Great Britain, as had Tecumseh's northern Indians, a course which could prove of incalculable value were Great Britain to win the war. Or they could maintain a stubborn neutrality, clinging to an attitude permitting later negotiation with whoever proved the victor. They adopted neither of these courses but instead elected a third. They joined the American invaders and vigorously assisted in the destruction of their Creek neighbor.

The Cherokee debate had been the most protracted and their decision of by far the most consequence. They possessed a significant residue of their traditional military power. Their determination was precipitated by the persistent arguments of Ridge,[2] one of their more influential chiefs. Unlike many Cherokee leaders, who were the part white descendants of early intermarriages

---

[2] Indian names ordinarily appear in contemporary records in the form of their contemporary white nicknames. Ridge's actual Cherokee name was "Walking the Mountain Tops." He was usually cited as Major Ridge to distinguish him from his equally prominent son, John Ridge.

between Cherokee women and colonial officers or traders, he was a full blood. His record of patriotic devotion to Cherokee territorial integrity was unassailable. Five years before he had assisted in the execution of a fellow chief, Doublehead, who had been accused of a land sale unauthorized by the Cherokee National Council. In this greater crisis the burden of Ridge's argument was that every future Cherokee hope of maintaining possession of their homeland depended upon American favor and that the Creek War offered an extraordinary opportunity to cultivate it. He advocated, therefore, a full scale Cherokee association with the American attack on the Creek. The distracted Cherokee Council hesitated but, with the assistance of a coincidental Creek murder of a Cherokee woman, his earnest plea finally carried the day.

Of the three American armies striking at the heart of the Creek country in central Alabama, the most important was the column of regulars and militia from Tennessee commanded by Andrew Jackson. Nearly a thousand Cherokee warriors flocked to his standard. The Creek, forced into unity by the extremity of this external danger, defended themselves with despairing valor. Frustrated by the unreliability and misbehavior of his militia, Jackson was twice compelled to retreat to his base while the weight of his campaign was carried by his Cherokee allies. His eventual victory at Horseshoe Bend, where more than a thousand Creek died in the flames of their central stronghold, was won, after his frontal assault by white troops had been repulsed, by the impetuosity of his Cherokee battalions who swam the river to take the defenders in the rear.

Jackson's Indian allies had won for him those first victories which had in turn opened to him his sensational opportunity at the ensuing Battle of New Orleans where in one fearful half hour he gained the military reputation which made him the west's great hero. These services the Indians began immediately and bitterly to regret. As in every former instance of white victories gained with Indian assistance the fruits of victory were reserved entirely for whites. Jackson's response to the allegiance of his Indian allies was to appoint himself their chief adversary. At the peace conference ending the Creek War he dictated a cession opening a wide corridor to white settlement leading through the center of the Indian country from the Tennessee to the Gulf. Thereafter he began at once to insist that not only the Creek but all southern Indians take themselves off forthwith to the far west. He pressed this insistence with a relentless vigor that was made irresistible by the executive power he wielded during the eight years he occupied the White House.

The pit the southern Indians had dug for one another had become a chasm engulfing them all.

3

The American Dream probably most nearly approached realization on the borders of the nearer west of the 1820's. People of the valleys of the Tennessee, the Cumberland and the Wabash could feel that they had found much of what their fathers and grandfathers had crossed the Appalachians to seek. Opportunity appeared unlimited. Freedom knew few restraints. There remained latitude for a full expression of any individual's most individualistic inclinations. The macabre horrors of the earlier period of the Indian wars had become dimming memories. Tranquillity, privacy and personal independence prevailed in a pleasant land which retained much of its original appeal. The railroad had not yet distorted the landscape. Mining had not yet scarred the hills. Industry had not yet polluted the streams. Much of the forest remained. It was still a beautiful country.

The average family was poor. But it was not a painful poverty. Unemployment could not become an overriding anxiety, for jobs were few and the lack of one of little moment. The family subsisted by its own efforts within its own vicinage. The most straitened had an abundance of food. The meanest corn patch provided a year round staple. Pigs and cattle could range for natural forage. The great herds of buffalo, elk and deer were long since gone but sufficient game remained to supplement the basic domestic diet. Wild fruits, nuts and greens supplied seasonal variety. All members of the family spent most waking hours out of doors. There was much to be done but so much time in which to do it that intermittent idleness exacted slight forfeit. Theirs was a sun-warmed, wind-cooled, rain-washed natural world.

It was a world in which every aspect was pleasing to the boy roaming a creek bottom with his dog, savoring the smells, sights and sounds of marsh, woodland and meadow, of swimming hole, trout pool and muskrat pond. Nor were these pleasures withheld from him after he became a man. All his life he could remain as susceptible to the sensory satisfactions of his natural surroundings. He was more apt than not as the years rolled on to find himself continuing to spend as much time with rod and gun as with hoe and scythe. These were also pleasures a man could afford. The headlong development of the country was increasing the value of whatever anybody owned at a rate unknown in any older country and therefore if he worked with even occasional diligence he was assured of doing more than well enough to underwrite his leisure. If he worked hard he could hope to become rich.

It was this personal freedom that was the essence of the Dream. The course of a man's life was subject to his own direction. Whether he idled more than he worked or attempted a nice adjustment between the two, the gratifications were certain and prompt. There was always the principal gratification that the choice had remained his. There were few pressures to narrow it. Most communities were sparse and dispersed. A man could make his neighbors his boon companions or ignore them and their opinions. Neither his conduct nor his livelihood was at the mercy of his social or economic environment. The solitude of seclusion was always available. He could as readily turn to the comforts of sociability. The most common tasks, butchering, quilting, cloth-fulling, corn-shucking, were occasions for those convivial expressions of mutual assistance known as bees. Muster day, court day, election day and the 4th of July drew wider and more boisterous assemblages of like-minded celebrants. Finally, there was the apogee of gregariousness, the camp meeting, in which throngs of thousands shared the heady mingling of social exuberance and religious ecstasy.

Whatever the limitations of his way of life, the inhabitant of the nearer western border could be certain of one proposition. It was a way that worked. It was a proven success. A man could hunt or fish or get a poor price for his corn or just sit and whittle a stick and still nourish the comfort of that reflection. He could see that the whole west around him was developing at a prodigious rate. Whatever his present fortunes or deserts there was perpetually the assurance of future improvement. It was this constant anticipation as an antidote to every present disappointment or discouragement that was the second most essential part of the Dream. Progress was a certainty. And the prospect was no longer distant. Westerners needed no longer to resent the easterners' galling assumption of superiority. Their numbers had increased until the meteoric rise of the west had been capped by its achievement of political power. Westerners had seized control of Congress and placed one of their own in the White House. With success had come self-consciousness. They could regard themselves as a people set apart, as a chosen people. Their new confidence enabled them even to view themselves with a sense of humor, an attitude to which national attention was drawn by the political and literary career of Davy Crockett.

Near the white border, sometimes at no greater distance than across a stream or over a ridge, were Indian communities. Once red men and white had been antagonists compelled by common defense needs to dwell hundreds of miles apart. Now they were neighbors who displayed more similarities than distinctions. The Indian, too, was a part-time farmer who hunted and fished and indulged his personal inclinations. Upon his existence played many bright reflections of the same Dream. Indians east of the Mississippi in the 1820's knew a measure of the Arcadian gratifications early observers had imagined all Indians to have enjoyed in their pre-white original state. Peace was their paramount blessing. Two centuries of nearly perpetual conflict had ended. They had been relieved of the haunting terrors of surprises and assaults, of burned villages and cornfields, of the continually recurring threat of death, torment, slavery, flight, which had characterized those hundreds of years of wars with whites and with each other. The maintenance of this peace which they had never before known was assured by the concern of federal authorities and the vigilance of federal arms. Indians could plant their fields, rear their children, play their ball games, attend their festivals, hold their councils, without the constant apprehension of violence which had formerly shadowed their lives. Their one-time boundless hunting range had been sadly restricted but there was still room for Indian day-to-day living to proceed much as it had, with the added advantage that it had been made easier as well as safer. Every tendency to augment their food supply by a more diligent application to food raising was encouraged by federal advice, tools and seed. Federal annuities, in payment for earlier land cessions, were largely sequestered by chiefs but some of the largess trickled down to the family level. Most Indians found reason for feeling that times were better than they had ever known.

In the north some smaller nations had succumbed to past misfortunes and degenerated into shiftless and drunken beggary. But most had retained enough of their ancient customs and traditions to constitute a degree of tribal integrity. They were being continually jostled and crowded by demands for new land cessions but behind them still stretched the wilderness in which they might still roam and hunt. For the Indian so inclined, there was still the opportunity to remain an Indian.

In the south, even after the island of Indian occupancy had been riven by Jackson's corridor, the areas held by Indians were still commodious. The Chickasaw and Choctaw occupied most of eastern and all of northern Mississippi. The Cherokee-Creek area was even more extensive. It stretched 350 miles from north to south, from near Knoxville almost to the Gulf, and 100 miles from east to west, from near the present Atlanta to near Montgomery. There was ample room in these twin areas, each larger than many of the original thirteen states, for Indians to continue their quickening transition toward civilization and meanwhile to live under circumstances of their own choosing.

Another essence of the Dream was a recognition by people who had lived long on the border that all men were entitled to acceptance as individuals. This had become a tolerance that did not reject even Indians. By the 1820's the friction between the races was least evident in those border areas where Indian and white communities were most in contact. In the earlier period of the Indian wars settler and Indian had been inveterate enemies. Cumulative outrages of which both had been guilty had bred passionate hatreds. It had been a conflict in which the adversaries had sought no other outcome than the other's complete extermi-

nation. But with the end of the wars it was the men who had
personally fought them who, as has so often been the case, were
more ready to adjust to peace than were others who had never
fought. White backwoodsmen who lived near Indians were soon
perceiving how many problems and inclinations they shared with
their red neighbors, in how many ways their traits and personali-
ties were similar. Interracial friendships developed. White men
gained permission to live in Indian communities where their
presence was doubly welcomed were they able to teach Indians
craft skills such as metalworking and woodworking or how to read
and write. Indians readily found employment on the white side of
the border or were as readily received as respected guests in white
homes. Even Jackson, who enjoyed warm personal relations with
many individual Indians, kept what amounted to an open house
for Indian visitors.

The two most notable frontier figures of the period, Davy
Crockett and Sam Houston, were representative of this new
border attitude.[1] Both became lifelong champions of Indian
rights. As a congressman from Tennessee's most primitive district,
Crockett did not hesitate to speak out as boldly in defense of
Indian interests as in those of his own people. Even when his stand
became a flagrant defiance of Jackson, he did not falter. In advocating Indian rights he was striking a chord which did not offend
too many of his backwoods constituents. Though Jackson was their
idol they twice re-elected Crockett. Houston, whose imprint on
the course of American history in his time was matched by no
other man save Jackson, carried his regard for Indians to the
extent of a personal identification. His career presented a continuing demonstration of the interplay of instinctive sympathies between red and white hunter-farmers along the southern frontier of
the 1820's. In his youth Houston ran away from home to spend
three years among the Cherokee, forming lasting friendships
among their young warriors, courting their girls, winning the
affectionate regard of their chiefs. Through all the rest of his life
he recalled those years as the happiest he had ever known. Then,
as he put it, he had been privileged to look "wistfully around on

1 Two of Crockett's grandparents had been killed by Cherokee and two of his uncles
had been held for 17 years in Cherokee captivity. Houston's family had held a
frontier stockade throughout the period of the Indian wars which had been repeatedly attacked by Cherokee.

all things for light and beauty" and then his heart had been "vacant to every fresh form of delight." Later when he dramatically resigned the governorship of Tennessee, in despondent reaction to his young bride's flight from his roof, he returned to live again with the Cherokee, this time on the Arkansas. He became a citizen of the nation, married a Cherokee woman and continued to devote his energies to his advocacy of Indian interests until, in the third stage of his public service, he moved on to Texas to become the architect of Texan independence.

The compulsions dictating Indian removal were therefore not generated along the line where the two races were in most intimate contact. By the 1820's white settlers and their Indian neighbors were realizing how many of their difficulties and aspirations were common. The Indians were meanwhile improving their condition at a rate comparable to that everywhere in evidence on the white side of the line. They, too, were clearing more land, building roads, mills and ferries, accumulating property, expanding their trade and sending their children to school. The missionary movement had gained such momentum that even the religious difference was fading. Had this live-and-let-live tolerance that was developing in areas where the two races were in actual contact been permitted to run its natural course there was increasing reason to suppose that the monstrous tragedies that had formerly characterized their relations might be henceforth escaped. Many Indians were already demonstrating as valid a preparation for citizenship as were their white neighbors. That this solution was to be postponed until nearly our own day was a consequence of larger and more inexorable forces than any then visible to either.

These were forces that threatened the way of life on the white side of the border as irretrievably as on the red. Foremost among them were population and industrialization. During the 20 years preceding 1830 the white population north of the Ohio increased by 1,199,594 and that south of the Cumberland by 1,545,605. Roads, steamboats, factories and mines were multiplying. Villages were becoming cities. The railroad was in the offing. The immediate impact of the surging increase in population was upon the value of land. Of land east of the Mississippi still unoccupied by whites the largest tracts were those reserved to Indians by earlier treaties. The Indians had already been stripped of most of what they once had claimed but the little to which they still clung had taken on a greater value than all that they had lost.

Formerly the great threat to Indian territory had been represented by the perpetually encroaching frontiersman. The Indian had at worst been able to resist physically, which he had, long and bitterly, in wars in which both adversaries paid the honest price of personal fortitude and personal sacrifice. The new threat was infinitely more difficult to resist for it was primarily political and the Indian had neither vote nor influence. The central threat sprang from southern statehouses where the demand for Indian removal was politically popular and from congressional caucuses where regional political favors could be traded. Party managers and land speculators manipulated the growing excitement. Candidates for office from local constable to the presidency fished for votes in the troubled waters. The public was bewildered by extravagant slogans. Press and pulpit whipped up the frenzy. National parties sought political advantage by their stands in the controversy. Sectional bigotry was galvanized. Congress became a sounding board in which charges and countercharges vied in virulence. Prejudices were aroused, both for and against the Indian cause, among distant millions who knew nothing about Indians or their case and whose every opinion of the issue had been derived from partisan oratory.

The Indian question was involving more than the fate of the Indian. It was becoming a vital testing ground for the responsible processes of democracy.

4

The Cherokee, whose resistance to removal was to provide the most searching test of these processes, had special reason to cling to their ancient homeland. They were the only Indians east of the Mississippi who dwelt in a mountain country. To it they were attached with the fierce devotion so often evidenced by mountain dwellers of every clime and every age. They inhabited the southern shoulder of the Appalachians, an area radiating from the Great Smokies where the range attains its most impressive heights. It was a region with an immense natural appeal that had entranced every early traveler and visitor. William Bartram, who saw it in 1776, was captivated. He wrote lyrically of its "cool, sequestered, rocky vales," of the "celebrated beauties of the hills," of its ridges "rising grandly one above another . . . whilst others far distant, veiled in blue mists, sublimely mount aloft with yet greater majesty," of its "stately columns of superb forest trees," of its "flowers and . . . green meadows and strawberry fields," of "flocks of turkeys" and "herds of deer" and "companies . . . of Cherokee virgins . . . bathing their limbs in the cool fleeting streams." If attractive to alien observers, to the Cherokee themselves their country was without any possible question in every way superior to any other. Here their ancestors had lived since the earliest times of which memories remained and here they were determined to stay.

They had had abundant opportunity to compare their country

with others. Like most mountain peoples they had always been warlike, predatory and venturesome. For countless generations they had issued from their mountain fastnesses to prey upon inhabitants of the lowlands, emboldened by the confidence that whenever pressed by coalitions of their enemies they could with-draw to the security of their peak-encircled strongholds. Their war parties had not hesitated to seek out adversaries as distant as on the headwaters of the Susquehanna or the upper reaches of the Ohio. Their hunting parties had ranged westward across the Mississippi. As a result of their habitual venturing they had become familiar with the continent from the Great Lakes to the Gulf and from the Atlantic to the edge of the Great Plains. But always their wanderers had returned to their mountain homeland. Their devo-tion to it was more than a simple nostalgic response to the place of their birth, or a sentimental appreciation of its magnificent land-scape. It was one deepened by their religion. In Cherokee myth-ology the West was the region ruled by evil in which even the sun died, the abode of the Black Man, the personification of death. Their country in the East on the other hand was the Sun Land, where light was reborn, presided over by the benevolent Red Man, the personification of life, and peopled by innumerable lesser gods and the spirits of their ancestors.

There was one insistent Cherokee legend that once a consider-able party of Cherokee warriors, with their families, had crossed the Mississippi to hunt and thereafter had never been heard from again. In Cherokee folklore they were regarded as having been doomed to wander endlessly and hopelessly in the western dark-ness. The first Cherokee migration of record, occurring in 1794, the last year of war between Cherokee and Americans, was not by choice but a flight from danger. In the course of the perennial guerrilla warfare that had tormented both white and red frontiers for the past 20 years a Cherokee subchief, Bowl, had with his small band assaulted the flatboat of William Scott at Muscle Shoals. Scott was on his way down the Tennessee en route to Natchez with a party that numbered 6 white men, 3 white women, 4 white children and 21 Negro slaves. The white men were killed and the others carried off captive, though there was some later indication that at least one of the women was eventually released. Bowl was at the time more concerned than elated by his success. He knew

that the principal Cherokee chiefs were engaged in peace negotiations and he feared their turning him over to American ven-
geance. He therefore kept on with his band, his loot and his
captives down the Tennessee to find a sanctuary which became a
new home in the west, first on the St. Francis River, next on the
lower Arkansas and then in Texas. As a consequence of this first
permanent, though involuntary, lodgment of Cherokee west of the
Mississippi there developed a continuous intercourse between the
small but presently growing western colony and the parent nation
in the east, along with a constant comparison of conditions in the
two widely separated regions.

The second migration in 1809 was the first deliberate decision
by any considerable number of Cherokee to exchange their residence in their ancient homeland in the east for a new location in
the west. It came after long and uneasy consideration of the
question. After the Louisiana Purchase the federal government
had begun exerting every pressure short of force to persuade the
Cherokee, along with all other southern Indians, to move west
into the immense new wild space that had been made available.
Innumerable conferences had been held. Federal and state agents
and commissioners had argued, cajoled and threatened. Presents
had been lavishly distributed. Chiefs had been bribed. Indian
delegates had been glutted with food and addled by drink. Still the
stubborn resistance to the proposal had persisted.

A people can be confronted by no more difficult, critical and
fundamental decision than to contemplate the complete abandonment of its native land. So total a change in their environment
arouses forebodings of as sweeping a change in their character.
Many other Indians had been compelled by the force of circumstance to wander widely. Many of these wanderings had preceded
the white era. Some had become quasi-nomads and increasingly
adaptable to changing conditions. For some it had meant rapid
degeneration, for others an improvement in their condition. In
the notable cases of the Shawnee, Delaware and Wyandot repeated
migrations had been survived without a fatal impairment of tribal
discipline or national coherence. But the Cherokee had been
wedded to their native mountains for centuries. To migrate to a
distant region meant for them a severance of the deepest roots

sustaining their religion, their traditions and their identity as a people.

Yet by 1809 there were plainly perceptible advantages in a move that were far more compelling than the specious arguments of time-serving federal officials. In the ten years preceding 1809 the Cherokee had been required to cede to the United States nearly a half of their remaining land. There was every indication that this was a process that might be expected to continue. The perimeter of white settlement, backed by an immeasurably more numerous white population, was slowly and inexorably strangling Cherokee living space. On what Cherokee land was left game was becoming progressively more scarce. Subsistence was becoming increasingly dependent upon other means than hunting and to the still primitive Cherokee majority the unfamiliar irksomeness of farming or working for hire was still repellent. On the Arkansas, however, as Bowl's band and various eastern Cherokee who had made an excursion there had discovered, game was as plentiful as it had ever been on the Tennessee. It was also a country that was as beautifully wooded and watered as the Tennessee, a still un-broken wilderness in every way suitable for Indian occupation and enjoyment. Towering above all its other advantages was the su-preme blessing that there were as yet no white settlers on the Arkansas. Indians contemplating the move were solemnly assured at every level of federal authority that this was an advantage that would persist. There Indians might roam and hunt, live and die, forever undisturbed by the proximity of white neighbors. The federal government was determined, they were told, to forbid perpetually the advance of white settlement to the Arkansas. This would therefore be the last move Indians would ever be asked to make.

The vastly troubled Cherokee sent a deputation to Washington to implore President Jefferson's advice. Jefferson had always mani-fested a humanitarian regard for Indians. But he was also possessed by a President's natural anxiety to tidy up regional problems in the struggling young republic wherever that was at all possible. There could be no swifter and more complete solution to the supremely vexing Indian problem than Indian consent to move forthwith across the Mississippi and this he earnestly counseled them to do. The gist of his advice was that if they wished to continue to be Indians, uncontaminated by white contacts, they could only hope to manage this in the unspoiled western wilderness. He indicated that those who chose to go at once would receive federal assistance in making the move, though funds for this proved not forthcoming.

The combination of allurements, represented by better hunting, more room, escape from white neighbors and official assurance of federal protection of Indian land rights in the west, was impressive. One principal chief, Tahlonteskee, decided to take the plunge. He had an added personal motive in that he had been a co-signer of the 1807 land cession treaty, a betrayal of Cherokee national interests for which the other signer, Doublehead, had been executed by fellow chiefs. Tahlonteskee set out in the late summer of 1809 with a following of some hundreds of families, most of them from the more primitive element among the Cherokee who had retained an unquenchable aversion to the resort to farming they must accept were they to remain in the east. During each of the next several years other hundreds of such primitives made the break. On the Arkansas they found the wilderness they had sought and regained the wilderness way of life for which they had yearned. They also excited the resentment of the resident Osage whose hunting range they had invaded. This caused them no great concern. Cherokee had always felt able to take wars with Indian enemies in stride. Presently there were three to four thousand Cherokee on the Arkansas who were becoming known as West Cherokee to distinguish them from the great majority of their fellow countrymen, the East Cherokee. The Cherokee had become in effect two nations, each with its council of chiefs and its federal agent.

The third major migration, and the last to be voluntary, came in 1818. Jackson's victories in the Creek War and at New Orleans had made him by far the most influential figure in the American west. This influence he was devoting to his determination to drive all Indians from the south. He was pressing his campaign with such vigor that he did not hesitate in 1818 to pursue hostile Seminole into Spanish Florida where he precipitated an international crisis by capturing two Spanish forts and hanging two Englishmen. Negotiations in which Jackson took a dominant part as United States Commissioner had extracted new land cessions from all southern Indians. The Cherokee had been forced to withdraw from all but two small corners of Tennessee and North Carolina. The one large holding still remaining to them was in northeastern Alabama and northern Georgia. The constricting ring of Indian dispossession was steadily tightening. Cherokee resistance to these exactions was handicapped by their isolation after their assistance in the overthrow of their Creek neighbors, by divisions in their councils and by the venal irresponsibility of some of their chiefs.[1]

Impressed by these depressing developments, another principal chief, Oolooteskee (better known by his more euphonious white name, John Jolly), became convinced of the virtue of yielding in good time to what he had come to consider the inevitable. His decision was assisted by two personal concerns. Tahlonteskee, head chief of the West Cherokee, was his brother. And Sam Houston, new sub-agent to the Cherokee, was his foster son. Houston had spent the years of his boyhood sojourn with the Cherokee in John Jolly's home on idyllic Hiwassee Island. Houston's wounds and services in the Creek War had made him a border hero second only to Jackson. The intimacy of his personal ties with the Cherokee made him in Jackson's eyes eminently fitted to promote the removal campaign. Houston accepted the appointment and performed what was expected of him. Appearing at Hiwassee Island in Cherokee costume, he was able, with undoubted sincerity, to persuade John Jolly that the move west was in the Indians' own best interests and the only possible escape from the sea of troubles flooding over them. John Jolly set out for the Arkansas in February of 1818 with some 300 followers. The same federal government which had so often urged Indians to turn to farming so that they might require less land was now furnishing the migrants with new rifles so that they might return to their former dependence upon hunting.

But John Jolly's party were not nomad-hunters seeking a more extensive wilderness. In descending the Tennessee they required 13 flatboats and 4 keelboats to transport their property. Most of them were from the more progressive element in the nation who

---

[1] In one report to the Secretary of War on expenses incurred during negotiations Jackson explained: "In concluding the treaty with the Cherokees, it was found both well and polite to make a few presents to the chiefs and interpreters."

had already accumulated considerable wealth in cattle and slaves. They were true colonists seeking new land to develop. In outlook and intention they were scarcely to be distinguished from John Donelson's flotilla of white pioneers which had descended the same river in 1780 to found the Cumberland settlements. On the Arkansas the Cherokee immigrants found good land which immediately they began to clear, fence and cultivate and upon which they built substantial houses, barns and granaries.

It was not, however, a country that any longer presented many of those aspects of an Indian Promised Land which had a few years earlier appealed to the warrior-hunters of Bowl and Tahlonteskee. It had instead already become a land distracted by every sort of uncertainty and menace. The white frontier had been advancing at a rate unforeseen in Washington or even by the border families participating in it. The Mississippi which had so recently appeared a providential barrier to the divisive dispersion of the American people had not provided the slightest deterrent. It had on the contrary facilitated the passage by flatboat of white settlers to any location of their choice. Their surge into eastern Arkansas after the War of 1812 had been preceded by an unruly horde of white trappers, traders and squatters intermingled with horse thieves, liquor dealers, outlaws and assorted frontier riffraff. By 1818 the apparently inexhaustible supply of game was disappearing. Professional white hunters were killing buffalo by the thousands for the sake of their readily transportable tallow.

These western white encroachments conformed to the pattern so long familiar in the east. As early as 1813 Missouri Territory had incorporated the region of the Arkansas as a county. Missouri authorities, backed by Missouri public opinion, refused to recognize the right of the United States to allocate land to Indians within its borders. The influx of settlers into the *de facto* county mounted. They came by water or overland from the Missouri by wagon or filtered through the forest on foot. After the establishment of Arkansas Territory in 1819 its legislature was as little disposed to recognize Indian land titles as was Georgia's or Alabama's. The federal government, guiltily mindful of its vows in persuading the Indians to emigrate, made sporadic efforts to protect not only the Cherokee but similar adjoining colonies of Creek, Choctaw, Chickasaw, Delaware and Shawnee. Detachments

of the army marched and countermarched, evicting swarms of
illegal settlers. The intruders returned on the heels of the withdrawing soldiery or circled to nearby locations. The white frontier
was a tide. If held at one point it broke through at another. By the
mid-twenties there were white settlers seizing upon choice locations hundreds of miles *west* of the Indian colonies. To the general
tumult were added the alarms and excesses of the continuing and
spreading war between the transplanted eastern Indians and the
Osage and plains Indians.

Thus the West Cherokee, along with their companion Indian
immigrants, were finding none of the peace and quiet and room
which had been their primary incentives in consenting to abandon
their eastern homes. They were being subjected to the same white
population pressures from which they had hoped to escape along
with the added harassments of extremes of violence formerly
unknown. Already vastly outnumbered by surrounding white
settlers of which new waves were pouring in each year, the conclusion had become inescapable that wherever there existed fertile
soil endowed with wood and water its inundation by white settlement was certain. The one recourse still open to Indians appeared
to be the acceptance of land too barren and arid to be coveted by
whites. It had become as certain that however well-intentioned
may have been the federal government's promises it had not the will
or possibly the power to fulfill them. Years of the Arkansas Indian
colonies' unavailing protests and petitions had demonstrated this,
as it had been so often demonstrated before on the Holston or the
Tennessee, the Scioto or the Wabash.

In 1828, in grim recognition of these portents, a deputation of
chiefs representing a minority of the Cherokee colony journeyed
to Washington to negotiate another land cession. New federal
promises of even more impressive solemnity than those that had
persuaded them to leave the Tennessee were made the despairing
Indians to prevail upon them to evacuate Arkansas Territory by
another move still further west. This new location, the government earnestly pronounced, would become:

a *permanent home* . . . which shall, under the most solemn guarantee of the United States, be and remain theirs forever—a home that
shall never, in all future time be embarrassed by having extended

around it the lines, or placed over it the jurisdiction of a new territory, or a state, nor be pressed upon by the extension in any way, of any of the limits of any existing territory or state.

The majority of the Cherokee colony bitterly denounced the treaty and its makers but possessed no means to resist its injunction. Wearily they abandoned their so recently developed properties and moved on west to their next "permanent" home at the edge of the plains beyond the western boundary of Arkansas Territory which they found already occupied by some hundreds of white settlers.

These tribulations and disasters afflicting the West Cherokee had not escaped the absorbed attention of the parent nation in the east. It had become glaringly obvious that no relief was to be gained by a flight to the west in quest of freedom and opportunity. The remaining East Cherokee, still numbering some three fourths of the nation, resolved henceforth to hold their ground, to defend their country as long as they were able.

5

The Cherokee had been long acquainted with the demands of self-defense. For 20 generations they had repelled invaders of their mountain homeland. But the possibility of physical resistance no longer existed. Their country had become an island in an engulfing sea of white humanity. In 1820 they numbered less than 13,000 while the population of the United States had mounted to nearly 10,000,000, of which their immediate and aggressive white neighbors in Tennessee, Alabama and Georgia totaled nearly 900,000. The imbalance in military power had made any thought of resistance preposterous and had consigned them to the status of prisoners wholly dependent upon the will of their captors.

Tied hand and foot by the obvious absurdity of even the most frantic appeal to arms, their one recourse appeared an appeal to reason. They resolved, in these desperate straits, to cease to behave like Indians and instead to conform to the white way of life. By self-education, by self-improvement and by an earnest application to every art, skill, craft and attitude of civilization, they conceived they might earn their own niche in the structure of the republic. In the next ten years they made such progress in this direction as no other people has ever made in so short a time.

The seeds of this total revolution in Cherokee society had been providentially planted 20 years earlier by three obscure Protestant missionaries. The Cherokee were the only Indians east of the Mississippi whose condition had been, or was to be, materially affected by the proselytizing efforts of the Protestant church. In the Spanish and French penetration of North America the crucifix had everywhere accompanied the sword and the flag. But, with the sole exception of the New England mission to the Oneida during the Revolution, an attempted Christianization of Indians had nowhere been a significant factor in the Anglo-Saxon advance. Incipient impulses to convert Indians had invariably been smothered by the recurrence of wars with Indians. The Moravian Brethren was the first Protestant sect, and for long the only one, to consider the evangelization of Indians a primary duty of the church.

Possibly prepared by their own sufferings and near extinction in Germany's Thirty Years War, from the moment of their appearance in North America the Moravians had manifested a deep sympathy for Indians together with a conviction that Christianity offered the one future hope for Indians. In Pennsylvania they had begun at once to instruct the nearest Indians, the Delaware. They taught their protégés not only to sing and pray, to keep the peace and accept the faith but also to sow and reap, to spin and weave, to read and write. Their mission flourished in spite of persistent attacks by white settlers, always incensed by any attempt at Indian improvement. To escape this interference the Moravians moved their Delaware mission to the sanctuary of the distant Ohio wilderness where again it flourished until the burning of their towns and the butchery of their converts by American frontiersmen in 1782.

After their initial lodgments in Georgia, Pennsylvania and New York, the migrant Moravians had in 1752 located another station on the Yadkin in North Carolina with a view to establishing a mission to the Cherokee.[1] Their intentions were frustrated by the anti-white prejudices excited among the Cherokee by the wars stretching in an almost unbroken series from the French and Indian War and Pontiac's Rebellion to the Revolution and its long aftermath of border conflict. Even after the general Indian peace of 1795 they found new difficulties in the language problem and continuous Cherokee suspicion of white motives. Finally, in 1801 Abraham Steiner and Christian Schweinitz gained the per-

[1] In a remarkable burst of evangelical activity the Moravians were during this same period founding missions in South America, Africa and the Far East.

mission of the Cherokee Council to found a mission at Spring
Place in northern Georgia. There was in these proceedings a
startling augury of the coming revolution in Cherokee opinion.
Among the approving Cherokee councilors attending the opening
ceremonies were many who had formerly been the nation's most
violent war chiefs, including Bloody Fellow who had on innumerable occasions justified his name, and Doublehead, the inveterate
white-hater who was especially noted for having once with his own
hand dispatched all 13 members of a settler's family after their
stockade had been surrendered. A new sense of what the future
might demand was beginning to stir among the Cherokee. The
councilors admitted little interest in the missionaries' religion.
What they were seeking was the instruction of their children. This
the Moravians cheerfully undertook to provide.

The third pioneer missionary to devote his services to the
Cherokee was Gideon Blackburn, a Presbyterian frontier minister
whose Maryville, Tennessee, parish bordered immediately on the
Cherokee country. For years he had been troubled by the beckoning need to convert his Cherokee neighbors not only from
heathendom to Christianity but from savagery to civilization. His
acquaintance with them had, however, led him to realize the full
difficulty of persuading adult Cherokee to renounce their lifelong
devotion to war, hunting and their inherited religious beliefs. But
on every visit to their country he was struck anew by the bright-
ness and alertness of Cherokee children. Their receptivity represented, he became convinced, the most hopeful opening for any
effort to save the Cherokee. Having gained the Council's permission to establish a school for very young children, he raised funds
for it during a tour of the north, from President Jefferson, who
directed the War Department to support the project, from the
Presbyterian General Assembly, and from contributions by many
churches.

His school, opening in the spring of 1804, proved an astonishing
success. A year later, on July 4, 1805, he was able to display his
pupils' progress before an assemblage of chiefs, councilors and
distinguished visitors, one of whom was Governor John Sevier of
Tennessee. The children, dressed in white clothing donated by
Blackburn's Maryville congregation, read aloud from English
books, sang hymns in English and demonstrated their proficiency

in arithmetic. Sevier, who in his long and militant career had commanded forces of American frontiersmen in 35 recorded battles with Cherokee, was moved to tears by the spectacle.

A second school was established. The Cherokee were so pleased by their children's progress that they were disposed to heed Blackburn's counsel that they develop self-government. This brief flare of improvement was quenched, however, by Cherokee dissatisfaction with the federal government's continuing insistence on further land cessions. When Blackburn's health failed his schools were closed. But his theory had been unquestionably proved. The Cherokee were not only ready to learn but eminently able to learn.

After a lapse during the alarms and confusion of the War of 1812, mission work among the Cherokee was resumed as a more active and better organized effort. The renewed zeal in Protestantism accompanying the rise of Methodism, accompanied in America by the religious revival on the frontier at the turn of the century, was also accompanied by a suddenly pronounced concern for the salvation of distant heathen. With American missions being established or projected in the farthest corners of Africa, Asia and the South Seas the so much nearer Cherokee opportunity did not escape attention. In 1816 the American Board of Commissioners for Foreign Missions, with the sanction and support of the federal government, delegated Cyrus Kingsbury, a young Brown graduate, to reactivate the work that had been initiated by Blackburn. At the Turkeytown conference at which Jackson was placing new boundary and removal pressures on the Creek and Cherokee, Kingsbury gained the approval of Cherokee chiefs. His project was sponsored by Jackson, who for all his determination to dispossess Indians as nations often exhibited a warm regard for individual Indians as persons.

The Chickamauga Creek site selected for the new mission was clothed with a special significance. There was no more historic spot in the Cherokee country nor one with which the barbaric past of the Cherokee was more closely associated. Here during the Revolution had been the central Cherokee citadel from which countless war parties had sallied to devastate the American frontier. The farm and trading post headquarters of John McDonald, who as resident British agent during the Revolution and as Spanish agent thereafter had for 20 years promoted and supplied Cherokee belligerence, was purchased to house the mission. Chickamauga, the storied stronghold of Dragging Canoe, most fiercely dedicated of all Cherokee war chiefs, which once had been the fountainhead from which had radiated relentless hostility to everything American, had become a source from which flowed new influences calculated to transform every aspect of Cherokee society and thus, the nation was beginning to hope, eradicate the differences between the races.

The new school, called Brainerd Mission in honor of David Brainerd, a New England missionary to the Indians of the Susquehanna 70 years earlier, was an immediate and continuing success. It was more than a primary school for children or a trade school for boys. On its faculty were graduates of many northern universities. Young women were offered the same courses as young men. The one limit to the school's educational program was Cherokee ability to learn. Once more it was demonstrated that Cherokee aptitude in this respect was prodigious. Catherine Brown, first Cherokee to be baptized at Brainerd on January 25, 1818, was soon teaching in a school of her own. By 1825 her brother, David, had finished translating the New Testament directly from Greek into Cherokee. Other denominations were founding other mission schools. The Cherokee people were embracing education with all the excited fervor with which once they had raised the war whoop.

When the Moravians, Steiner and Schweinitz, had made their first tour of the Cherokee country in 1799 they had everywhere found their survey handicapped by the necessity of depending upon interpreters, most of whom knew either too little English or too little Cherokee to find expression for religious ideas. By the middle 1820's English had become a second Cherokee language. The effect of education which has come to most societies as a gradual permeation, a process measured by the passage of generations, had come to the Cherokee like the sudden all-pervading light of a rising sun. Pupils and students from the schools carried home sparks of learning which were kindled anew in their awed and bewildered yet eagerly receptive communities. The whole Cherokee outlook was shifting, almost overnight. Fears and superstitions never before questioned were suddenly subject to question. The man who had always believed that to point his finger at a rainbow was sure to cause the finger to swell was led to wonder if this could really be so. A people who had believed implicitly that all events were under the control of wizards, witches, spirits, supernatural animals, the Great White Rabbit, the Old White Bear, the Little Men, and the invisible, invulnerable Little Deer were being obliged to speculate instead upon the possibility that the principle of cause and effect might offer a likelier explanation.[2] They blinked with many painful misgivings in the strange glare but only the most stubborn among the traditionalists covered their eyes. A primitive people who had always before regarded whatever was most ancient with the deepest reverence had developed a tendency to regard whatever was newest as inherently superior. The conviction had become fixed that the overwhelming success of their white adversaries had been achieved by the magical powers with which they had been clothed by their education.

This extraordinary widening of the Cherokee intellectual horizon had been accompanied by an equally extraordinary metamorphosis in Cherokee manners, customs, occupations and living conditions. More and more Cherokee families were descending from their isolated mountain glens to cultivate river bottom farms. More and more Cherokee youths were becoming blacksmiths, carpenters, masons. An 1826 count of Cherokee property disclosed 22,000 cattle, 7,600 horses, 46,000 swine, 726 looms, 2,488 spinning wheels, 172 wagons, 2,943 plows, 10 saw mills, 31 grist mills, 62 blacksmith shops, 8 cotton machines, 18 schools, 18 ferries and many roads. The ambitious young Cherokee who once had dreamed of the number of scalps he might take or horses he might steal was now dreaming in terms of a two-story brick house, a hundred slaves and a 500 acre plantation.

Amazing and promising as were the Cherokee steps toward civilization during the early 1820's, a note of portentous warning was being struck in far off New England, presumably the traditional center of sympathetic support for Indian advancement. The same year that Brainerd Mission was founded a companion institution with a wider purpose was being established in Cornwall,

2 See James Mooney's *Myths of the Cherokee* (Part I, 19th Annual Report, Bureau of American Ethnology) Washington, 1900 and *Sacred Formulas of the Cherokee* (7th Annual Report, BAE) Washington, 1891, for detail on Cherokee superstitions.

Connecticut. New England ships sailing the seven seas were returning with occasional alien sailors recruited in distant lands.
The sight of these flesh and blood denizens of remote pagan climes
gripped New England attention. The Puritan conscience was
disturbed. With so many strange peoples unaware of the truth, the
obligation to extend Christian enlightenment was inescapable.
Among many responses to this impulse was the founding of a
mission school at Cornwall under the sponsorship of Lyman
Beecher, who since the recent death of Yale President Timothy
Dwight was acknowledged to be the most distinguished of Connecticut clergymen. The new academy was open to all comers,
whether Polynesian, Asian, African or American Indian. Cornwall
was a typical New England town, built about a green, with
church, school and town hall its principal edifices, whose inhabitants' chief interests, aside from making a better living, were
centered in education and theology. Such a climate of intellectual
righteousness would seem to have provided an ideal atmosphere
for such a soul-saving undertaking. Nobody could have foreseen
the ensuing catastrophe.

The first contingent of Cherokee students, seeking the more
advanced education offered at Cornwall, was escorted north by
Elias Boudinot, a philanthropic Philadelphia clergyman who had
long taken a personal interest in Indian improvement. There was
a pause at Washington where the young Cherokee were received
by the President. At Cornwall they were warmly welcomed by the
school and the community. Among the new arrivals were Major
Ridge's son, John, and his nephew, Buck (or Stag) Watie. Indians
were accustomed to change their names at will whenever some
event or achievement in their careers seemed to invite such com-
memoration. Buck was so impressed by the expedition and by
their illustrious conductor that he elected to change his name to
Elias Boudinot as a mark of his gratitude and respect. He was to
make the name so much better known in American history that
the original may never be mentioned without an explanatory
asterisk.

The Cornwall school was already attracting such widespread
and approving attention that it was receiving donations and visita-
tions not only from many sections of America but of the world.
The young Cherokee took their place in the babel of languages

and mingling of races that characterized the student body. With their Brainerd and Moravian school backgrounds they gained quick recognition as exceptional students. The school's purposes were being fulfilled at a rate that exceeded its well-wishers' fondest hopes when an extra-curricular incident produced the first slight tremor of the coming collapse. Given an opportunity by the surface cordiality of interracial social relations in the Cornwall environment, a romantic attachment developed between John Ridge and Sarah Bird Northrup, daughter of the school steward.

John felt no hesitation in asking for his beloved's hand in marriage. The Cherokee had not yet been made to suffer by any sense of racial inferiority. For generations their men had fought white men with results of which they had never needed to feel ashamed and as recently as their last war their military prowess had excelled that of Jackson's white militia. For as many generations their women had been sought in marriage by so many distinguished white officers, officials and traders that through the veins of many Cherokee leaders ran more white than Indian blood. John had witnessed his father being acclaimed by white generals as a great soldier and had himself been received by governors, senators and presidents. Since coming to Cornwall there had been no home unready to accept him as an honored guest. There was some evidence that Sarah's mother had actively encouraged his courtship. The Northrup family's initial hesitation appeared to rest not so much on the ground that their daughter's suitor was an Indian as that he had been attacked by an illness that required him to use crutches. There was the temporizing suggestion that the young lovers wait until the prospective bridegroom had recovered his health.

John Ridge withdrew to his father's plantation home to recuperate. When he returned to Cornwall in January, 1824, he was accompanied by his statuesque, broadcloth-clad, beaver-hatted father. The Indian statesman-commander and his heir made their entry in state in an ornate coach with four white horses driven by a liveried coachman. These evidences of wealth and rank impressed Yankee viewers. There were few surface indications of community disapproval when the marriage was forthwith solemnized. If there was some covert uneasiness about this ultimate flaunting of racial tolerance there was also a practical inclination to conclude that Sarah had made a sensible choice inasmuch as she had married a fortune.

The newlyweds set out by coach for the bridegroom's ancestral home in Georgia. It was not until some weeks after their departure that the slowly gathering storm suddenly broke. Conservative Isaiah Bunce, editor of *The American Eagle* of neighboring Litchfield, had for some time been increasingly troubled by the missionary craze which seemed to him to be becoming an improvident depletion of New England's substance and a violation of New England's common sense. The Ridge-Northrup nuptials appeared to him an opportunity to strike a long-invited blow at what he considered to be the excesses of the missionary movement. In raising the explosive miscegenation question in his issue of March 22, 1824, he directed his attack not on the participants but on the august sponsors of the Cornwall school. The opening editorial in his campaign was a thunderous, sensation-seeking blast that convulsed Connecticut opinion:

The affliction, mortification and disgrace, of the relatives of the young woman, who is only about sixteen years old . . . will, it is believed, on examination be found to be the fruit of the *missionary spirit,* and caused by the conduct of the clergymen at that place and its vicinity, who are agents and superintend the school. And though we shrink from recording the name of the female thus throwing herself into the arms of an Indian yet, "daring to do all that may become a man or a christian," we hesitate not to name those believed to be either mediately or immediately the cause of the unnatural connection; they are, Rev. Dr. Lyman Beecher, Rev. Timothy Stone, Rev. Charles Prentice, Rev. Joseph Harvey, and Rev. Hermann Daggett . . . And the relatives of the girl, or the people of Cornwall, or the public at large, who feel indignant at the transaction, some of whom have said that the girl ought to be publicly whipped, the Indian hung, and the mother drown'd, will do well to trace the thing to its true cause, and see whether the men above named, or their system, are not the authors of the transaction as a new kind of *missionary machinery.*

This undisguised appeal to race prejudice and even to mob violence elicited no remonstrance from the community so flagrantly indicted. Bunce appeared to have shrewdly estimated the effect of his timing and his subject, along with the temper of the Connecticut public. Lyman Beecher and his fellow members of the school's Board of Agents who had been directly assaulted made no move to defend their conduct and instead hastened to agree with Bunce's thesis. Whether or not this was their intention, the eminent clergymen were conforming to the reaction of their flocks. Whoever read *The Eagle* had been compelled to take stock of his moral and spiritual principles. The missionary enthusiasm that had recently swept New England had been dedicated to the saving of heathen souls. The endeavor had been endowed with a special piquancy in that it had been devoted to people of another color who inhabited remote, exotic lands. But the calculated virulence of the editor's charge had startlingly revealed that the Puritan heart harbored other passions than piety. Once forced to face all the implications of the ethical problem, both congregation and community realized by how far their recognition of the brotherhood of the church fell short of an acceptance of the brotherhood of man. The Agents' reply was therefore hailed as a justified expression of the only point of view possible. Their formal statement deplored racial intermarriage, characterized the one that had occurred as an isolated phenomenon which the Agents could assure the public would not be repeated, and sternly forbade any future contemplation of such unions by any person in any way connected with the Cornwall school.

With most of the wind spilled from his sails, Bunce still persisted in his harassment of the missionary movement with the published charge that "females" of Cornwall were "receiving" foreign students "as the most favored gallants, and beaux, and the topknot of gentry; while the young men of the town, poor white boys, were often cast into the shade by their colored and tawny rivals." The somewhat tepid retort of the young men of Cornwall was to hold a meeting in which they passed a resolution, stating: "we do not fear that . . . imputed partiality on the part of the young ladies here . . . will . . . compel us, Isaac-like, to go out of town for female helpers" and "though we do not profess to be 'ladies' men, still we spurn at (sic) the intimation that we have been cast into the shade, by our rivals, white or tawny." A more serious counter to the charge that Cornwall girls were continuing to prefer the companionship of non-white students was advanced in an open letter signed by eight heads of leading Cornwall families, declaring: "With the best opportunity to know the truth in this case, we fully believe that such assertions as have appeared in your paper upon this subject are not *facts;* we deny that they are facts; and, in our turn, assert that they are *base fabrication.*"

One of the signers of this letter was Benjamin Gold, a prosperous farmer-merchant, who had two marriageable daughters. His father had been a minister, a son had been educated for the ministry at Yale, two of his daughters had married clergymen and he himself was a deacon and a member of the Board of Agents of the Cornwall mission school. The letter of indignant protest had scarcely been published before his 19-year-old daughter, Harriet, asked his permission to marry Elias Boudinot. Elias had completed his term of instruction at Cornwall three years before to go on to Andover and then home to his people but he and Harriet had continued to correspond. The gist of her appeal to her parents was that she was determined to become a missionary and could conceive of no more appropriate field than among the Cherokee as the wife of a leading Cherokee to whom she was personally devoted.

Gold was thunderstruck. Both he and Harriet's mother expressed their adamant opposition. That winter Harriet became so ill that she seemed at the point of death. In the hope of reviving her desire to live, her distracted parents promised to consent to the marriage were she to recover. During her long convalescence the project was kept a closely guarded secret but the necessity of preparing the various connections of the Gold family for the eventuality led to a disclosure of the situation in June of 1825. Revelation of Harriet's intentions provided a far greater sensation than had Bunce's editorial denunciation of the already half-forgotten Ridge-Northrup marriage. The community seethed with disapproving fury. The Board of Agents of the Cornwall mission school, where the two had met, with no hesitation and great indignation pronounced their sweeping judgment. Lyman Beecher and his clergyman associates issued a special report, declaring:

We . . . feel it to be our duty as honest men, to say to the public, that we have recently become acquainted with the fact, that a negociation for a marriage has been carried on secretly between Elias Boudinot, a young Cherokee, who left school with a good character, almost three years since, and has never returned, and Harriet R. Gold of this village; and that this negociation which has been carried on by secret and covered correspondence, has now become a settled engagement between the parties . . . we feel ourselves bound to say, that after the unequivocal disapprobation of such connexions, expressed by the Agents, and by the christian public universally, we regard those who have engaged in or accessory to this transaction, as criminal; as offering insult to the known feelings of the christian community; and as sporting with the sacred interests of this charitable institution. For those who have been guilty of this outrage upon public feeling, we can offer no apology; all we have to request is that the christian public will not condemn the innocent with the guilty: nor associate in their just censure, those who have been laboring to prevent this evil, with those who have thus induced it.

During the ensuing months, while Harriet's health improved and her plans matured, frantically insistent pressures were imposed on her by her family and relatives, by friends of the family, by fellow inhabitants of the region and by representative members of the Connecticut clergy, including all of the teachers and ministers with whom she had been since childhood associated. Distant strangers wrote her long letters denouncing her wickedness. No single voice, near or far, was raised in her defense. The chorus of vituperation stressed particularly the imperative necessity that she realized that what she was doing constituted a monstrous disservice not only to the missionary movement but to the cause of Christianity itself. She remained not only unmoved but serene. Her father, though he continued to disapprove of her course as strongly as when he had first learned of her resolve, declined to retract the promise given on what he had thought was her deathbed. When in the early spring of 1826 Elias Boudinot came north to claim his bride Cornwall's excitement had become frenzied. Members of the choir in which Harriet had once sung wore crape. An effigy representing her corpse, intended to indicate that in the estimation of the community she was dead, was burned in the village square, her own brother lighting the fire. Demonstrations and protest meetings became so turbulent that the Golds feared physical attack. Harriet was for a time hidden in the house of a friend. But the community's fury appeared spent by the time the actual marriage took place. The ceremony, March 28, 1826, in the Gold home was not interrupted. Still fearful of violence, Benjamin Gold accompanied the young couple as far as Washington on

their journey homeward.[3] The Cornwall mission school had been
consumed in the flame of its supporters' emotions. It was never
again to open its doors. For the people of Cornwall and Litchfield
the episode soon receded into the past to be all but forgotten. But
for the Cherokee people it had provided a grim portent of the
multiplicity of future dangers besetting the road toward their
acceptance as citizens of the republic. Perceptive and articulate
Elias Boudinot was carrying to his homeland more than a white
bride. He was also carrying a warning that, when subjected to the
stress of personal involvement, racial prejudice could become as
rampant among their declared friends in the north as among their
avowed enemies in the south.

If in her last months in her former home Harriet had endured
strains and torments which must have crushed any young woman
of less spirit and purpose, she was rewarded and reassured by her
experiences in her new home in her husband's country. Instead of
being confronted by the pagan scenes and heathen customs she
had expected she found herself in an intellectual atmosphere
reminiscent in many ways of her own New England. Her closest
associates were fellow teachers and fellow missionaries. The preoccupation of all around her, as well as of all Cherokee she met,
was with the self-improvement possible by reliance on education
and religion. Many of her Cherokee friends, particularly those of
her generation, were well enough educated to have developed
similar cultural tastes and to turn as eagerly as she to the latest
arriving package of new periodicals or new books. At the Cherokee
churches she attended she sat with congregations, dressed in conventional clothing, who had come in carriages to listen to Cherokee preachers and Cherokee choirs with the services usually conducted in English. Meanwhile by correspondence and a constant
stream of sympathetic visitors she was able to keep in touch with a
widening circle of church workers, educators and well-wishers in
the north who were beginning to regard her career with as much
approbation as they did Cherokee aspirations. Her dwelling was a
mission and a school as well as a home. In it she found her
opportunities for missionary service both more pleasant and more
successful than she had dared hope. Even in worldly details she
found her new existence reminiscent of her past. She lived in a

---

3 See Ralph Henry Gabriel's *Elias Boudinot*, Norman, 1941, for much fascinating
detail on this early 19th century outbreak of racism in New England.

comfortable, well-furnished frame house. Food was plentiful and varied. Her husband's means permitted the frequent entertainment of 18 or 20 guests. Everywhere beyond her threshold the stir of progress was evident. New mills, ferries, bridges, taverns and homes were under construction. Heavily laden freighters' wagons, the 12-horse semi-weekly stage, droves of cattle and throngs of travelers crowded the Federal Road crossing the Cherokee country from Nashville to Augusta. Most of her Cherokee neighbors in and around the Cherokee capital, New Echota, lived under conditions as comfortable as did her household and were as intent on their own improvement and the education of their children as could be the most thrifty and forward-looking New Englander. Several were more prosperous than the Ridges or the Waties. They owned even larger plantations and finer houses and were served by greater numbers of slaves, servants and retainers. Her parents, paying a dubious visit to learn how she was doing, discovered all of their concern relieved and, during a prolonged stay, wrote family and friends in Connecticut highly approving comment on the success with which both Harriet and the Cherokee were managing their affairs. Finally, in her choice of a mate she could not in New England or anywhere have found one with whom she had more interests in common. Elias Boudinot was as literate and devout as she, a graduate of Andover, an accomplished orator and a public-spirited servant of his people who had in the first years of their life together become a distinguished editor with a nationwide reputation. Hers was a happy and successful marriage in which she bore her husband six children before her untimely death after ten years of service in the field she had chosen.[4]

Harriet Gold's Cherokee experience vividly highlighted the amazing advance made by the Cherokee in the 1820's. By the intensive education of their children and their versatile readiness to adapt themselves to a totally different way of life they had undertaken to become Americans. They had very nearly succeeded.

[4] After Boudinot's death his white second wife, Delight Sargent Boudinot, took all of his children, with the encouragement and assistance of the Gold family, to New England to be educated. Some remained in New England and others returned to the Cherokee. Several contracted New England marriages. As a result there were Boudinots serving on opposite sides in the Civil War. One was killed before Richmond. Another was a delegate to the Confederate Congress.

No people may hope to retain that vitality which alone can preserve their essential qualities as a people once their development has become totally dependent upon a borrowed culture. The threat becomes the more ominous when the foreign culture they have elected to assimilate is borrowed not from friendly neighbors but from a mortal enemy. Yet, in spite of the avidity with which they had sought white education and white religion, the Cherokee managed to avoid the fatal pitfall. A sudden renaissance of their national self-esteem gave them the virility to survive the terrifying ordeal that was approaching. This saving grace was entirely due to the emergence among them of an authentic genius, Sequoyah. Unprepared, unadvised and unaided, after years of lonely, dedicated effort, he invented, developed and perfected a system of signs and letters by which the sounds and meanings of Cherokee speech might be transcribed as a written language. In all human history there is recorded no example of innate and untutored intellectual capacity to parallel this extraordinary achievement.

Sequoyah was as representative of Cherokee mind and character as a single individual could be of any people. If in blood he was part white, as were many upper-class Cherokee, in background, training and experience he was traditionally Indian to an almost aboriginal degree. His mother was Wurteh, sister of Old Tassel, head chief of the Cherokee during the Revolution, and of Doublehead, successor to Dragging Canoe as most violent exponent of implacable antagonism to white settlement. Among her nephews were Young Tassel (John Watts), Cherokee field commander in the culminating campaigns of the Indian wars and Bench, notorious along the American frontier from the James to the Mississippi for his terroristic exploits. Old Tassel himself had on the other hand devoted his influence as political spokesman for the Cherokee to the seeking of peace, thus carrying on the tradition of his great predecessor, Attakullaculla, who had striven for 40 years to keep the peace between the races. Old Tassel's pacific labors had been tragically terminated in 1788 when, after entering American lines by invitation under a flag of truce to discuss peace terms, he, together with four companion ambassadors, had been axed by American frontiersmen. It was perhaps indicative of Sequoyah's political philosophy that while there remains no record of his ever having expatiated on the subject of his uncle's murder he was reported to have been inordinately fond of describing in emotional detail the occasion, which he had been privileged to witness as a child, of an Iroquois-Shawnee delegation's visit to the Cherokee in 1776 to confirm the alliance which had succeeded three quarters of a century of war between northern and southern Indians. To him Indian history was more deeply concerned with relations among Indians than with relations with alien whites.

On his paternal side his white lineage was as distinguished as his Indian. His grandfather was Christopher Gist, famed explorer of Kentucky and companion of Washington's winter journey to warn the French away from the Ohio. His father, Nathaniel Gist, was dispatched by Washington after Braddock's defeat to summon Cherokee help against their then avowed enemies, the northern Indians. As a consequence of his embassy a contingent of more than a hundred Cherokee warriors under the command of Ostenaco, later noted for his visit with Timberlake to London, came north to aid Washington in his desperate defense of Virginia's northwest frontier.[1] For the next 15 years Nathaniel Gist periodi-

[1] The vagaries of Cherokee diplomacy bear comparison with the eccentricities of Europe's international relations. They were hostile to Spain from De Soto's time, Spain's ally after the Revolution, contracted alliances with the earliest English colonists in the Carolinas, engaged in war with the northern Indians from 1710 to 1770, opposed French penetration south of the Ohio from 1740 to 1763, were England's ally from 1730 to 1759, fought a violent war with England in 1760–61, became England's ally again during the Revolution, fought the United States from 1776 to 1794, became an ally of the United States in 1813–14 and had meanwhile fought innumerable sporadic wars with their Creek and Chickasaw neighbors.

cally left his North Carolina home on the Yadkin to trade with the
Cherokee. He won their affection as had no other white man
except John Stuart, the remarkable British administrator who had
survived the Fort Loudon massacre to become the vigorous champion of Indian rights. It was during one of these visits, some of
which lasted for years, that Gist contracted the marriage with
Wurteh which produced Sequoyah.[2] At the outbreak of the Revolution, Gist, devoted to both sides, strove for Cherokee-American
peace with a diligence that for a time gained him the suspicion of
both. With the onset of the American-Cherokee War in 1776 he
entered the American service in which he became colonel in
command of a regiment known as Gist's. At the end of the
Revolution he married Judith Cary Bell of Virginia and in 1793
moved to Kentucky to lands granted him for his Revolutionary
services. There was other testimony than the intellect of Sequoyah
to the vigor of the Gist blood line. Among Nathaniel Gist's white
descendants were Montgomery Blair, postmaster general in Lin-
coln's cabinet, Francis Preston Blair, Jr., United States Senator,
Civil War major general and 1868 Democratic candidate for vice-
president and B. Gratz Brown, 1872 Democratic vice-presidential
candidate.

The date of Sequoyah's birth has never been satisfactorily established. It has generally been set as early as 1760 though so early a
date, as Grant Foreman, his principal biographer[3] pointed out
critically, would have meant that he was 53 when he enlisted in
Jackson's Creek campaign and 55 when he married in 1815. At the
other possible extreme he must have been born long enough
before Nathaniel Gist left the Cherokee country at the outbreak of
the Revolution to have witnessed the 1776 Iroquois-Shawnee-
Cherokee conference which made so profound an impression upon
him. In whatever event he was reared by his mother with whom he
lived alone in an isolated cabin near the ruins of Fort Loudon. He
had grown to manhood long before the establishment of the
earliest mission school and at no time in his career did he make
any attempt to learn either spoken or written English. All of his

2 For long there was doubt about Sequoyah's paternity. Gist family records appear,
however, to offer conclusive evidence. There are mentions, for example, of visits
paid by Sequoyah in later life to the Gist home in Kentucky upon which occasions he was acknowledged as Nathaniel's son.

3 Foreman, Grant. *Sequoyah*. Norman, 1938.

more formative years were shadowed by the terrors and privations of the 18-year-long war between the Cherokee and the Americans, by the periodic invasions and devastations of the Cherokee country by American armies and by the retaliatory raiding of the American frontier by Cherokee war parties. There is no record of his personal participation in these campaigns but his service in the Creek War clearly indicated that he must have had prior military experience. At some unrecorded stage of his career he had suffered an injury, whether from disease, battle wound or hunting accident, which caused him to walk with a pronounced limp.

He was not, however, by preference a warrior and only in moments of national emergency did he accept the responsibilities of political leadership. His personal predilection was for the arts. Early in life he became a skilled silversmith, the first accomplished practitioner of the craft among the Cherokee. His designs ran to embossed armbands, gorgets and other ornaments highly prized by his fellow Cherokee. He was also a talented painter. Having never seen a camel's hair brush or a tube of paint, he had contrived his own brushes by using the hair of wild animals and his own pigments from concoctions of earth and plants. He was noted for his spirited picturization of animals though his portraits were also described as true and lively. But in spite of his artistic bent, which represented a novelty in Cherokee culture, he remained in all other respects firmly committed to Cherokee traditionalism. As long as it was possible he supported his family by hunting and trapping and only turned to farming with the greatest reluctance. In the early years of the century, when there was a bitter cleavage among Cherokee between progressives and conservatives he adhered to the more primitive faction which was opposed to the adoption of white ways. To escape the solicitations of the more civilized Cherokee who were concentrated in the northern section of the Cherokee country he moved to Cherokee lands in Alabama where he could feel more detached from white contacts. For all his devotion to the Cherokee past and his accompanying patriotic regard for the Cherokee homeland he sympathized with the tendency of the more primitive Cherokee to migrate to the west in order to withdraw a still greater distance from white associations. In 1818 he himself joined the migration and after 1821 made his permanent home among the West Cherokee.

It was this instinctively primitive Indian, who had led a secluded life shielded from all outside influences, who proved capable of one of the most original intellectual achievements of all time. It was an achievement rooted in the depths of his devotion to his people. Indians had long been acutely aware that the most decisive advantage possessed by their white adversaries was their ability to transmit their words to any distance, to pool the accumulation of their knowledge for the benefit of all and to maintain a permanent record of their more productive acts and ideas. There was even a popular Indian myth that in the beginning the Creator had bestowed a book on his first and favorite creation, the Indian, and that his secondary work, the white man, had stolen the book and left in its place the bow and arrow for the use of his deprived rival. In spite of his deliberate avoidance of white associations Sequoyah's native intelligence made him painfully conscious of this supreme advantage enjoyed by the white man. According to one Cherokee account, he became so irritated by the boasting of a nephew who was learning to write the white man's language at the Moravian school that he declared Indians were just as capable of learning to write their own language were they to choose to make the effort.

Whatever the immediate incentive, in 1809 he dedicated himself to the enormous task of proving this assertion to be true. The difficulties standing in his way were increased to the verge of impossibility by the peculiar complexities of the Cherokee language which had developed from antiquity as a haphazard conglomeration of sounds each referring like a pointing finger to a thing, an action, an attribute or a sensation. Its vocabulary extended over an almost infinite range of ramifications. There was a different word for every aspect of any object. Verbs had many excessively variant forms, some more than 200. The Moravians, with world-wide and century-old experience in dealing with strange languages, had been unable after years of effort to hit upon any pattern that might lead toward a transposition of spoken Cherokee into an intelligible written form. The early New England missionaries, armed by their linguistic training in Latin and Greek, were likewise baffled. It was left to Sequoyah, without the slightest background of formal training, to solve a problem that had so long confounded professional etymologists.

In the initial stages of his 12-year-long struggle he resorted to the representation of each spoken word by a pictograph. This was a process the preliminary rudiments of which were not totally unknown to Indians. Most Indians north of Mexico were accustomed, to a limited degree, to record simple and easily identified ideas by crude, usually representational, drawings. Likewise, in the almost universal Indian sign language manual gestures and facial grimaces, also imitative, were used to express thoughts visually. Sequoyah's growing array of pictographs was an immensely elaborated extension of these simple efforts in representationalism. He had never seen or heard of Egypt's hieroglyphics or China's characters but he was instinctively taking the course by which those early written languages had evolved. His work was handicapped by a lack of writing materials such as pens and paper and he was obliged to scratch his symbols on sheets of bark. He was not discouraged as the dimensions of his task began to become increasingly apparent and the multiplicity of Cherokee words continued to indicate that he must rely upon a totally unworkable multiplicity of pictographs. He was not content, as must have been the original Egyptian and Chinese scribes, to develop a writing so complex that it could be mastered only by scholars. He was seeking an ordinary language for ordinary Cherokee people.

He became so absorbed in his effort that he neglected his farm and his family. To escape his scolding wife he built a hut some distance from his home and made this his study, his solitary laboratory. Gradually word of what he was attempting had spread through the nation. He became the butt of general scorn and derision. He was believed to have lost his wits. The idea that an unlettered Cherokee could presume in the privacy of his cabin to learn to write a language that had never before been written was considered utterly preposterous. He became a national joke. People trooped to his threshold not to voice interest or encouragement but to laugh. Some of his neighbors became more seriously concerned. Conceiving that his preoccupation must be devoted to witchcraft, they burned his hut together with his entire accumulation of records, studies and experiments. He rebuilt it and patiently resumed his work.

His labors were interrupted by his 1813–14 service in the Cherokee army, by his 1816 attendance at Jackson's Turkeytown

conference and by his 1818 journey to see for himself the nature of
the Arkansas country. But always he returned to his single-pur-
posed concentration on his project. He at last was beginning to see
some light. By a triumph of analytical reasoning he had determined that all Cherokee spoken words were composed of various
combinations of some 80-odd phonetic syllables. A list of symbols
representing these syllables could therefore, he was beginning to
believe, approximate a functional alphabet permitting the transposition of spoken Cherokee into written Cherokee. Though he
had still paid no attention to English he had chanced to come into
possession of an English speller. From this he copied the English
letters, added to the list by using some of the letters in reversed or
inverted positions and further added to it symbols of his own
contrivance until he had built his table of characters to the
required 85. A particularly ingenious refinement in his syllabary
permitted the discretionary attachment of the character representing the "s" sound, so frequent in spoken Cherokee, to any other
character.

In 1821 he was at last prepared for a public revelation of his
success. A number of leading Cherokee assembled to watch the
performance. All had come prepared to scoff. He had taught no
one his novel learning, but his six-year-old daughter had glimpsed
his work with enough attention to have gathered its meaning. She
proved able to stand at a distance and read with ease any message
given to her father by the observers for written transmission to
her. The examiners were astounded but not convinced. It was felt
some sort of trickery must be involved. A more conclusive test was
organized. A group of youths unacquainted with Sequoyah was
recruited. After a few hours of his instruction they proved as able
as had been his daughter to understand his written messages. The
incredulous chiefs were converted by this conclusive demonstration. The sensational news spread through the nation. There was
no Cherokee who did not feel the impulse to stand straighter. The
stupendous advantage enjoyed by the white man was no longer
unique. From now on the Cherokee, too, could read and write, not
in a borrowed language but in his own native tongue.

What immediately ensued was no less a miracle than had been
Sequoyah's achievement. Within a matter of months Cherokee by
the hundreds and then by the thousands had learned to practice

the new knowledge. The speed with which use was made of the invention was largely due to a special facet of Indian intelligence. The way of life the Indian had inherited from countless generations of ancestors had led him to rely on memory by visual association. All the demands upon his perceptivity involved in the pursuit of game, the tactics of war in a forest, the practical make-do incidentals of daily existence had developed in him a facility in detecting the functional relationships among everything that he handled or observed or sensed. Once he had noted the relationship between one of Sequoyah's symbols and a meaningful sound he himself had been from infancy accustomed to utter it became fixed in his memory. There were recorded instances of Cherokee becoming proficient in the new technique in several days. The dullest neophyte needed no more than a few weeks.

No language schools were organized. None was needed. The aspiring student required only a single sheet upon which Sequoyah's syllabary was inscribed. He took it home with him to share the fascinating accomplishment with his family and his community. The English education available in the mission schools had been most often sought by the offspring of the more progressive and prosperous. It was among the less advanced two thirds of the nation that Sequoyah's gift was received as a supreme boon. Within three years the ability to read and write their own language was general among even the most backward Cherokee. Returning to the Arkansas, Sequoyah disseminated the new learning among the migrant colonists who had tended from the beginning to stem from the more primitive elements of the nation. One of the first and most significant consequences of his accomplishment was that soon East and West Cherokee were able to communicate in writing, to keep each section informed of the other's problems and thus to coordinate their relations with the United States.

By a remarkable coincidence Sequoyah's invention had become available to his people at the very moment the sudden Cherokee interest in English education was becoming manifest. Thereafter these two main currents of Cherokee self-improvement proceeded in conjunction, each serving the other. The missionaries were quick to realize the value of the new capacity. Formerly they had been unable satisfactorily to translate religious writings into Cherokee. Now this could be done. Formerly they had been almost hopelessly impeded in carrying their message to more primitive Cherokee communities by the language barrier. Now this had been lowered. Sequoyah had envisaged his work as a contribution to the revitalization of Cherokee native culture. In this he had succeeded but he had also inadvertently succeeded in materially assisting the collateral processes of English education and Protestant evangelism.

The attitude of American missionaries was of the utmost importance to Cherokee aspirations. Backed by funds raised by churches and by federal support, they were presiding over many current phases of Cherokee advancement. Most were sincerely and primarily devoted to Cherokee interest. Of the many who had dedicated their energies to Cherokee improvement Samuel Austin Worcester was to have the greatest impact on Cherokee fortunes.

He was a graduate of the University of Vermont who, like Elias Boudinot, had taken his religious training at Andover but who, unlike his fellow alumnus, whose immediate ancestors had been savages, had sprung from an unbroken line of eight Congregational clergymen. His uncle, Samuel Worcester, had been one of the founders of the American Board of Commissioners for Foreign Missions who had died at Brainerd on an 1821 inspection tour. The younger Samuel Worcester had long contemplated his personal call to the Cherokee mission field with a zeal as enthusiastic and as resolute as had been Harriet Gold's. Accompanied by his bride, Ann Orr, he reached Brainerd October 21, 1825, shortly before his Andover classmate, Elias Boudinot, set out on his venturesome expedition north to claim his New England bride. Sensing the potential advantage of working in collaboration with an influential Cherokee as literate as Boudinot, Worcester in 1827 arranged a transfer to New Echota where the two like-minded young couples were neighbors embarked upon an intimate association as personally congenial as it was professionally effective. It was a relationship particularly comforting to Harriet whose direct participation in educational and missionary work was so frequently impaired by the regularity with which she was bearing children.

In coming to the Cherokee, Worcester had been obsessed by the need to succeed, where all others had failed, in developing a

Cherokee written language so that instruction, both religious and secular, might become so much more available than it could be if restricted to English. He was overjoyed to discover that the key fashioned by Sequoyah was already awaiting his hand. In collaboration with Boudinot he foresaw the succession of doors it might unlock. The two young enthusiasts began to plan a project involving the eventual translation of the best of the world's literature into Cherokee. As a start, Worcester successfully petitioned the American Board for funds to cast the characters of Sequoyah's syllabary in type so that the Bible might be printed in Cherokee.

The Cherokee Legislative Council had a more immediate and practical view. In 1825 it voted an authorization to establish a printing press in New Echota for the primary purpose of publishing a Cherokee newspaper. The Council had at its disposal insufficient funds for the project, however, and in 1826 delegated Boudinot to make a tour of the north, particularly of his religious and educational contacts, to seek contributions under an arrangement that stipulated early repayment by the Council. His effort proved a striking success. Large audiences in Philadelphia and New York were enthralled by his eloquent accounts of Cherokee progress. Donations poured in. Worcester procured a press in Boston. The eagerly awaited mechanical blessing at length arrived by sea and wagon. Paper was brought from Knoxville. A deerskin bag stuffed with wool served as inking pad. The imported journeyman printers knew neither a word of Cherokee nor the meaning of the Cherokee characters. But the urgent effort persisted and the first issue of the *Cherokee Phoenix,* printed in both English and Sequoyah's Cherokee, appeared February 21, 1828. Boudinot was its editor and Worcester his principal advisor.

In this first issue the *Phoenix* defined its editorial policy by announcing in both languages that:

The laws and public documents of the Nation, and matters relating to the welfare and condition of the Cherokees as a people, will be faithfully published in English and Cherokee.

Then it added succinctly:

We will invariably state the will of the majority of our people on the subject of the present controversy with Georgia, and the present removal policy of the United States Government.

This first newspaper to be published by Indians in an Indian language aroused intense and sympathetic interest generally in the United States and throughout the world. In adjoining Georgia and Alabama this new evidence of Indian presumption stirred new animosities. In every area it signalized as could have no other event the extraordinary progress toward enlightenment being made by the Cherokee. But for the Cherokee the achievement had a deeper meaning. The publication of books and newspapers on their own press and in their own language was a monument not only to Sequoyah's intellect but to their intellect as a people. They were immensely reassured. Their national confidence was reinvigorated. They felt that they had justified their demand to be recognized as a distinct and free people. They had been reminded as no success in war had reminded them that they need feel no compulsion to recognize any inherent inferiority to whites. No one had ever doubted that they were as brave. Now no one could doubt that they were as intelligent. All the meanings and nuances of their ancestral language, all the common memories that made them a people and all the accumulated traditions of their native culture could henceforth be captured and preserved with the fidelity that had always before been reserved to the whites. There had been left no field in which they could not feel that they had demonstrated that they were the white man's equal.

7

The Cherokee were engaged in an unprecedented effort to move from barbarism to civilization in the brief span of half a generation. They were taking incredibly effective steps in that direction. They were managing the irksome transition to a subsistence based on agriculture and commerce. They had opened their minds to education. The invention of their own written language had preserved them from sacrificing to the effort their self-respect as a people. One even more difficult step remained to be taken were their striving not to falter in midcareer. They must learn to govern themselves. Their freedom as a people could be kept secure only by the just care with which their citizens' freedom was guarded, yet defined and limited to an extent permitting united and coherent action. This required a scrupulous balancing of values which no people has ever fully achieved and in which no people had ever so signally failed as the Indian.

The foundation principle of Indian government had always been the rejection of government. The freedom of the individual was regarded by practically all Indians north of Mexico as a canon infinitely more precious than the individual's duty to his community or nation. This anarchistic attitude ruled all behavior, beginning with the smallest social unit, the family. The Indian parent was constitutionally reluctant to discipline his children. Their every exhibition of self-will was accepted as a favorable indication of the development of maturing character. From his childhood onward the Indian was schooled by his every experience to consider his most passing whim the one criterion to which his conduct need conform.

It was grudgingly admitted that a certain degree of extemporized accommodation and collaboration was necessary if people were to live together in even the loosest sort of association. The political device to meet this necessity was the intermittent assembling of a council which might be attended by the fellow inhabitants of a community, by the representatives of the several communities comprising a nation or by delegates from two or more nations obliged to deal with diplomatic relations among friends or enemies. Whoever attended a council was eligible to raise his voice though there was a natural disposition to listen with more respect to the elder who had acquired wisdom by long experience, to the warrior who had proved his martial capacity, to the orator who had the gift of forceful expression or to the conjuror who was conceived to have demonstrated the efficacy of his magic. The primary function of the council was to provide a forum for a general exchange of views relative to any current problem so that each individual attending might have the assistance of this information in coming to his own decision on what he should do under the circumstances. There were no means other than the influence of public opinion by which the council's consensus, even when supported by an overwhelming majority, could be made binding upon any individual. The shrewdly observant Moravian missionary, John Heckewelder, left an appreciation of the effectiveness of Indian government under original and ideal conditions:

Thus has been maintained for ages, without convulsions and without civil discords, this traditional government, of which the world, perhaps, does not offer another example; a government in which there are no positive laws, but only long established habits and customs, no code of jurisprudence, but the experience of former times, no magistrates, but advisers, to whom the people, nevertheless, pay a willing and implicit obedience, in which age confers rank, wisdom gives power, and moral goodness secures a title to universal respect.

The Indian was not totally unaware of the need for more practical leadership to deal with the requirements of certain occasions. The community required a spokesman for its interests when they chanced to conflict with those of neighbors. No war party could hope for success without the direction of a captain. The cure of sickness sometimes required the application of a specialist's skills. Even a deer drive needed a head huntsman to coordinate the effort. Leaders at all of these levels of responsibility were elevated by common recognition of their apparent merit. They fell into three major categories.

There was the political chief who conducted the community's relations with other communities. There was the war chief whose former victories had led his companion warriors to conclude he might continue to prove fortunate. And there was the prophet or conjuror whose claimed supernatural powers were deemed capable of dealing with illness, witchcraft and divination. No chief gained his distinction by formal selection or inherited rank. He gained it by common consent as a result of the force of his personality or the example of his deeds and he retained his eminence only so long as he could command willing followers. Indian government included no laws to require obedience to leaders, no courts or judges to regulate the behavior of the individual. If any citizen elected to continue his private pursuits in an hour of community crisis this was considered his privilege. In the rare instances of personal offenses or breaches of the peace such as theft or assault, the duty to punish, usually on an eye for an eye scale, devolved upon the aggrieved victim's kinsmen. By no exercise of authority by council, chiefs or public opinion could the individual's freedom of decision and action be abridged. If offended by community ostracism, he had only to pack up his few belongings and set off with his family to another hunting ground or another community. Due to a low birth rate's restrictions on the normal growth of population even enemy nations were ordinarily glad to welcome and adopt such migrants.

The indulgence of a political system which subjected the citizen's conduct to no guidance more peremptory than his own wish to find favor in the eyes of his neighbors was well enough adapted to Indian needs during the pre-discovery period when he was the continent's sole occupant. Probably in recent millenniums a people has never lived under circumstances permitting each person to lead a life rendered so pleasantly satisfying by freedom from those restraints which in most societies circumscribe the individual's self-expression. With most nations separated from their neighbors by hundreds of miles of wilderness there was ample room for such freedom. But there was no room for these indulgences after the arrival of the white man presented threats with which only an organized and authoritative response could cope. These were no longer crises which could be met either by a community, only a fraction of whose warriors chanced at any given moment to feel inclined to rally to the community's defense, or by a nation which could seldom summon the resolution to move to the assistance of an ally. The new danger which the Indian was failing to repel was from an altogether new enemy capable of preparing plans long in advance, accumulating stores of supplies and then launching attacks by disciplined armies under trained commanders invested with absolute authority. The rate of Indian downfall was possibly as much accelerated by his nearly total lack of political discipline as by the superiority of the white man's weapons and the deadliness of the white man's diseases.

The traditional forms of Cherokee government had from the earliest white contacts with them been comparable to those of other Indian nations. They held the same town and national councils, with no authority more compelling than that arising from the provision of a forum for the exchange of views. They acknowledged the same two principal leaders, a political chief and a war chief, each elevated to his position of influence by a general recognition of his virtues. There was some difference in the Cherokee political and social system in the relatively high station afforded women. As with most Indians, pedigree was traced through the mother's line. But the Cherokee woman could also own property. At marriage her husband came to live in her house. Their children were considered more hers than his. She was in effect the head of the family. She had been free to choose her husband, could change husbands at will and was subject to no penalty for adultery. She could speak as an equal in council. Exceptional women became influential councillors, noted warriors and even military commanders. Such memorable women were invested with the title *Gighau* which possessed the combined connotation of War Woman, Beautiful Woman and Beloved Woman. The relative equality of Cherokee women in rank and privileges probably contributed to the sustained vigor with which the Cherokee for centuries maintained their independence in their mountain homeland. They had in a sense doubled the manpower of the Cherokee state. Their personal freedom also permitted the prevalence of intermarriages with white officers and traders which introduced an important element of strength into Cherokee society.

The Cherokee had had one early experience with the more sophisticated and authoritative principles of white government in a form actually more intricate than had ever been practised in Europe. In 1736 Christian Priber, a German Jesuit who had successively failed to find asylum for his political and social theories in Germany, England and South Carolina, turned up among the Cherokee. He was already fluent in Latin, Greek, German, French, Spanish and English and he quickly learned to speak Cherokee. The Cherokee were captivated by his novel doctrine, which, after all, represented not too many departures from many of their own economic attitudes, and for several years his advice was sought and accepted on every occasion. A visiting French trader described the idealized communal system Priber was pressing upon the Cherokee:

. . . in his republic there would be no superiority; that all should be equal there; that he would take superintendence of it only for the honor of establishing it; that otherwise his condition would not be different from that of the others; that the lodging, furniture and clothing should be equal and uniform as well as the life; that all goods should be held in common, and that each should work according to his talents for the good of the republic; that the women should live with the same freedom as the men; that there should be no marriage contract, and that they should be free to change husbands every day; that the children who should be born should belong to the republic, and be cared for and instructed in all things that their genius might be capable of acquiring; that the law of nature should be established for the sole law, and that . . . the individual was to have as his only property a chest of books and paper and ink.[1]

Priber accompanied his preaching of his communistic doctrine with a recommendation that the Cherokee recognize their principal chief as an "emperor" endowed with absolute authority. For himself he took the title "His Majesty's Secretary of State" and

---

[1] See *Journal of Antoine Bonnefoy* in Samuel Cole Williams' *Early Travels in the Tennessee Country*. Johnson City, 1928.

attempted diplomatic exchanges with France, Spain and England. English traders and Carolina authorities became apprehensive that Priber might be bringing the Cherokee under French influence. He was unquestionably obstructing English trade. The entranced Cherokee were scoffing at the remonstrances of English traders who had until his appearance been their bosom friends. They rallied so enthusiastically to his defense that a Carolina military column sent to arrest him was compelled to withdraw ignominiously under his safe conduct. Eventually he was seized by English traders while en route to consult with French authorities at Fort Toulouse and died soon afterward in a Carolina prison.

The Priber experiment in wilderness communism provided striking evidence of the un-Indian readiness of the Cherokee to consider unfamiliar ideas but the episode had no lasting influence upon their political development. An ensuing smallpox epidemic halved their population and in the terror inspired by the visitation his advocacy of a more authoritative and centralized government was forgotten. Through all the stresses of the next 80 years of intermittent war with the northern Indians, with the Creek, with France, with Spain, with England and with the United States they clung to their traditional form of government by powerless council with all the erosions of national strength by vacillation and factionalism that this entailed. It was not until the twin crisis of 1817–19, the migration of a significant portion of the nation to the Arkansas coupled with a new urgency in American demands for the cession of more land, that their more perceptive leaders began to realize that were their people to be saved from extinction a more effective form of government must be devised. Having once embarked upon this total departure from Indian political dogma Cherokee progress was as remarkable as that made by the inspired designers of a more effective American government during the period from the First Continental Congress through the Confederation to the Constitutional Convention.

The guiding hand in this extraordinary achievement was that of John Ross, who, after accepting responsibility then, continued to preside over Cherokee fortunes for the next 50 years. Though more essentially Cherokee and more single-mindedly devoted to the nation than were many of his full-blooded rivals, he himself was by birth only one-eighth Cherokee. His grandfather was John

McDonald, deputy British agent under John Stuart with station at Chickamauga, who had married Anna, the half-Indian daughter of the interpreter, William Shorey, who after surviving the Fort Loudon massacre had died while en route to England with Timberlake. The father of John Ross was Daniel Ross, a Scotch trader who had taken residence with the Cherokee before the Revolution and eventually married Mollie, John McDonald's quarter-Indian daughter. John Ross was educated at Kingston, Tennessee, by a private tutor engaged to teach the Daniel Ross children. His leadership potential won early recognition. At the age of 19 he was entrusted with a mission to the West Cherokee and at 23 he was adjutant of the Cherokee regiment serving with Jackson in the Creek War. In his youth he was briefly engaged in the business of conducting a store and operating a ferry and early in the missionary period he joined the Methodist Church, one of whose ministers, Nicholas Scales, had married his niece, Mary Coody. But from 1818 on his paramount preoccupation was public service, a service which continued during all the agonies of the removal, of the fratricidal strife between East and West Cherokee following the removal and of the Civil War which divided the Cherokee Nation as fearfully as it did the American Nation. After his death at Washington in 1866 the Cherokee in formal memorial resolutions framed his people's tribute:

No danger appalled him. He never faltered in supporting what he believed to be right, but clung to it with a steadiness of purpose which alone could have sprung from the clearest convictions of rectitude. He never sacrificed the interests of his nation to expediencey. He never lost sight of the welfare of the people. For them he labored daily for a long life, and upon them he bestowed his last expressed thoughts. A friend of law, he obeyed it; a friend of education, he faithfully encouraged schools throughout the country, and spent liberally his means in conferring it upon others. Given to hospitality, none ever hungered around his door. A professor of the Christian religion, he practiced its precepts. His works are inseparable from the history of the Cherokee people for nearly half a century, while his example in the daily walks of life will linger in the future and whisper words of hope, temperance, and charity in the years of posterity.

During the year 1817 Alabama was established as a territory and Mississippi admitted to the union as a state. Henceforth there was no white man living within hundreds of miles of the Cherokee homeland who was not assured of the protection of his local and responsible government in addition to the general protection afforded him by the United States. To the more influential class of better informed Cherokee the need to furnish comparable political guardianship to their own beleaguered people had become imperative. The first great departure from age-old Indian conceptions of government was the establishment of a permanent and functioning executive authority. On May 6, 1817 the National Council of Chiefs and Warriors representing 54 towns provided for a National Committee, of which 27-year-old John Ross was the first president, to be *elected* every two years and which during the intervals between meetings of the National Council was to have charge of "the affairs of the Cherokee Nation."

This establishment of executive power, without precedent in Indian political attitudes, coincided with the sudden eruption of Cherokee impulses to seek education and economic advancement. The nascent executive strongly encouraged this wave of progress. On October 26, 1819 the National Committee by a unanimous vote permitted residence in the nation of "schoolmasters, blacksmiths, millers, saltpetre and gunpowder manufacturers, ferrymen, turnpike keepers and mechanics."

But the great task of the newly strengthened government was to resist the pyramiding pressures of state and federal demands that all Cherokee lands in the east be exchanged for lands in the west. It was too late to stem the sweep of the tide already under way. By the February 27, 1819 treaty with the United States the Cherokee was stripped of more than half of their remaining land in North Carolina and Tennessee. The new government was resolved, however, to resist further cessions and to create a situation in which their resistance might prove effective. Resistance had formerly been stultified, as in all other nations, by the willingness of a minority or faction to negotiate sales or treaties disapproved by the majority. By an 1820 law the death penalty was provided for the unauthorized sale of land or the unauthorized negotiation of land cessions. These new-style Cherokee leaders further realized that the mere enactment of a law was not enough, that unless enforced it remained as meaningless as the majority recommendation of an old-style Indian council. They were determined that the formal laws that were for the first time being enacted by elected Indian legislators would likewise be for the first time obeyed by Indian citizens. To implement this determination, on October 20, 1820 the National Council and National Committee, assembled together in a legislative body thereafter known as the General Council, theoretically comparable in authority and responsibility to a state legislature or the Congress of the United States, provided for the division of the Cherokee country into eight districts, each with a local council house and district judge, for four circuit judges and for a "company of light horse" to enforce laws and regulate behavior. For the first time in Indian history an Indian nation had contrived a fully functioning democratic government armed with the police power to compel its citizens' obedience to its will.

The headlong rush of the Cherokee into a new world that was daily changing, a world revolving ever faster under the thrusts of education, material prosperity, the emergence of their own press, and a spate of political improvisation, was producing many unforeseen trends, some conflicting and all bewildering. One trend was that the abrupt turn toward authoritative government soon began to exhibit the moralistic tendencies that have so often marked enthusiastic reform movements. On November 18, 1822 the National Committee, "being fully convinced that no nation of people can prosper and flourish, or become magnanimous in character, the basis of whose laws are not found upon virtue and justice," prohibited bringing alcoholic spirits within three miles of National Committee meetings or court sittings and forbade card games or the introduction of cards into the country. This venture into the field of regulating the daily and ordinary behavior of individuals represented an even more fundamental revolution in Indian political thinking than had the recent vesting of authority in elected legislators, administrators and judges.

Another trend was revealed by a reassessment of the Negro's place in the nation. Having erected a functioning republic, the Cherokee were aware that a primary factor in the maintenance of a republic must be an efficacious definition of the right to citizenship. This brought to the fore the Negro problem and along with it the familiar tendency of an oppressed minority to reject tolerance of lesser minorities. The Cherokee solution of the problem represented another departure from Indian thinking. The Negro had always enjoyed a favored position in Indian regard. In every Indian nation there was a considerable proportion of Negroes. For centuries runaway slaves had found ready sanctuary in Indian towns. Thousands had been adopted and through intermarriage had merged into Indian society. Much of the instinctive sympathy between the two strains was due to the color factor. Both Indian and Negro had learned to regard the white race as their common adversary. More was due to the ingrained Indian abhorrence of slavery as an institution. In the Pittsburgh Treaty of 1775, the first between Indians and Americans, the Indians agreed in principle to the demanded return of white captives, stolen horses and runaway slaves but refused to return the children of Negro women by Indian fathers on the grounds that it was unacceptable that persons of Indian blood be subjected to the degradation of slavery. In the past Cherokee sympathy with Negro fugitives had paralleled that of other nations and assimilation had been countenanced as readily. However, the recent increase in Cherokee wealth had cast a different light on the situation. To the number of Negroes who had been so long resident that they had been tacitly accepted as members of the Cherokee nation had been added the far greater number of slaves legally purchased to work newly developed Cherokee farms and plantations. The 1825 census of the East Cherokee showed: native. Cherokee, 13,563; white men married into the nation, 147; white women married into the nation, 73; Negro slaves, 1,277. Other considerations than the purely economic bore upon the question. The Cherokee country was encircled by slave-holding American states. Slavery was a long established American institution. It appeared to the Cherokee government that a clearly necessary preliminary to American recognition must be to conform to American practice by a denial of the rights of citizenship to Negroes. A first step was taken in 1824 when the National Committee forbade intermarriage between Cherokee, whether red or white, and Negroes and the possession by Negro slaves of horses, cattle or hogs.

But the central problem overshadowing all others was to find means to preserve to the Cherokee possession of their country. Even were the Nation to succeed in rejecting the reiterated demands of the United States for additional negotiated land cessions Cherokee land was being frittered away piecemeal at an alarming rate. By various legalistic devices white men were gaining title to Cherokee farms, stores, mills and ferries or marrying Cherokee women to gain title. Heedless Cherokee were mortgaging their land to white money lenders. Immigrant Cherokee were exchanging their land in the east for promised titles to land in the west. The Cherokee government was realizing that the very ground under Cherokee feet was dissolving like quicksand. On June 15, 1825 the National Committee, of which John Ross was president, and the National Council, of which Major Ridge was speaker and Elias Boudinot clerk, declared all land in the nation under the sole control of the nation. All annuities from the United States were declared the property of the nation. The right of Cherokee citizens to sell even improvements to citizens of the United States, a common feature of the persistent federal effort to persuade Cherokee to migrate, was denied. Further to strengthen the government's hand, additional limitations were placed upon the influence of regional chiefs over the courts.

The remarkable surge of the Cherokee people along a strange new course had not been merely instinctive or impulsive. It was a course that had been for ten long years under constant discussion. There had been nothing unusual about this approach to any Indian decision. Indians had always been born talkers, loved talking for its own sake, and set the highest value on the clarity, force and eloquence with which any speaker could present his views. Innumerable Indian councils of the past had debated for weeks and months, with the manner in which arguments were delivered often considered more significant than the substance of the issue. The great departure in these Cherokee discussions had been that they had reached decisions which upon being affirmed by a majority had been considered binding upon all. These decisions had moreover been painful and most un-Indian, forcing the Cherokee people into an unfamiliar arena upon which beat the threatening glare of unknown dangers which at the very least restricted the individual's ancient freedoms and committed every Cherokee to repellent tests and demands along with a renunciation of fundamental traditions, customs and beliefs delivered to him intact by his ancestors. Yet, upon being informed by discussion so long and earnest, the Cherokee people had proved resolutely ready to take so enormous a risk.

They had been strongly influenced by those of their leaders who had been educated in white schools and who had become acquainted with the mysterious workings of white government, industry and religion. But this was not the whole answer. A majority of the Cherokee were still ignorant hill people. They were still Indians, as conservatively resistant to change as most primitive peoples have always been. Many others among the nation's most respected leaders were without formal education and, like Major Ridge, had still not learned to speak, read or write English. There was even a decided opposition, led by the venerable and widely esteemed chief, Whitepath. He and his faction of fellow traditionalists had fiercely objected to every progressive novelty, from the speaking of an alien language to the erection of courthouses, as a shameful preference for the white man's way of life which could only lead to the total decay of Cherokee integrity. Nevertheless, the Cherokee people, with all these divergent elements among them, listened to the years of soul-searching discussion, participated in it, and at length made up their minds. By essentially democratic processes an overwhelming majority reached the conclusion that a Cherokee conformation to the outer world represented the best Cherokee hope for survival in their own.

The time had now come, were the pace of Cherokee progress to be maintained, for the Cherokee government's new authority, improvised to man the nation's defenses, to be identified, defined and organized as a permanent political structure. The years of discussion, experimentation and indoctrination of the people had prepared both the nation and its leaders for the task. On October 13, 1826 the General Council provided for the election of delegates from each district to meet in convention the following July 4th to draft a constitution. The delegates were elected, assembled at the newly established Cherokee capital, New Echota, chose John Ross president of the convention, engaged in three weeks of earnest debate and on July 26, 1827 adopted a constitution. Its preamble, setting the tone of the document, declared:

We, the Representatives of the people of the Cherokee Nation, in Convention assembled, in order to establish justice, ensure tranquillity, promote our common welfare, and secure to ourselves and our posterity the blessings of liberty; acknowledge with humility and gratitude the goodness of the sovereign Ruler of the Universe, in offering us an opportunity so favorable to the design, and imploring His aid and direction in its accomplishment, do ordain and establish this Constitution for the government of the Cherokee Nation.

Article I, Section 1 grappled straight off with the basic issue of a defensible definition of the right of the Cherokee to consider themselves a nation. Upon this all else depended as directly as did the identity of the United States on the Declaration of Independence. Since there could be no question that the Cherokee were a distinct people it was the integrity of their territory that lay at the root of the matter. The section defined the boundaries of the Nation as "embracing the land solemnly guaranteed and reserved forever to the Cherokee Nation by the Treaties concluded with the United States."

The governmental structure erected by the Cherokee constitution followed in most respects the pattern set by the constitutions of the United States and the several states. There was provision for separate legislative, executive and judicial departments. The legislature, termed the General Council, consisted of two houses, a National Committee composed of two members from each district and a National Council of three members from each, in both cases elected for two-year terms. Each house had a veto power over the enactments of the other. Executive power was vested in a Principal Chief to be elected by the General Council to serve for four years. There was provision for a Supreme Court, circuit courts and district courts.

In defining the privileges of citizenship, including primarily the right to vote, there was general conformation to contemporary American constitutional practices. During the recent years of governmental experimentation the traditional privileges of Cherokee women had been impaired and this impairment was now made permanent. In the new government they could not, any more than Negroes, vote or hold office. Membership in the General Council was limited to free, male Cherokee of 25 who were descendants of Cherokee men by free women or Cherokee women by free men and denied to any in whom Negro parentage was identifiable. All free male citizens except those with identifiable Negro blood were eligible to vote.

The religious question was one of exceptional delicacy. Though many Cherokee, particularly those who had been prepared for leadership by white education, had become Christians, the great majority of the nation remained unconverted. The drafters of the constitution skated on this thin ice with the utmost care. Article VI, Section 1 declared:

Whereas, the ministers of the Gospel are, by their profession, dedicated to the service of God and the care of souls, and ought not to be diverted from the great duty of their function, therefore, no minister of the Gospel, or public preacher of any religious persuasion, whilst he continues in the exercise of his pastoral functions, shall be eligible to the office of the Principal Chief, or a seat in either house of the General Council.

The negation expressed in this section was balanced by an affirmation in the next:

No person who denies the being of a God, or a future state of rewards and punishment, shall hold any office in the civil department of this Nation.

Other sections provided for complete freedom of worship, established the right of trial by jury and declared "schools and the means of education shall forever be encouraged in this Nation."[2]

The Cherokee Constitution represented the first erection by an Indian nation of a complete political structure providing for the government of its people under laws enacted by wholly democratic processes. By its promulgation the Cherokee felt that they had taken the last necessary step in proving their right to recognition as a free people. They felt that they had demonstrated that they were as capable as whites of accepting the enlightenment of education and religion, as adaptable as whites to the demands of agriculture, industry and commerce and now that they were as fitted as whites to govern themselves. They felt that they had proved their right to be considered not only as a distinct ethnic unit but as a distinct economic and political unit. Their homeland, even after all the treaty reductions, was greater in size than several of the seaboard states. In population they were approaching the point eligible under the American constitution for recognition as a territory. Some Cherokee even dreamed of eventual

[2] For textual detail in development of Cherokee self-government see Starr, Emmett. *History of the Cherokee Indians.* Oklahoma City, 1921.

admission as a state. The more perceptive foresaw no possibility of this but regarded the establishment of the District of Columbia as a precedent indicating a constitutional device by which Indian rights in a case so special as theirs might be protected. All believed that even were they to be afforded no added privileges they must at worst be permitted to retain those they already held.

The Cherokee had made a stupendous effort but the issue was not one over which they could exert the slightest control. Their future, together with that of their fellow Indians, depended altogether upon the will, good or ill, of the United States.

8

The American attitude toward Indian rights in 1830 was an end product of the pragmatic attitudes of many earlier generations of white men who had since their first contacts with Indians been primarily devoted to Indian dispossession. The basic Indian claim to consideration had always been the circumstance of prior occupancy. The basic white rejection of this thesis had been the equally undeniable circumstance that the Indian had been making little or no use of vast regions which could become highly productive under white development.

To the European nations seeking footholds along the Atlantic shores of North America in the second half of the 16th century the Indian inhabitants were invested with no shadow of national or community title to the territory they chanced to occupy. A continent that had been for many thousands of years the home of an entire branch of the human race was considered a "new world," a treasure trove destined by God and nature to benefit a more deserving race. Implementation of this attitude sprang from the assumption that only a politically developed nation with an organized government, army, navy and diplomatic service could aspire to sovereignty over any portion of the earth's surface. This assumption was supported by the current theological opinion that Christians had obviously been ordained by providence to inherit the earth and that Indians, being heathen, could not hope to oppose the process. Legitimate opposition to any European nation's territorial claims in North America could therefore only come from another European nation.

Rival European claims were largely based on right of discovery. It was standard procedure for a white explorer coming upon a previously unknown river to claim for his government the entire territory it drained. Another standard procedure was the assertion in the name of a newly founded seaboard colony of title to all territory extending indefinitely westward from the occupied coastal strip. Soon all known or presumed portions of North America were encompassed by the overlapping and conflicting claims of European nations. In the peace negotiations concluding Europe's frequent wars these claims became pawns which were from time to time exchanged among nations, with the Indian occupants of the regions concerned considered items in the transaction as transferable as the wild animals, the rocks and the trees.

In practice the physical occupation of North America by Europeans, as distinguished from their assertions of national claims, took a course that deviated considerably from their original assumptions of predestined sovereignty. The violence of Indian resistance threatened the survival of the early colonies founded by the French on the St. Lawrence, the Dutch on the Hudson, the Swedes on the Delaware and the English in Massachusetts, Virginia and South Carolina. Meanwhile experience had demonstrated that a major economic return from the colonies depended upon the fur trade with the Indians. Under the pressures of these two most practical considerations, the costs of war and the profits of trade, the local representatives of European nations were authorized to undertake the negotiation of treaties with adjoining Indian nations, thereby admitting that the Indians were endowed with at least some of the aspects of sovereignty. The twin pressures were enormously accentuated as the territorial rivalries of England, Spain and France continued to develop in the first half of the 18th century. The military potentiality of the Indian nations occupying the intervening wilderness had become a nearly determining factor and alliances with them were earnestly sought by all three powers through treaties, gifts, protestations of friendship and explicit recognitions of Indian independence and equality. For generations England and France competed for the favor of the Iroquois, for example, as assiduously as either might have sought the support of prospective allies in Europe. The same year that England came by virtue of military conquest into sole and undisputed possession of the entire region east of the Mississippi witnessed a pronouncement of imperial policy reiterating a recognition of coexisting Indian rights of occupancy. By the Proclamation of 1763 white settlement was limited to the area east of the Appalachians and the Indians guaranteed undisturbed use of the area west of the mountains.

Throughout this period of imperial rivalry when Indian favor had been necessarily courted, Indian rights of possession at a legal level just below the jurisdictional level of each colonial power's assertion of general sovereignty had been repeatedly and consistently recognized. This recognition had been extended not only to territory which they inhabited but to territory over which they hunted and, in the case of the Iroquois, to even wider regions that they once had ravaged in their wars with other Indians. After the middle of the 17th century no foot of ostensibly Indian land had been taken for white use except after the negotiation of a treaty according to the terms of which there had been a voluntary Indian relinquishment. Many of these treaties had been fraudulent or the cessions extracted by threats of force. Some had been negotiated with unauthorized minorities or with delegates who had been bribed or debauched. But always white commissioners had gone through the motions of seeking a legal extinguishment of Indian title. Always the principle that Indians were invested with a title to their ancestral lands had been accepted as a preliminary basis for negotiation. In innumerable treaties during the two centuries before 1830 a clear distinction had been made between lands of which whites could be considered to have come into legal possession and those of which Indians could be considered still to retain legal possessions.

Again in practice there had been a wide departure from legal theory and political policy. Many of the most decisive advances of the frontier had been in violation of treaties and of governmental dictates. Impatient settlers had seldom proved subject to the control of their own governments. Painfully negotiated agreements between Indian nations and provincial or imperial authorities had often been broken before the ink was dry. The problem posed the Indian by encroaching settlement was baffling. The approach of settlement ruined hunting and even those Indians engaged in war upon the trespassers were compelled to continue to retreat. The immediate and disproportionate increase in white population in every newly settled area soon left the Indians no possible response that was sufficient. The advance of the white frontier had as a consequence proceeded at a pace that had been little affected by treaties or juridical determinations and never delayed for long except when repulsed by the vigor of Indian military resistance.

Meanwhile, from the beginning there had been occasional white reflection upon the ethical issues involved. Invasions and conquests had been common enough throughout human history. But never before had an entire continent occupied by one race been suddenly subjected to the intrusion of another. The physical superiority of the trespassers highlighted their moral responsibility. The primitive innocence, or at any rate the aboriginal ignorance, of the native tenants appeared to most conscientious observers to raise the possibility that the newcomers could be inflicting a fundamental wrong rather than asserting an inherent right. There was an early English examination of this moral problem in the 1630 sermon delivered by Cotton Mather to the Puritan company departing from Southampton to found Massachusetts Bay Colony:

Now God makes room for a people in three wayes: First, when he casts out the enemies of a people before them by lawfull warre with the inhabitants, which God cals them unto. . . . But this course of warring against others, & driving them out without provocation, depends upon speciall Commission from God, or else it is not imitable. Secondly, when he gives a forreigne people favour in the eyes of any native people to come and sit downe with them either by way of purchase, as Abraham did obtaine the field of Machpelah; or else when they give it in courtesie, as Pharoah did the land of Goshen unto the sons of Jacob. Thirdly, when he makes a Countrey though not altogether void of inhabitants, yet voyd in that place where they reside. Where there is a vacant place, there is liberty for the sonne of Adam or Noah to come and inhabite, though they neither buy it, nor ask their leaves. . . . If therefore any sonne of Adam come and finde a place empty, he hath liberty to come, and fill, and subdue the earth there. . . . So that it is free from that common Grant for any to take possession of vacant Countries. Indeed no Nation is to drive out

another without speciall Commission from heaven, such as the Israel-
ites had, unless the Natives do unjustly wrong them. . . . This may
teach us all where we doe now dwell, or where after wee may dwell, be
sure you looke at every place appointed to you, from the hand of God:
wee may not rush into any place, and never say to God, By your leave;
but we must discerne how God appoints us this place. There is poore
comfort in sitting down in any place, that you cannot say, This place
is appointed me of God. Canst thou say that God spied out this place
for thee, and there hath setled thee above all hindrances? didst thou
finde that God made roome for thee either by lawfull descent, or
purchase, or gift, or other warrantable right? Why then this is the
place God hath appointed thee; here hee hath made roome for
thee. . . . This we must discerene, or els we are but intruders upon
God.[1]

The violence of Indian resistance to the encroachments of seaboard colonists soon subordinated the moral question. Titles to
land were being decided not by reason but by force of arms.
Adversaries who were fighting not only for land but for their lives
had little leisure to entertain compunctions. In the ensuing effort
to limit hostilities by resort to wilderness diplomacy there was a
tacit recognition of the Indian's title to his land in return for his
intermittent relinquishment of a portion of it. Only among the
pacifist Quakers of Pennsylvania was there a genuine regard for
the Indian rights as such. But even in Pennsylvania's outwardly
benevolent land purchase policy there were anomalous expedi-
ences. The later and larger acquisitions were purchased not from
the unwilling Delaware occupants but from their Iroquois over-
lords who had no direct interest in the land that was being delivered into white possession.

The outbreak of the French and Indian War in 1754 swept
away all moral or legal concerns by ushering in a desperate ten-
year conflict. The Indians had ceased to appear victims of aggression, even to the most sympathetic. They had themselves become
the aggressors. The chief sufferers were white settlers who had
occupied lands to which the Indians still claimed their ancestral
right. In the ensuing brief and uneasy peace the Iroquois at the
1768 Treaty of Fort Stanwix, once more selling Indian title to

---

[1] For this and other selected documents related to the white man's historic attitudes
toward the Indian see Washburn, Wilcomb E., ed., *The Indian and the White
Man.* Garden City, 1964.

regions they did not themselves occupy, negotiated with English imperial and provincial authorities a monumental land cession which permitted the sudden surge of settlement into southwestern Pennsylvania and central Kentucky. Though this tremendous abandonment of Indian territorial claims was eventually to prove fatal to Indian hopes it nevertheless once more underlined an international acceptance of the validity of Indian title. At the highest diplomatic level it had again been recognized that Indian land rights existed and could only be extinguished through the formalities of Indian consent.

Seven years later the newborn government of the United States, beginning to breathe on the floor of the Continental Congress, was compelled to consider relations with Indian nations more important than those with any other power except England and France. The Indian threat massed along the wilderness border of the infant republic represented the gravest among the many dangers to which the American people were being subjected. In a desperate attempt to avert it by gaining Indian neutrality American commissioners were instructed to promise permanent acknowledgement of Indian land rights. In the first treaty of record between the United States and Indian nations, at Pittsburgh in 1775, the United States guaranteed the major Indian boundaries previously defined by the Proclamation of 1763 and redefined by English-Indian negotiation at the Treaty of Fort Stanwix.

The neutrality bid failed. Every Indian nation of consequence became a military ally of England during the Revolution. The Indians had elected to defend their remaining land by force of arms in company with Englishmen who, unlike Americans, appeared no longer bent upon possessing it. The struggle was in essence a continuation of the border conflict of the French and Indian War and Pontiac's Rebellion. A generation of American frontier people was growing from infancy to middle age in almost constant peril. Thousands of settlers, their women and children, lost their lives to Indian attacks. A war made more appalling by inhuman practices and outrageous excesses of which both sides were guilty generated furious hatreds. Yet in the midst of these flames of passion people were still driven by the nagging need to justify in some fashion the white man's continuing dispossession of the Indian. Henry Brackenridge, a prominent resident of Pittsburgh, then a frontier village, in a 1782 covering letter transmitting to Philadelphia eye witness reports of the frightful death by torment of George Washington's friend and agent, Colonel William Crawford, voiced a contemporary view:

With regard to the narrative enclosed, I subjoin some observations with regard to the animals, vulgarly called Indians. . . . Having an opportunity to know something of the character of this race of men, from the deeds they perpetrate daily round me, I think proper to say something on the subject. Indeed, several years ago, and before I left your city, I had thought different from some others with respect to the right of soil, and the propriety of forming treaties and making peace with them. . . . On what is their claim founded?—Occupancy. A wild Indian with his skin painted red, and a feather through his nose, has set his foot on the broad continent of North and South America; a second wild Indian with his ears cut in ringlets, or his nose slit like a swine or a malefactor, also sets his foot on the same extensive tract of soil. Let the first Indian make a talk to his brother, and bid him take his foot off the continent, for he being first upon it, had occupied the whole, to kill buffaloes, and tall elks with long horns. This claim in the reasoning of some men would be just, and the second savage ought to depart in his canoe, and seek a continent where no prior occupant claimed the soil. . . . The whole of this earth was given to man, and all descendants of Adam have a right to share it equally. There is no right of primogeniture in the laws of nature and of nations. . . . The member of a distant society is not excluded by the laws from a right to the soil. He claims under the general law of nature, which gives a right, equally to all, to so much of the soil as is necessary for subsistence. . . . What use do these ringed, streaked, spotted and speckled cattle make of the soil? Do they till it? Revelation said to man, "Thou shalt till the ground." This alone is human life. It is favorable to population, to science, to the information of a human mind in the worship of God. . . . I would as soon admit a right in the buffalo to grant lands, as in Killbuck, the Big Cat, the Big Dog, or any of the ragged wretches that are called chiefs and sachems. What would you think of going to a big lick . . . and addressing yourself to a great buffalo to grant you land? . . . I am so far from thinking the Indians have a right to the soil, that not having made a better use of it for many hundred years, I conceive they have forfeited all pretence to claim, and ought to be driven from it.[2]

2 For detail on the burning of Col. Crawford see *Indian Atrocities: Narration of the Perils and Sufferings of Dr. Knight and John Slover, among the Indians, during the Revolutionary War.* Cincinnati, 1867 or Connelley, William Elsey, ed. *The Heckewelder Narrative.* Cleveland, 1908.

On the seaboard the Revolution ended with the recognition of American independence. There was a general American feeling that the Indian allies of England had lost the war as decisively as had England. Having subjected the issue to arms the Indians were considered now obliged to accept the consequences. The Continental Congress proclaimed them a defeated enemy who had by their belligerent actions forfeited every right except such as might be restored them by the sufferance of the victors. Congress, however, was equipped with no military power to enforce its decrees. The Indians, encouraged and supplied by England and Spain, formed their own confederation which continued to fight for the boundary to their country that had been recognized in 1763, 1768 and 1775. Beyond the mountains the border war of the Revolution continued more violently than ever for 13 years after Yorktown.

The new central government of the United States provided by the Constitution came into existence in the midst of that border war. Washington, taking office as first President, was compelled to consider the Indian problem the most thorny of the many confronting his harassed administration. His was a more responsible government than had been possible under the Confederation and the rush of events was requiring that it formulate a coherent Indian policy. His Secretary of War, Henry Knox, who had in the same capacity long dealt with Indian affairs under the Confederation, offered his recommendations on the nation's most appropriate attitude toward Indian rights in his report of June 15, 1789 to the President:

In examining the question how the disturbances on the frontiers are to be quieted, two modes present themselves, by which the object might perhaps be effected; the first of which is by raising an army, and extirpating the refractory tribes entirely, or 2ndly by forming treaties of peace with them, in which their rights and limits should be explicitly defined, and the treaties observed on the part of the United States with the most rigid justice, by punishing the whites, who should violate the same. In considering the first mode, an inquiry would arise, whether, under the existing circumstances of affairs, the United States have a clear right, consistently with the principles of justice and the laws of nature, to proceed to the destruction or expulsion of the savages. . . . It is presumable, that a nation solicitous of establishing its character on the broad basis of justice, would not only hesitate at, but reject every proposition to benefit itself, by the injury of any neighboring community, however contemptible and weak it might be, either with respect to its manners or power. . . . The Indians being the prior occupants, possess the right of the soil. It cannot be taken from them unless by their free consent, or by the right of conquest in case of a just war. To disposses them on any other principle, would be a gross violation of the fundamental laws of nature, and of that distributive justice which is the glory of a nation. But if it should be decided, on an abstract view of the situation, to be just, to remove by force the Wabash Indians from the territory they occupy, the finances of the United States would not at present admit of the operation. . . . Were the representations of the people of the frontiers (who have imbibed the strongest prejudices against the Indians, perhaps in consequence of the murders of their dearest friends and connexions) only to be regarded, the circumstances before stated, would not appear conclusive—an expedition, however inadequate, must be undertaken. But when the impartial mind of the great public sits in judgment, it is necessary that the cause of the ignorant Indians should be heard as well as those who are more fortunately situated.

Having with some eloquence expounded the moral view, along with a pungent reminder that the United States could for the moment afford no other, Knox proceeded to an examination of the jurisdictional principles involved in the Indian question:

The time has arrived, when it is highly expedient that a liberal system of justice should be adopted for the various Indian tribes within the limits of the United States. By having recourse to the several Indian treaties, made by the authority of Congress, since the conclusion of the war with Great Britain, excepting those made January 1789, at fort Harmar, it would appear, that Congress were of the opinion, that the Treaty of Peace, of 1783, absolutely invested them with the fee of all the Indian lands within the limits of the United States; that they had the right to assign, or retain such portions as they should judge proper. But it is manifest, from the representations of the confederated Indians at the Huron village, in December, 1786, that they entertained a different opinion, and that they were the only rightful proprietors of the soil; and it appears by the resolve of the 2nd of July, 1788, that Congress so far conformed to the idea, as to appropriate a sum of money solely to the purpose of extinguishing the Indian claims to lands they had ceded to the United States, and for obtaining regular conveyance of the same. This object was accordingly accomplished at the treaty of fort Harmar, in January, 1789. The principle of the Indian right to the lands they possess being thus conceded, the dignity and interest of the nation will be advanced by making it the basis of the future admininstration of justice toward the Indian tribes.[3]

The Knox view of the Indian legal position was strongly supported by the formal opinion of Secretary of State Thomas Jefferson who August 10, 1791 wrote the Secretary of War:

I am of the opinion. . . . That the Indians have a right to the occupation of their lands, independent of the states within those chartered limits they happen to be: That until they cede them by treaty, no act of a state can give a right to such lands: That neither under the present constitution, nor the ancient confederation, had any state or person, a right to treat with the Indians, without the consent of the general government . . . That the government is determined to exert its energy for the patronage and protection of the rights of the Indians, and the preservation of peace between the United States and them; and that if any settlements are made on the lands not ceded by them, without the previous consent of the United States, the government will think itself bound, not only to declare to the Indians that such settlements are without the authority or protection of the United States, but to remove them also by force.

The Knox report to the President in the opening weeks of Washington's first administration became the cornerstone upon which the Indian policy of the United States rested for the next 40 years. But any hope that there might be prompt and dispassionate consideration of the inherent validity of Indian title was swept away by a flood of political necessities. The President and Congress, with all the new powers with which they had been invested by the Constitution, had little opportunity to balance right and wrong or to consider measures that time might prove wise or reason pronounce just. The Indian attitude of the first strong central government of the United States was as a result hammered into shape by immediate dangers that dictated resort to immediate expedients. Continuation of the Indian war was driving the outraged western settlers toward secession from the United States. On the other hand federal offensive moves against the Indians on a scale promising to regain the settlers' allegiance appeared certain to bring on a war with England or Spain or both which the struggling young republic was in no condition to wage.

Faced by these fearful alternatives Washington first assayed

[3] *American State Papers,* Indian Affairs, Vol. I, p. 12.

limited punitive expeditions which spawned terrifying Indian victories and then embarked upon a course of calculated appeasement. Every accommodation short of a total surrender of the American position was offered the belligerent Indians. New peace commissioners were dispatched into the wilderness after their predecessors had been murdered.[4] The most distinguished American plenipotentiaries waited in vain for a hearing at Indian councils. Only the sophisticated Iroquois could be persuaded to send representatives to the American capital to discuss American views. Knox and Washington earnestly begged them to carry to the great Indian council on the Maumee the message that the United States wanted only peace. For three years the confederated Indians were assured by every available means, at times frantically, that were they to make peace no further relinquishments of land would ever be required of them. The one American demand was a recognition of the validity of the Treaty of Fort Harmar which had provided for the opening to settlement of a portion of southeastern Ohio but which had been repudiated by the confederated Indians on the ground that it had been signed by unauthorized Indian delegates. The Indians, encouraged by their English advisors, elected to continue to fight for their original Ohio boundary.

Even after the decisive military defeat of the Indians at Fallen Timbers in 1794, where at the climax of the battle they were abandoned by their English allies, their title to the lands they had not yet ceded was not questioned. The 1795 Treaty of Greenville, imposed by the victors and accepted by the vanquished, reinforced the principle of American sovereignty by providing for military roads and posts throughout the Indian country but at the same time provided for continued Indian occupancy of all other lands beyond the Fort Harmar boundary until the occupying Indians chose voluntarily to relinquish their right of use.

Again in actual practice the renewed definition of Indian land rights proved no more effective than in earlier instances. The extraordinary increase in population in the west produced pyramiding pressures. Each Indian nation, obliged to deal singly with requests for local tracts, tended to yield piecemeal cessions in return for annuities, bribes, promises and other inducements. The

4 See Dale Van Every's *Ark of Empire*. New York, 1963, for detail on this troubled period.

settlement line continued to thrust northwestward across Ohio and into Indiana and Illinois. Only in the south were these 1795–1811 pressures less insistent. There Indian territory was for the moment sheltered by Spanish possession of the Gulf coast, a curb on economic development which made the intervening region less desirable for settlement.

By the time Jefferson had assumed the presidency the white population west of the mountains was approaching 700,000 and each year was continuing to increase at an ever faster rate. The frontier was pressing outward from its original perimeter in Kentucky and Tennessee toward the Great Lakes and down and across the Mississippi. The Indians of the region, outnumbered 8 to 1 by their perennial adversaries, the western settlers, were confronted by perpetually renewed demands that they consent to new cessions. Force was not used or threatened but the federal agents entrusted with the guardianship of their rights were generally the first and most vociferous in counseling that those rights be yielded. Jefferson's personal attitude toward the Indian question was humanitarian in principle. He approved in theory of various schemes to civilize the Indians so that they might become ordinarily self-sufficient inhabitants who required less land for subsistence. But he was naturally much more vitally concerned with the problems of American citizens. He acquiesced in the negotiation of the 1802 Georgia Compact which committed the federal government to promote the future removal of the Creek and Cherokee and he did little to restrain the Indian-baiting aggressiveness of Governor William Henry Harrison of Indiana Territory.

The tremendous alteration in the situation produced by the unexpected purchase of Louisiana appeared to Jefferson to offer the first satisfactory solution that had yet been hit upon. Since he did not foresee extensive white settlement of the new American territory west of the Mississippi he considered it a perfect sanctuary for eastern Indians who might there find a welcome escape from their increasing difficulties. Indian acceptance of the opportunity was still to be voluntary. There was as yet no hint of federal compulsion in the constant reiterations of federal advice that they move west for their own good. This moderation did not spring altogether from moral or ethical considerations. The military power of those long time patrons of the Indians, England and Spain, was still entrenched on either flank of the American west.

In the gathering shadows that forecast the War of 1812 the Indians of Tecumseh's confederation saw one final opportunity to set up a military resistance to American territorial demands. It was a foredoomed course. At the end of the way they were abandoned by their English allies as they had been at the end of the Revolution. Then they had been able to fight on but this time they were powerless. Now, for the first time, the United States was in a position to formulate an Indian policy upon which no outside considerations could impinge. English influence had been neutralized in the nearer northwest. On the Gulf coast Spain had become impotent. The Indians themselves possessed no residue of effective military force. They had become the helpless wards of the United States.

The new federal policy rapidly took an increasingly defined shape. In the face of the nation's fresh memory that 37 of the last 60 years had known all the horrors of a border war waged at an untold cost in lives and money the official attitude toward Indians was marked by more than a token regard for justice to Indians. The peace being established was not a punitive peace. Indian rights were still recognized. As a first step in the implementation of the policy the regular army was given police power to maintain order on the border. Posts were established and military roads constructed. The army was directed not only to regulate Indian behavior but equally to assure that Indians were not molested by settlers. When further land cessions were sought the negotiations were to be conducted under strict federal supervision with the greatest care that Indian consent had not been gained by unfair pressures.

Yet this effort to maintain the rule of law on the border represented no more than a stopgap. The fundamental problem remained and appeared daily more difficult. The white population west of the mountains had by 1820 increased by another million. Each new state and territory was impatient to speed the process of gaining cession of Indian lands within its borders so that they might be available for development. At the same time the comforts and satisfactions enjoyed by Indians in their occupancy were being increasingly abridged by the contiguity of white settlement. Many Indians, particularly in the north, were still primitive and the contrasts in the way of life between adjoining communities were embarrassing to both races.

John C. Calhoun, of South Carolina, Secretary of War in the cabinet of James Monroe, the fifth President, undertook an exhaustive study of the country's population problem as it was compounded by the continued expansion of the settled area and further complicated by racial frictions along the borders between white and Indian lands. Calhoun's primary responsibility was his official guardianship of the nation's Indian wards who were harassed by so many difficulties the foremost of which he epitomized as:

One of the greatest evils to which they are subject is that incessant pressure of our population, which forces them from seat to seat. To guard against this evil . . . there ought to be the strongest and most solemn assurance that the country given them should be theirs, as a permanent home for themselves and their posterity.

There was, of course, in no existing state or territory an area which it was willing to regard as a permanent home for Indians. It was upon this dilemma that Calhoun was focusing his study. His report to the President, the second great step after Knox's 1789 report to Washington in the formulation of a definitive United States Indian policy, embodied recommendations which purported to offer a complete and final solution to the Indian problem. It was transmitted to Congress January 27, 1825 and won the approval of Congress, of later presidents, of state authorities and of public opinion. This Monroe doctrine dealing with the nation's internal affairs appeared at the time of far more consequence to the future of the United States than did his ultimately more famous doctrine dealing with the international affairs of the hemisphere.

The basic thesis of the doctrine was the proposition that for the sake of the nation's stability and cohesion some limit ought to be placed on the dispersion of its population as a consequence of the continuing headlong advancement of the white frontier. A natural limit to this divisive expansion appeared to be the edge of the western plains beyond which lay an area believed unsuitable for civilized occupation. The doctrine involved the establishment by federal fiat of a line, running north from the Mexican border along the western borders of Arkansas and Missouri and thence to and along the Mississippi to its source, to be known as the Indian Line. White settlement would be permitted only in the area east of it while the area west of it would be reserved for Indian occupancy. It represented a reenactment in principle, purpose and practice of the Proclamation Line of 1763 which had for 30 years served by its definition of Indian rights to restrain and channelize white settlement. Beyond this new line the western Indians already inhabiting the area would be forever protected from white encroachment. Eastern Indians who elected to migrate beyond the line would equally be guaranteed on the faith of the United States a permanent asylum.

There was no suggestion as yet that eastern Indians would be forced to move. But three powerful inducements were expected to incline them to take advantage of the opportunity. There would be federal assistance in transit, an increase in annuities, a liberal exchange of new land for old and the assurance that peace would be maintained in the new sanctuary by the regular army. In their new homeland there was the prospect that they would have escaped the irritation of white proximity and once more could live their own lives in their own way. The third inducement was the most attractive. By the most solemn promise of the United States they were guaranteed perpetual possession of their new homes. Never again would they be required to move.

For some years the new doctrine appeared to have provided at last a solution to the Indian problem which for so long had seemed inherently insoluble. There were as yet no population pressures against the Indian Line for beyond it the natural environment appeared to defy agricultural development. The expansionist energies of white settlement were instead directed to the southwest toward normally wooded and watered east Texas. More and more Indians, particularly from the numerically weaker nations in the north, were submitting to their agents' earnest solicitations that they embrace the only available improvement in their situation by accepting the proffered sanctuary in the west. Even among the more numerous and tradition-minded southern Indians there was a growing disposition to feel that there might be more to gain in escaping the known exasperations visited upon them by their white neighbors than they were likely to lose among the unknown risks of existence in a new country. Soon considerable segments of more than 30 eastern nations were ranged along the western flank of the Indian Line. With such promising early progress there seemed every reason to expect that in the near future the rearrangement of the country's population would have been completed in full conformance with the ordered plan prepared by Calhoun and approved by the President and Congress.

But Georgia could not wait. In Georgia's history there was some justification for Georgia's impatience. It had been the last of the thirteen colonies to be founded and its late start had denied it the early opportunity to develop that had been afforded older colonies. In its early years it had been obliged to serve as a buffer between hostile Spaniards in Florida and more valued English colonies. The advance of its settlement line had for generations been obstructed by the proximity along its western border of the Creek, the most numerous of all Indian nations who had long known the added advantages of Spanish and French alliances. Not until after the Revolution were Georgians able to push their settlement much beyond the immediate vicinity of the seacoast and the Savannah River. During a period Pennsylvanians, Virginians and North Carolinians had advanced to the Kentucky and the Cumberland, the Georgians' advance had fallen far short of the present Atlanta.

It was with an acute awareness of this long retardation of its growth that Georgia in 1802 had negotiated a release to the federal government of its claim to western lands. This claim was based on its original colonial charter which had described its territory as extending indefinitely westward from the seacoast. The significance of the claim was shadowed by the several circumstances that throughout most of the period since Georgia's founding the region in question had been claimed by France or Spain, that Spain still possessed that portion of it south of the 31st parallel, that Indian nations still occupied all of it except the Natchez littoral and that since the earliest days of the Continental Congress the determination of Indian rights had been generally regarded as within the province of the federal government. Nevertheless, in ceding its western claim, reducing its limits to those of the present state by the instrument known as the Georgia Compact, Georgia took astute advantage of unwary federal authorities, including Jefferson, by extracting from them a promise that as soon as was "peacefully" and "reasonably" possible the federal government would arrange for the conveyance to Georgia of title to all remaining Indian lands within the state's borders.

No other state in ceding its western land claims to the federal government had had the foresight to demand a similar guarantee. Georgia's perspicacity, however, earned no reward. During the next 20 years after the Compact's signing the federal government negotiated extensive cessions of Indian land for the benefit of Ohio, Indiana, Illinois, Kentucky, North Carolina, Tennessee, Alabama and Mississippi but none for Georgia. In the middle of the 1820's much of west and northwest Georgia, nearly a third of the state, was still in the possession of Creek and Cherokee. Georgia's mounting resentment was taking on explosive proportions. The state's internal politics were frequently marked by bitter factionalism but on this proposition all parties and all candidates and all officials were united. Indian expulsion had become a standard to which all Georgians had repaired. Race antipathies, the value of Indian lands, the larger slaveholders' pressing need for wider acreage and the federal government's apparent discrimination against Georgia's interests were among contributions to popular emotion. But the fiercest and most enduring element in the intensity and unanimity of public opinion was state pride. Georgia had become absolutely determined to prove it was master on its own soil.

In reply to Georgia's increasingly insistent and indignant demands that the United States fulfill the promise made in the Georgia Compact the administrations of James Monroe and John Quincy Adams returned answers which if rational seemed evasive: The federal government had been doing all that could be reasonably expected to comply. Commissioners had repeatedly been sent to the Indians to persuade them to cede their lands. The federal government was no less anxious than Georgia to get the Indians moved west. All sorts of pressures such as the sequestration of their annuities and the flagrant bribery of their leaders had been exerted. It was not the fault of the federal government that the Indians had proved obdurate and there was no provision in the Compact committing the United States to the use of force.

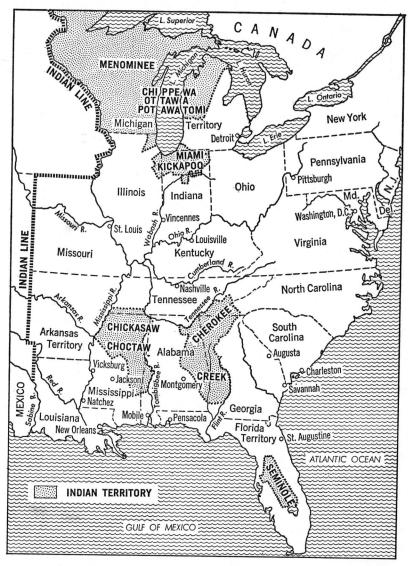

Shaded areas represent major Indian holdings east of the Mississippi
not yet ceded to the United States, January 1, 1825. On January 27,
1825 President Monroe recommended to Congress implementation
of the proposal of his Secretary of War, John C. Calhoun, that all
Indians be required to move west beyond what was thereafter known
as the Indian Line and that as an indispensable component of this
new national policy, white settlement be forever prohibited west of
that line.

The Cherokee, with the rapid development among them of political discipline, had proved specially obstinate. In 1823 their Council pronounced flatly:

It is the fixed and unalterable determination of this nation never again to cede one foot more of our land.

The next year they took the initiative by sending a delegation to Washington where it declared:

The Cherokee are not foreigners, but the original inhabitants of America, and that they now stand on the soil of their own territory, and they cannot recognize the sovereignty of any state within the limits of their territory.

The Indian delegation had attracted much flattering public notice in the nation's capital and had been officially received with diplomatic courtesies and honors. The incensed Georgia congressional delegation denounced the administration's exhibition of preference for Georgia's adversaries. The federal government's considered position in the mounting controversy was taken in Monroe's assertion in his March 30, 1824 message to Congress that the United States was not obliged to use other than peaceable and reasonable means to remove the Indians from Georgia.

Cherokee unity had offered no legal opening of which Georgia could take advantage but the Creek were not so well organized. A minority, under the tutelage of William McIntosh, a sub-chief who was given to boasting of the large sums secretly advanced him by the United States, negotiated an agreement relinquishing Creek lands in Georgia. McIntosh was killed by his indignant fellow Creek. President Adams belatedly questioned the validity of the treaty and ordered its renegotiation. Georgia refused to admit the President's authority and commenced a survey preparatory to white occupation. Adams, deeply troubled by what he conceived to be the fundamental constitutional question involved, took the issue to Congress in his message of February 5, 1827:

It ought not, however, to be disguised, that the act of the Legislature of Georgia, under the constructions given to it by the Governor of that State, and the surveys made, or attempted, by his authority, beyond the boundary secured by the treaty of Washington, of April last, to the Creek Indians, are in direct violation of the Supreme Law of this land, set forth in a Treaty, which has received all the sanctions provided by the constitution, which we have been sworn to support and maintain. Happily distributed as the sovereign powers of the people of this Union have been, between their General and State Governments, their history has already too often presented collisions between these divided authorities, with regard to their respective powers. No instance, however, has hitherto occurred, in which this collision had been urged into a conflict of actual force. No other case is known to have happened, in which the application of military force by the Government of the Union has been prescribed for the enforcement of a law, the violation of which has, within any single State, been prescribed by a legislative act of the State. In the present instance, it is my duty to say, that, if the Legislative and Executive Authorities of the State of Georgia should persevere in acts of encroachment upon the territories secured by a solemn Treaty to the Indians, and the laws of the Union remain unaltered, a superadded obligation, even higher than that of human authority, will compel the Executive of the United States to enforce the laws, and fulfil the duties of the nation, by all the force committed for that purpose to his charge.

In Congress, even during the preliminary consideration in each chamber of the committee to which it might most appropriately be referred, the question immediately kindled flames which revealed the intensity of sectional antipathies that had been excited. In the Senate John Berrien of Georgia, who later became Attorney General in Jackson's administration, took the floor to deliver a castigation of the President:

He has told you . . . of his determination, under a sense of higher obligations than any which Congress can impose, if in his view it shall become necessary, to call out the military force of the United States to carry this act of Congress into effect, according to *his* understanding of its meaning and intent. . . . The feeling of indignation, of abhorrence, which such a measure would excite, would be so strong, so universal, that, happily for us, no man in the times in which we live, would dare to resort to it. Or, if he had the audacity to do so, he would bring down upon himself the merited execrations of the whole American people.[5]

In the more volatile House threats of a general resort to arms, a quarter century before the Civil War, were exchanged with studied effrontery. John Forsyth of Georgia stigmatized the conduct of the federal government:

[5] *Abridgment of the Debates of Congress* (hereafter cited as ADC), Vol. IX, p. 301.

There was nothing to be apprehended if the General Government did not interfere, and, under the semblance of protection, stimulate the Indians to a resistance of the authority of the State. All the difficulties which had existed from the beginning of this business, had been created by this interference. Those unfortunate beings would long since have done their duty to the country, and to themselves, if it had not been for the base interference of infamous white men, who exercised an influence over them.[6]

With the voice of measured resonance soon to become famous in other constitutional debates, Daniel Webster of Massachusetts rose to pronounce his rebuke:

The gentleman from Georgia must know that there were two sides to this question between Georgia and the United States; and he would tell the gentleman from Georgia that there existed two opinions also, not only on that question, but on the conduct which that gentleman had designated as "base and infamous." This, Mr. W. said, was strong language but it was not argument. The gentleman had told the House that nothing had prevented every thing going right in Georgia but the interference of the General Government. . . . But, Mr. W. said, he would tell that gentleman, that if there were rights of the Indians which the United States were bound to protect, that there were those in the House and in the country who would take their part. If we have bound ourselves by any treaty to do certain things, we must fulfil such obligations. High words will not terrify us—loud declamation will not deter us from the discharge of that duty. For myself, said Mr. W., the right of the parties in this question shall be fully and fairly examined, and none of them with more calmness than the rights of Georgia. In my own course in this matter, I shall not be dictated to by any State, or the representatives of any State on this floor. I shall not be frightened from my purpose, nor will I suffer harsh language to produce any reaction in my mind.

Forsyth gave no ground.

The honorable member from Massachusetts indeed might very well be calm and unmoved; he did not reside near the scene of action; the people of his State were far removed, and had no reason to dread the bayonet at their throats. It was quite natural that the gentleman should be calm and dispassionate, and prepared to take a cool and composed view of the subject; but the Representatives from Georgia did not feel so. We feel very differently, said Mr. F., and when I feel, I

[6] For February House debate see ADC, IX, pp. 412–13.

will not attempt to conceal my feeling. Our rights have been violated and their violation has been made known to this House; and our appeal has not been regarded.

William Haile of Mississippi then interposed to add his fuel to the incipient conflagration:

Several of the States had already exercised their rights over the Indians within their chartered limits, and Mississippi intended shortly to follow the example, and he could assure the gentleman from Georgia that, if the bayonets of the General Government should on this account be turned against any of the States, it would speedily find its friends rallying around it.

To which Webster retorted:

But he must tell the gentleman from Mississippi, that the States would act on their own responsibility, and at their own peril, if they undertake to extend their legislation to lands where the Indian title has not been extinguished. If any such measure was contemplated in the State which the gentleman represented, Mr. W. hoped that gentleman would lose no time in warning his friends against making any such attempt.

The gathering of so threatening a storm was dispelled when further congressional consideration was made academic by the dispatch and resolution with which Georgia acted. Its legislature authorized the use of Georgia militia. The overawed Creek recognized the inevitable. Adams, with somewhat less grace, made no further protest. The federal government did not resist and the Creek could not resist Georgia's immediate occupation.

Having got rid of the Creek, Georgia's attention was now concentrated on the dislodgment of the Cherokee who still held the state's northwestern section. The extraordinary progress of the Cherokee during the 1820's, their economic advancement, the proliferation of their schools, their invention of their own written language, their development of a responsible government, which had excited so much admiration elsewhere in the world, served only to inflame Georgia's resentment, spur Georgia's impatience and harden Georgia's determination. Cherokee adoption of a constitution was viewed as a final provocation made more nearly intolerable by its presumption that a permanent and independent state could be maintained within the borders of Georgia. Losing hope of gaining a sympathetic hearing from the administration or that the shrewd Cherokee might provide a legal opening of which advantage might be taken, Georgia decided to accept all the unforeseeable risks of subjecting its case to consideration by Congress. On December 13, 1827 Wilson Lumpkin, Georgia congressman, introduced a resolution in the House:

Resolved, that the Committee on Indian Affairs be instructed to inquire into the expediency of providing, by law, for the removal of the various tribes of Indians who have located within the States and Territories of the United States to some eligible situation, west of the Mississippi River.

Then, to make Georgia's position so clear that no one could possibly mistake it, on December 27, 1827 its legislature resolved:

That the policy which has been pursued by the United States toward the Cherokee Indians has not been in good faith toward Georgia.

Lumpkin's resolution represented an attempt to take the Indian question over the head of the President to the floor of Congress where it might become a factor in the complex interplay of partisan and sectional politics. Through the next year Congress contributed an intermittent and always embittered discussion that was more often marked by the indignant outcries of Cherokee sympathizers than by the emergence of a sufficient band of supporters of Georgia's program. Then the 1828 election of Andrew Jackson to the presidency cast a blazing new light upon the situation. Unlike all former presidents he had been since his arrival on the Tennessee frontier in 1788 a zealous advocate and personal dictator of Indian dispossession. Henceforth the judgment of the White House would weigh in the balance against not for the Indian. Congress could no longer procrastinate. The Cherokee-Georgia controversy had become a national issue which must be debated and decided not only by Senators and Representatives but by the American people.

It was an issue impregnated with the most fundamental bearings on the evolution of the American form of government under the Constitution. Inherent in the painful and unavoidable decision were pronouncements upon the duty of the President, the authority of the Supreme Court, the responsibility of Congress, the balance between federal and state powers and most of all upon the functioning of American democracy under the stresses of a crisis made more turbulent by sectional and racial animosities.

⑨

In 1830 the overwhelmingly most striking chapter of the American story had been the incredible rapidity with which an extemporaneous aggregation of minor maritime states had developed an extension of sovereignty over a land mass of continental proportions. The population of the United States which under the Confederation had not yet reached 4,000,000 was in 1830 about to pass 13,000,000. In so short a time the area opened to its people had been enlarged to two thirds the size of Europe, an area more than three times the combined area of England, France, Spain and the multiple principalities composing Italy and Germany. This prodigious augmentation had been rendered even more striking by its having been unplanned and unexpected. During the Revolution Congress had contemplated a United States limited to the coastal region between the Appalachians and the Atlantic. Instead, the few settlers who had crossed the mountains during the Revolution had been joined by others until within the span of one lifetime the migration had become a tide of settlement which had inundated most of the eastern half of the continent's great central valley. No nation in recorded history had ever been able in so brief a period to extend its contiguous borders to so immense a distance or to leap so suddenly to the status of a world power.

The perpetual availability of new land awaiting settlement had become the dominating eventuality in the American experience. The effort and peril involved in its occupation had been a major influence in the shaping of American character. A readiness to accept any risk for the sake of wider opportunity had become so general that individual initiative had become an attribute that was taken for granted. No young man was required to admit that his prospects were necessarily limited by his environment. No head of a family was denied the hope that his children's lot could be improved. The opportunities offered by a constantly advancing frontier had generated a fluidity in American society which had as constantly reduced economic, political and social distinctions as it had promoted the development of democratic institutions.

All of this unparalleled growth and development had been at the expense of the Indian. Everywhere the Indian had been forced to give way, always against his will and always in abrogation of earlier white engagements. Until 1768 the entire region west of the Appalachians had been declared reserved to Indian occupancy at the highest jurisdictional, diplomatic and international levels. The later expansions of the original settlers' lodgment in Kentucky had invariably been accomplished through the application of force, the threat of force or the breaking of treaties. Of the 11 states admitted before 1830 to the union of the original 13 all but Vermont and Maine had been erected in territory from which Indian nations had been recently dislodged or were still in the course of being dislodged. This process of Indian dispossession had been under way since the first halting steps in the white occupation of the continent but in 1830 had been made to seem more conspicuous by the fact that during the past 30 years it had been accelerated to a pace so many times more rapid than during the preceding two centuries.

Throughout those centuries the existence of the Indian had had a primary bearing on the existence of the white man. Always there had been the shadow of the wilderness upon every outlying settlement. Always there had been the sporadic emergence from the wilderness of Indians bent upon burning and slaying. Always there had been the necessity of subjecting white armies to the fearful and often fatal risks of campaigning in the wilderness. Always there had been the sense that white advancement could only be measured by Indian retreat. Always there had been the perpetually renewed white vow that the next land cession would be the last ever to be required of the Indian. For generation after generation relations with Indians had necessarily remained a principal consideration for every white inhabitant. For those near the frontier they had represented a question of life and death. They had impinged almost as vitally on residents of coastal cities kept relatively safe by distance and numbers for of perpetual concern to urban residents were profits of trade with Indians and taxes to support wars with Indians. In every wider war between England and France or England and Spain or England and the United States Indians had been major participants. The Indian role in early American history had permeated American memory and imagination. Songs and tales of wilderness encounters, exploits, depredations, marches, torments and captivities had become a principal element in American folklore. The schoolboy was as familiar with the names of Powhatan, Pocahontas, King Philip, Pontiac, Cornstalk, Brant and Tecumseh as with those of Virginia Dare, John Smith, Miles Standish, Henry Bouquet, Daniel Boone, George Rogers Clark and William Henry Harrison. It had not been until after the War of 1812 that the Indian danger had receded into the dimness of the past. Even in 1830 the sonorous roll of Indian oratory and the chilling scream of the Indian warwhoop still echoed.

Yet, after all these generations of preoccupation with Indians, it was not until 1830 that the American people were obliged for the first time to face up to a decision upon what place in North America, if any, the Indian was henceforth to be permitted to have. No longer was there need to take into account the resistance either of Indians or of foreign powers with whom they had so often been allied. The United States had reached a position of strength which made any disposition of the Indians dependent solely upon its own will. This in turn defined and enlarged its responsibility for the future welfare of its helpless wards. The question had as a result ceased to be what to do about Indians and had instead become the infinitely more perplexing question of what it was right to do about Indians. The American people had founded their own career upon a declaration of equal justice for all and this therefore appeared to many of them to be as fundamental a question as could be posed.

The moral aspects of the question soon began to prompt those who held opposing views to scorn the motives and doubt the sincerity of their opponents. The poison of sectional prejudice as soon began further to embitter every difference. The facts of geography spurred this trend. Only in the south were there great numbers of Indians still inhabiting established states. Southerners could assert that northerners could now find it convenient to favor Indians only because they were no longer troubled by Indians, that Massachusetts, Pennsylvania and Ohio had once been as bent on Indian dispossession as now were Georgia, Alabama and Mississippi. Northerners could retort that the Southerners' determination to expel their Indians represented the whole region's inherent callousness to human rights which was already evidenced by the practice of slavery.

The general public's preliminary acceptance of the Monroe doctrine of Indian removal drafted by Calhoun had been based on relief that so ostensibly sensible and humane an escape from the dilemma had been hit upon. The agreeable theory justifying the proposal relied on the assumption that the Indians were still childlike savages, that they could be saved from extinction only by their removal from contaminating contact with whites and that they would be happier as well as better off in the offered sanctuary in the far west. This comforting assumption was disturbed by the unexpected Cherokee grasp at civilization. Their miraculously sudden exhibition of economic, intellectual, political and religious progress captured the nation's fascinated attention. In response to their appeal for consideration a wave of sympathy swept the north. In the estimation of many northern observers it was as though a curtain had been parted to reveal the spectacle of a gallant handful of deserving Indians heroically resisting the invasion of an all powerful aggressor. The Cherokee stand suggested classic allusions to Leonidas at Thermopylae or Horatio at the Bridge. Pulpit and press began to voice support of the Indian cause. Mass meetings drafted memorials. Petitions were circulated. Georgia had had the misfortune to have become committed to a frontal attack upon the Indian case in the one instance, the Cherokee, in which that case was the least vulnerable.

When the House of Representatives in February of 1828 had undertaken preliminary consideration of the Indian removal program it was with some reluctance. The agitation of public opinion was already becoming apparent. There was even less comfort in the realization that it was not a question, such as the tariff or the national bank, likely to offer political advantage to any advocate of either side. Nevertheless, there was immediately evidenced a sense that this was indeed a basic issue and some willingness to come to grips with it.

Oliver H. Smith of Indiana led with the orthodox defense of the righteousness of the removal doctrine:

Sir, I consider the question . . . of momentous importance; it is of importance to the character of the United States, and of much greater importance to that most unfortunate and wretched people, that the future policy of the Government, in relation to them, should be marked with justice, humanity, and a magnanimity of purpose, that will atone, as far as possible, for the great injustice which we have done them. We cannot retrace our steps; we cannot affect the past; we cannot resuscitate or bring to life the thousands of this miserable people, who have wasted away and perished under the influence of our baneful policy. But, sir, we may, and I do most sincerely hope will, profit by the past experience of the nation, in the policy which has been pursued, and in our future legislation on this subject carefully avoid that course of policy which has produced such dire effects. . . . Then, sir, these people do stand in great need of the interposition of the strong arm of this Government to relieve them; and this Government is bound by every tie of humanity, justice, morality, and religion, to do all in her power to save the wreck of this people.[1]

Though an earnest advocate of removal, Smith's remarks, as was the case with most congressional debate on the subject during the next ten years, had been interspersed with frequent and equally earnest cries of *mea culpa*. Having succeeded in totally breaking the power of their one-time chief enemy and, in the process, in having destroyed the Indian world, Americans were becoming increasingly haunted by a sense of guilt. With the passing of the Indian so much of the original color had been erased from the American scene that people felt contradictory impulses to preserve such vestiges of it as could be retained. In his reply to Smith, John Woods, from the adjoining state of Ohio which had as recently as had Indiana known the trials of Indian war, approved Smith's confessions of national guilt but took a contrary view of the national atonement:

[1] For February 1828 House debate see ADC, X, pp. 18–43.

I am glad, Mr. Chairman, that this measure is thus brought forward, and that it stands before us in its proper form and nakedness, stripped of the pretence of disinterested humanity, which has been thrown around it. It is now presented in its true character, as a measure, not for the benefit of the Indians—not for their civilization and preservation—but for our interest, and only our interest. This appropriation is asked, as the means to effect measures for the removal of the Indians out of the limits of our States and Territories, that they may, by our aid, trail their bodies into the wilderness, and die where our delicacy and our senses may not be offended by their unburied carcasses. . . . We are told, sir, that this is a measure necessary for the happiness and preservation of the Indian—that we must adopt it, or they will perish, and become extinct as a people. I do not believe this is the only way in which we can save the Indians, or promote their happiness. In my opinion, this measure would effect more rapidly their extinction. Instead of being entitled "An act for the preservation and civilization of the Indian tribes within the United States," it should be called a scheme for their speedy extermination. . . . We are told by one of our sovereign states, while urging upon us her claims to the Indian country within her limits, that it belongs to her, and that she must and she will have it; that we are bound, at all hazards, "and without regard to terms, to procure it." . . . Shall we be told that Congress is to disregard the right of the Indians? That the lands on which they now reside shall be taken from them "without regard to terms?" That it is the interest—the determination—the settled policy of the United States, "at all hazards," to drive them from their country and homes? I hope not, sir; for the honor of my country, I hope not.

Samuel Vinton of Ohio joined his colleague in attacking the removal policy but his approach was on less emotional and more practical grounds:

. . . it must be obvious, that, if, in the prosecution of the proposed plan of removing and colonizing the Indians, you transfer them from one section, thereby relieving it from its pressure, and put them down upon the other, thereby adding to the pressure the latter already feels; or, if you transfer them from one section to the uninhabited regions adjacent to the other, and thus enlarge the sources of the future, but certain power and wealth of the former, at the expense of the latter— discontent and angry collision must inevitably spring up. Not to expect this result, is to shut our eyes upon all history, and upon the fixed laws and motives of human action. . . . With the State of Georgia the Government had become involved in a very delicate and embarrassing controversy. Perplexed by Georgia and pressed on all sides by the importunities of the new States to extinguish the small remaining remnant of Indian territory within their limits, the Executive sought by a great effort to give itself relief. At this crisis, Mr. Monroe sent in a message to Congress, breathing the language of the purest benevolence, but which, I hesitate not to say, proposes the boldest experiment upon human life, and human happiness, that is to be found in the history of the world. It proposes to take a whole people, nay, more, the remnant of forty nations, from their abodes, and place them down in the recesses of a distant and forbidding wilderness. . . . When the plan there marked out is understood by the people of the western country, it will fill them with alarm. . . . Such a disposition of the Indians greatly endangers the security of the whole western frontier, and renders the condition of Missouri, in particular, imminently perilous. . . . Place around Missouri on the north and west, in conjunction with the two hundred thousand that would be there besides, the sixty or seventy thousand Indians of the Southwest, and what have you done! You have executed, by a single movement, the great plan of Tecumseh, that carried terror and dismay to every cabin beyond the Alleghanies. . . . The policy we are now asked to adopt, of removing them without any previous governmental arrangement for their future regulation, will, if pursued, result in carrying them forward, at a single movement, almost half way to that ocean in which there is too much cause to fear they are destined, ultimately, to terminate their existence and their miseries together. . . . My colleague over the way (Mr. Woods) yesterday read an extract from a letter of General Clark, the Indian Superintendent beyond the Mississippi, written two years since, in which he speaks of facts within his own knowledge, and as such communicated here in an authentic shape. Speaking of the country where these Indians have been sent (and to which this appropriation is asked to send more) he says "during several seasons every year, they (the Indians) are distressed by famine, in which many die for want of food, and during which the living child is often buried with the dead mother: because none can spare it so much food as would sustain it through its helpless infancy." It is, sir, to increase the number of these miserable beings beyond the Mississippi, and thus to add new and increased distress to these regions of famine, that this appropriation, if granted, is to be in part applied. To sustain and relieve from suffering those whom we have reduced to distress, is our solemn duty, and so far as this appropriation is to be so applied, it will have, as I have already said, my hearty support. But, sir, the great object of this appropriation is the removal of the Indians. And I appeal to gentlemen to say, whether they can, in their consciences, go forward another step in this work of desolation.

Wilson Lumpkin of Georgia, presenting in his rebuttal the major statement for the bill's advocates, described his state's demands without any further effort to disguise the implacability of its intentions:

The best refutation which can be presented, to all that these gentlemen have said upon this important and interesting subject, will be found in the fact that they stand opposed to the wisdom, the experience, and benevolence, of the whole country. In opposition to all their opinions, doctrines, and reasoning, I will place those of James Monroe, John C. Calhoun, James Barbour, and a host of others, who are experienced and distinguished statesmen and patriots, and who have long deliberated and reflected upon the subject of our Indian policy and relations. These distinguished individuals have all arrived at the same results; that the only hope of saving the remnant tribes of Indians from ruin and extermination, was to remove them from their present abodes, and settle them in a permanent abode west of the Mississippi River. . . . I feel it my duty to warn this committee, and the nation, of the impending evils which must necessarily grow out of an imbecile course on the part of this Government. . . . The Cherokee Indians, who principally reside within the limits of Georgia, have, in the course of the past year, renewed their often-repeated declaration, that they will never—no, never—relinquish their present possessions. They have placed this declaration in a constitutional form; and, with all the formality of a sovereign and independent State, they have set up for themselves. They not only disregard Georgia, and the rights of Georgia, but they have actually enacted laws, and execute them, too, which are in direct violation of the laws of the United States. . . . This state of things cannot exist: something must be done, and the sooner it is done the better. It is high time these unfortunate people should know their destiny plainly and positively. They should know precisely what relation they do stand to the United States, and in what relation they do stand to the particular States in which they reside. A state of suspense is the worst of all cruelty that can be exercised toward this noble race of people. If they are to be resigned to the States and the State laws, I call upon this Congress to tell them so. If we determine upon their emigration to the West, the sooner they know it the better, that they may send their Calebs and Joshuas to search out and view the promised land: for situated as they now are, and where they are, there is no rest for the sole of an Indian foot.

This introductory congressional debate served chiefly to reveal how hopelessly irreconcilable was the divergence of opinion on the residue of rights claimed by and for the Indian. So sharp a

cleavage produced a reluctance to pursue so depressing a subject
and the question was not brought to a vote during the 20th Congress. But the next Congress, assembling December 7, 1829, could
no longer evade a decision. Its representatives and a third of its
senators had been elected in the same campaign which had swept
Andrew Jackson to the Presidency. In his first message, December
8, 1829, Jackson left no doubt of his views on the Cherokee
assumption of political rights:

The Constitution declares that "no new State shall be formed or
erected within the jurisdiction of any other State" without the consent
of its legislature. If the General Government is not permitted to toler-
ate the erection of a confederate State within the territory of one of
the members of this Union against her consent, much less could it
allow a foreign and independent government to establish itself there.
Georgia became a member of the Confederacy which eventuated in
our Federal Union as a sovereign State, always asserting her claim to
certain limits, which, having been originally defined in her colonial
charter and subsequently recognized in the treaty of peace, she has
ever since continued to enjoy, except as they have been circumscribed
by her own voluntary transfer of a portion of her territory to the
United States in the articles of cession of 1802. Alabama was admitted
into the Union on the same footing with the original States, with
boundaries which were prescribed by Congress. There is no constitutional, conventional, or legal provision which allows them less power
over the Indians within their borders than is possessed by Maine or
New York. . . . Actuated by this view of the subject, I informed the
Indians inhabiting parts of Georgia and Alabama that their attempt
to establish an independent government would not be countenanced
by the Executive of the United States, and advised them to emigrate
beyond the Mississippi or submit to the laws of those States.

The House returned to its discussion of the question, in the
form of a new removal bill, in February of 1830. Members were
acutely and painfully sensitive to the growing popular excitement.
They gingerly debated a procedural proposal to print additional
copies of the report of the Indian Affairs Committee favoring the
bill. James Buchanan of Pennsylvania, later to serve as President
at another period of sectional disturbance, assumed that there
must be much public misapprehension else there would not be so
much public disapproval of the administration's program:

Mr. Buchanan said this was a subject of great importance; the more, as he had no doubt, from the nature of the numerous memorials presented to the House, that great misapprehension prevailed in the country on the subject. It was commonly believed that the Indians were to be removed from the Southern States by force; and nothing was further from the intention of Congress, or of the State of Georgia either, than this.

Tristam Burges of Rhode Island received Buchanan's assertions with some skepticism:

The gentleman said nothing was further from the intention of this Government and of Georgia, than to remove the Indians by force. Mr. B. presumed that nothing of this sort was intended by the Government of the United States; but when he saw Georgia making laws to extend over the Indians her jurisdiction, and excluding them from the exercise of their own rights, he could not agree to the remark of the gentleman.

Burges was probing a tender point. The framers and proponents of the bill were at this stage still making every effort to assure Congress and the American people that they were not contemplating a resort to force. Richard Henry Wilde of Georgia, who had inherited Forsyth's seat when the latter had become Governor of Georgia in 1827, indignantly challenged Burges:

He denied that the State of Georgia entertained the project of driving the Indians from their soil by force; and he believed he had at least as good an opportunity of being informed as to the views and policy of that State, as the honorable gentleman from Rhode Island.

Buchanan rose again to reiterate a congressman's natural alarm when confronted by a sudden upsurge of public opinion. In this case, he continued to maintain, it could only be due to the public's misunderstanding:

The memorials which loaded the tables of this House proved this fact. He was satisfied that the fears of memorialists respecting the intentions of the Government, and of the State of Georgia, were totally groundless. The forcible removal of the Indians was thought in many parts of the country, to be resolved on—a great excitement prevailed on the subject—enthusiasts have been busy in scattering firebrands and arrows throughout the country relative to this subject, calculated to create discord, to sow the seeds of disunion, and to sever brethren, who ought ever to be united.

Henry Lamar of Georgia, who had assumed George Gilmer's seat when the latter had resigned to run successfully for governor of Georgia, hastened to share Buchanan's dismay that the public was being so grievously misinformed:

Mr. Lamar of Georgia said . . . it was true that great misapprehension existed in some parts of the country on the subject; the news papers had teemed with the statements and comments calculated to mislead the public mind; and he hoped that a large number of this report might be printed, and distributed among the people, to counteract the great misrepresentation on the subject.

John Sterigere of Pennsylvania, a northern Democrat who favored the bill, agreed with Buchanan and Lamar on this unforeseen development which was beginning to disturb congressmen almost as much as the main question was beginning to disturb the American people:

Mr. S. concurred in the opinion that the most erroneous impressions were entertained among the people on this subject. His own correspondence, as well as the numerous petitions received by this House, convinced him of the fact. He had received a letter lately from home, expressing surprise at a proposition now before Congress, as was honestly believed, for removing the Indians by force; and the people in his part of the country were actually holding meetings to petition Congress against such a measure.[2]

By the time the Senate had undertaken consideration of the removal bill public excitement in both north and south had become intense. The address in support of the Indian cause that won the most attention at the time was delivered April 9, 1830 by Theodore Frelinghuysen of New Jersey. It was a speech that made him famous throughout the north, gained him the lifelong title of the "Christian statesman" and led to his nomination for vice-president by the Whigs in 1844. He dealt at length with the legal status of Indian rights, citing treaties and acts of Congress and quoting the opinions of Washington and Jefferson, but the portion of his address in which he dwelt on what he considered the moral principles involved had the greatest impact on the public mind:

God, in his providence, planted these tribes on this western continent, so far as we know, before Great Britain herself had a political exist-

2 For February 1830 House debate see ADC, X, pp. 666–69

ence. I believe, Sir, it is not now seriously denied that the Indians are men, endowed with kindred faculties and powers with ourselves; that they have a place in human sympathy, and are justly entitled to a share in the common bounties of a benignant Providence. And, with this conceded, I ask in what code of the law of nations, or by what process of abstract deduction, their rights have been extinguished? Where is the decree or ordinance, that has stripped these early and first lords of the soil? . . . We have crowded the tribes upon a few miserable acres on our southern frontier: it is all that is left to them of their once boundless forests: and still, like the horse-leech, our insatiated cupidity cries, give! give! . . . Sir, let every treaty be blotted from our records, and in the judgment of natural and unchangeable truth and justice, I ask, who is the injured, and who is the aggressor? . . . Sir, let those who please, denounce the public feeling on this subject as the morbid excitement of a false humanity; but I return with the inquiry . . . Do the obligations of justice change with the color of the skin? Is it one of the prerogatives of the white man, that he may disregard the dictates of moral principles when an Indian shall be concerned? . . . Our fathers . . . successfully and triumphantly contended for the very rights and privileges that our Indian neighbors now implore us to protect and preserve to them. Sir, this thought invests the subject under debate with most singular and momentous interest. *We,* whom God has exalted to the very summit of prosperity—whose brief career forms the brightest page in history; the wonder and praise of the world; Freedom's hope and her consolation; about to turn traitors to our principles and our fame—about to become the oppressors of the feeble, and to cast away our birthright. . . . Sir, the question has ceased to be—What are our duties? An inquiry much more embarrassing is forced upon us: How shall we most plausibly, break our faith?

The principal reply to Frelinghuysen was made by Forsyth of Georgia, who, when a member of the House, had had the celebrated exchange with Webster and who had in the meantime completed a term as Governor of Georgia during which his legislature had enacted laws stripping the Cherokee of all civil rights:

I consider it a matter of conscience, before entering upon the discussion of the general subject of the bill, to relieve the Senator from any apprehension that it may be necessary to cut white throats in Georgia to preserve inviolate the national faith, and to perform our treaty engagements to the Indians. It is true, the gentleman displays no morbid sensibility at the idea of shedding the blood of white men in this crusade in favor of Indian rights. . . . Gentlemen may amuse themselves with the transfer by the United States of a power granted to them, and intended to be used by the United States only. They may prove it, if they choose, an act of injustice to the Cherokees—a violation of faith. We will not take the trouble to interfere with such questions. The United States obtained, by treaty, the power to legislate over the Cherokees, and transferred it to Georgia. The justice and propriety of this transfer must be settled by the United States and the Cherokee. In this settlement Georgia has her burthen to bear, as one of the members of the Union; but no more than her fair proportion. If any pecuniary sacrifices are required to do justice to the injured, let them be made: if a sacrifice of blood is demanded as a propitiation for this sin, to avert the judgment of Heaven, let the victim be selected. Justice having shown, if not to the satisfaction of the Senator from New Jersey, I trust to that of the Senate, that upon the principles assumed by the adversaries of the bill, Georgia stands justified in her course; I shall proceed . . . not merely with a view to relieve the mind of the Senator from New Jersey from painful apprehensions, but to show to the Senate that our opinions on the great subject of the aborigines were not formed to suit our interests, nor at all influenced by them; that there was no motive operating upon our minds to tempt us into erroneous judgments. The condition of the remnants of the once formidable tribes of Indians is known to be deplorable: all admit that there is something due to the remaining individuals of the race; all desire to grant more than is justly due for their preservation and civilization. Recently great efforts have been made to excite the public mind into an unreasonable and jealous apprehension in their behalf. The evidences of these efforts are before us in petitions that have been pouring in from different parts of the country. The clergy, the laity, the lawyers, and the ladies, have been dragged into the service and united to press upon us. But these efforts have been unavailing: the people are too well informed to be deluded; they have too much confidence in the justice and wisdom of the administration to be misled by persons who have united, at this eleventh hour, in opposition to a project which has been kept steadily in view by three administrations. . . . These delusions will pass away . . . all . . . who have been misled, will soon know that they misunderstood both our principles and our purposes, and have formed on this subject crude judgments without the knowledge of the facts necessary to a correct decision; and without due reflection upon the past and the future.[3]

The bill's proponents continued to insist that no use of force was contemplated and that the sole purpose of the legislation was

[3] For April 1830 Senate debate see ADC, X, pp. 519–34.

to provide federal assistance to facilitate the migration of those Indians who elected to remove to the west. Frelinghuysen put this profession to the test by offering an amendment:

Provided, always, that until the said tribes or nations shall choose to remove, as by this act is contemplated, they shall be protected in their present possessions, and in the enjoyment of all their rights of territory, and government, as heretofore exercised and enjoyed, from all interruptions and encroachments.

The amendment was rejected 27 to 20. This April 24, 1830 roll call was the decisive vote on the issue in the Senate. By it the Senate was committed to the application of all federal pressures upon the Indians short of force and to the withholding of federal protection from those Indians who persisted in declining to migrate. The sectional nature of the controversy had now become fully apparent. The south voted solidly against the amendment 18 to 0. New England voted for it 11 to 1. Of the 8 votes against the amendment cast by senators from states north of the Potomac and the Ohio 4 were from Indiana and Illinois, where Indian occupation was still a concern, and 2 were from New York, the northern citadel of Jackson's new Democratic party.

It had been expected that proponents of Indian removal would carry the day in the Senate where all states had an equal vote and the carefully maintained balance between northern and southern states would be weighted against the amendment by the votes of frontier senators from Indiana and Illinois and Democratic senators from New York. But all realized that the preponderance of northern population would invest northern public opinion with a greater influence in the House. Every member knew how narrow might be the margin and how acute was the country's attention to the discussion. The tension lent painful significance to every political maneuver and every word of argument. When the House undertook final consideration of the bill in May, 1830, advocates of Indian rights continued their dissertations on their opinions of applicable law and justice. The debate was made more notable by the premonitory candor with which the representatives of Georgia expressed Georgia's scorn of federal intervention. Wilson Lumpkin, presently to become governor of Georgia during the period Cherokee affairs reached the crisis, rose May 17, 1830, to say:

Sir, I blame not the Indians; I commiserate their case. I have considerable acquaintance with the Cherokees, and amongst them I have seen
much to admire. To me, they are in many respects an interesting
people. If the wicked influence of designing men, veiled in the garb of
philanthropy and christian benevolence, should excite the Cherokees
to a course that will end in their speedy destruction, I now call upon
this Congress, and the whole American people, not to charge the Georgians with this sin; but let it be remembered that it is the fruit of cant
and fanaticism, emanating from the land of steady habits, from the
boasted progeny of the pilgrims and the puritans. Sir, my State stands
charged before the House, before the nation, and before the whole
world, with cruelty and oppression towards the Indians. I deny the
charge. . . . Where do you find one solitary opponent of President
Jackson in favor of the measure on your table? I do not know one. Sir,
I have tried to prevent party considerations from operating on this
question; but our opponents are an organized band; they go in a solid
column. . . . Upon this question, our political opponents have availed
themselves of the aid of enthusiastic religionists, to pull down the
administration of President Jackson. Sir, pure religion will aid and
strengthen any cause; but the undefiled religion of the Cross is a
separate and distinct thing, in its nature and principles, from the noisy
cant of these pretenders. . . . Who compose this "christian party in
politics," here and elsewhere? Are they those individuals who are most
distinguished for morality and virtue? . . . While the smallest intrusion (as it is called) by the frontier citizens of Georgia on the lands
occupied by the Cherokees, excites the fiery indignation of the fanatics,
from one end of the chain of concert and coalition to the other, do we
not find an annual increase of intruders, from these philanthropic
ranks, flocking in upon the poor Cherokees, like the caterpillars and
locusts of Egypt, leaving a barren waste behind them? Yes, sir, these
are the intruders who devour the substance which of right belongs to
the poor perishing part of the Cherokees. . . . The inhumanity of
Georgia, so much complained of, is nothing more nor less than the
extension of her laws and jurisdiction over this mingled and mis-
guided population who are found within her acknowledged limits.
And what, I would ask, is to be found in all this, that is so very
alarming? . . . But if the heads of these pretended mourners were
waters, and their eyes were a fountain of tears, and they were to spend
days and years in weeping over the departure of the Cherokees from
Georgia, yet they will go.[4]

The basic statement of Georgia's legal position, including a
summarization of southern views on the constitutional issue, was

[4] ADC, XI, pp. 87–89.

made May 24, 1830, by James Moore Wayne who five years later was to be appointed to the United States Supreme Court:

Sir, we meet the honorable gentlemen who so fondly revert to the rights of these early and first lords of the soil, and deny that the Indian had either ownership, proprietary right, or tenancy by occupancy, to the lands over which he roamed. It is commonly said, our ownership exists by purchase from the Indian, and that he was proprietor and sovereign of the soil. But both are said, only because he was found upon the continent at its discovery. That he was in possessions of portions of land, which were in savage cultivation, over which he roamed for game and war—that several of the tribes had designated natural boundaries as the limits of their hunting grounds, and claimed such an exclusive use of it, against other tribes, no one will deny. But did the extent of their natural rights against each other give such a title or occupancy to all that they aggregately claimed, as to include a power to exclude others from seeking this continent as a resting-place from persecution and want, and making it the land of civilization and Christianity? Sir, they were proprietors of what they used, so long as it was used; but not sovereigns of any part. . . . Sovereignty over soil is the attribute of States; and it can never be affirmed of tribes living in a savage condition, without any of the elements of civilization, as they were exhibited in the nations of antiquity, or in those of modern times. . . . Without formal conventions to fix boundaries, the tribes in the neighborhood of each other, in the course of time, knew the hunting grounds as they were separately claimed. A trespass by either upon the grounds of another, was followed by individual contentions or tribal war. . . . When the relative strength of tribes prevented one from extirpating or enslaving another, the fears of each conceded to the other rights, not to the land or soil, but to the fish in its streams, and to the animals on its surface; and this usufructuary enjoyment was all that the Indian claimed. . . . What, then, becomes of the position, so vauntingly assumed and repeated in the course of this debate, that God, in his providence, planted these tribes in this Western World, and made them tenants of the soil by immemorial possession? The Indian the tenant of the soil! He never was so, in any sense of the word. . . . The assumption in behalf of the Cherokees is, that they are an independent people, having a political sovereignty over, and title in fee to, the lands which they claim; that they are neither subordinate to the United States, nor subject to the jurisdiction of any of the States in which they live; that they have the right to form a Government, which shall act not only upon themselves, but upon citizens of the United States who may transgress its laws; and that they have the ability to establish such relations between themselves and the United

States, in future, as their interest or convenience may dictate. . . . Sir, so monstrous a concatenation of construction it is only humane to strangle in its birth; and I trust it lies dead in all its deformity.[5]

Wayne's was the closing salvo in the exchanges of ideological broadsides that marked the debate. A preliminary vote on a question of parliamentary procedure had indicated how closely the House was divided. The first effort of proponents of the bill to move the previous question had been defeated 93 to 99. When after many hours of further debate a second effort was made it resulted in a tie vote of 99 to 99. The Speaker, Andrew Stevens of Virginia, cast the deciding vote. On the resulting move of the previous question the vote was another 99 tie again decided by the Speaker. The May 26, 1830 roll call on the main question, passage of the Indian Removal Bill, produced 102 yeas and 97 nays.

As in the Senate the vote was predominantly sectional with most northern votes for the bill coming from strongly Democratic areas where administration discipline could be imposed and most southern votes against the bill coming from border states where members felt free to vote their personal sentiments. New England voted 28 to 9 against and the north as a whole 79 to 42 against. The south voted 60 to 15 for and the western states, Kentucky, Tennessee, Ohio, Missouri, Indiana and Illinois, 23 to 17 for.

After long and impassioned consideration the American people had thus decided, through the instrumentalities of a duly elected President and Congress, that it was right as well as wise to require the Indians to migrate from their eastern homes to new homes in the far west. The bill did not prescribe the use of force and its central provision was the appropriation of funds to facilitate Indian migration but its effect was to leave to those Indians who continued to object to exile scant means to sustain their resistance. The federal government which in the name of the nation's welfare and the nation's reputation had formerly protected them from unreasonable demands had now been instructed by the nation to insist upon their expulsion.

[5] ADC, XI, pp. 96–105.

1O

The country had not long to wait to realize the consequences of its national government's difficult decision. Jackson signed the Indian Removal Bill May 28, 1830 and after the adjournment of Congress went home to Tennessee for the first summer vacation of his first term. He took with him General John H. Eaton, his Secretary of War, who headed the department charged with the conduct of Indian affairs, and General John Coffee, his nephew-in-law, who had been a prominent lieutenant in his Creek and New Orleans campaigns and since 1818 his co-speculator in ceded Indian lands. Jackson had for the past 17 years been energetically devoted to the expulsion of all Indians from the south and now as President, doubly armed by the specific authorization of Congress, was determined to bring the process forthwith to a conclusion.

The four nearer southern Indian nations were admonished to send delegations to confer with the President at Eaton's home in Franklin in order that they might learn what was expected of them. The Cherokee and Creek declined to attend on the grounds that they needed more time to consider their situation. The Choctaw were too agitated by internal dissensions to muster a delegation. Only the Chickasaw came. Their 21 chiefs were received by the President and then assembled in the Presbyterian church to listen to his administrators' explanation of the meaning of the new law. The Chickasaw had approached the conference with confidence that their long record of friendliness to the United States would entitle them to special consideration. Aside from a brief flurry of raids on the first Cumberland settlements they had never made war on Americans. They had again and again been active allies of the United States, furnishing contingents of their warriors to serve with the American commanders, St. Clair and Wayne, in their campaigns against the northern Indians, and with Jackson in his Creek invasion and his defense of New Orleans. They had made cooperation with the United States the keystone of their national policy and had consistently preferred the interests of the United States to those of their Indian neighbors.

But if they imagined their historic amity might have won them any indulgence they were soon disillusioned. Jackson's commissioners bluntly informed them that the United States was no longer in a position to guard either their civil or their property rights. They were told that their tribal government had been superseded by state governments, that all their affairs, including land tenure, commerce and behavior, were henceforth subject to the regulation of state laws and that the only protection that could still be afforded them by the federal government was the assurance of permanent possession of the new lands offered in the west upon which when occupied they might resume the practice of self-government. The troubled Chickasaw delegates, perceiving no avenue of escape, entered into a reluctant agreement to migrate if and when they were suffiently reimbursed for their eastern lands and if after inspection the proposed western location appeared to them suitable. The agreement was meaningless, other than as an entering wedge that weakened later Chickasaw resistance, inasmuch as it was repudiated by the majority of the nation and never ratified by the Senate.

Having been disappointed in hitting upon a quick and easy solution to the problem of gaining general Indian consent to migrate, the administration buckled down to the longer haul of developing those pressures which must leave Indians no other recourse than consent. It was felt that were one Indian nation once prodded into movement the example would open the way to requiring the others to follow suit. In casting about for this likeliest first victim the administration determined that the Choctaw situation afforded the most fruitful field for the exercise of the new powers and the expenditure of the large appropriations recently granted by Congress. Many factors influenced this selection.

The Choctaw were numerous, with a population of some 20,000, but politically much more loosely organized than were the Cherokee, Creek or Chickasaw. Their location in middle Mississippi presented them with a shorter migration distance than in the case of the Cherokee, Seminole or Creek. Many of them had long been accustomed to hunt in the region to the westward and they had early established scattered colonies in the very country to which now all of them were expected to migrate. They could be presumed susceptible to rational and legalistic appeals, since they had had enough contact with whites to have become accustomed to negotiation, during the more than a century of competition for their patronage among French, English, Spanish and, finally, American traders and of periodic solicitation of their favor by all four powers. Their location, furthermore, had been sufficiently remote from the earlier frontier to spare them armed conflict with American settlers or armies and they had had as a result far less experience with resisting white demands than had their neighbors. They were subject to another weakness in that long continued intermarriage with whites had in their case produced a class of mixed bloods who while becoming natural leaders had been spared the necessities of organizing resistance and had tended instead to become prosperous planters and merchants disposed to devoting their political influence to the improvement of their private economic positions. In the instance of the Choctaw even the counsel of their relatively few white missionaries favored removal. The missionaries' experience with local conditions had convinced them that the rapid deterioration in the nation's manners and morals could only be arrested by removing them from association with their white neighbors. But of all the factors arousing the administration's hopes, the virulence of factionalism among the Choctaw appeared to offer the most inviting opportunity. Their councils were divided into fiercely disputing cliques, each led by self-seeking spokesmen eager to grasp at any personal advantage at the expense of rivals.

When Jackson returned to Washington, his commissioners, Eaton and Coffee, descended upon the Choctaw. Dismally aware that they must face up to the threat, large numbers of chiefs and

warriors, still quarreling among themselves with much brandish-
ing of weapons, assembled for the conference. The commissioners'
task had been eased by a recent act of the Mississippi legislature
providing fines and imprisonment for any Indian who attempted
to direct, advise or influence his fellow Indians. Eaton and Coffee
were soon able to separate the sheep from the goats among the
leading delegates. Some 50 of those most disposed to listen to
reason were offered secret bribes of money and public rewards of
title to Mississippi land in tracts ranging from one to four sections.
It remained clear that a majority of the Choctaw opposed removal
but a sufficient number of their more prominent representatives
were persuaded to sign the Treaty of Dancing Rabbit Creek,
September 27, 1830, to give it the appearance of a negotiated
agreement.

It was set forth in the treaty's preamble that "the General Assembly of the State of Mississippi has extended the laws of said
State to persons and property within the chartered limits of same,
and the President has said that he cannot protect the Choctaw
people from the operation of these laws," though this singular
phrase was deleted by the Senate before ratification. By the treaty
the Choctaw ceded to the United States their remaining land east
of the Mississippi while the United States for its part undertook to
compensate the migrants for their property left behind, to arrange
transportation, to provide food for the first year in their new
homes and to guarantee the Choctaw nation the perpetual right of
self-government along with a companion warranty that they would
never again be required to move. To maintain the fiction that this
was not to be a removal by force the treaty also stipulated that any
Choctaw might remain in Mississippi if he wished to live under
the laws of Mississippi without the protection of the laws of the
United States.

Thus, sooner than anybody had foreseen during those recent
months of theoretical and moralistic debate in Congress, the
American people were presented with the spectacle that revealed
the reality of what they had ordained.[1] The fact that the bill

1 For exhaustive detail on the earlier stages of Indian removal see *Senate Document
512*, 23rd Congress, 1st session, a five-volume compilation of official correspondence
and reports furnished in response to the demand upon the administration for information in the Senate resolution of December 27, 1833. For a definitive secondary
treatment of the subject see Grant Foreman's *Indian Removal*, rev. ed. Norman,
1953.

which had purported to facilitate Indian removal had actually been a bill to compel removal could no longer be concealed. Any Choctaw who had felt the slightest inclination to migrate had left for the west during those recent years when conditions under which Indians in Mississippi had been obliged to live had become every month less endurable. The 20,000 who still clung to their ancestral homes were as unwilling to abandon them as they had been before the treaty but, deprived of the support of the United States and their native leaders and assailed daily by new rumors, alarms and threats, more and more of them became resigned to their fate.

Every circumstance conspired to undermine the resolve of those disposed to hold back. Foreseeing the imminence of Indian departure, whites were swarming in on Indian farms and homes. Many trespasses were on trumped up legal charges such as claims based on alleged debt or fraudulent bills of sale. Others were wholly illegal seizures of property from owners who had been persuaded they had no legal defense. Such state courts as were inclined to support the due processes of law were swamped by litigation with which in any event only those few Indians with the means to hire lawyers could deal. Indians who left their homes for even a few hours to attend community councils or confer with relatives were likely to find upon their return that their premises had been looted. Their country had been infested with wandering packs of white pilferers. The federal Indian agents who formerly had sought to maintain civil order within Indian borders were either standing aside or deciding that any effort to control the turmoil was useless. The remnants of Indian discipline were meanwhile breaking down. The abolition of tribal government had permitted the introduction of a flood of liquor into Indian communities. Whites peddled alcohol not only for immediate gain but to facilitate swindles. At every gathering of Indians assembled to discuss the problems of migration debauchery became a more immediate problem. A people who had lost all hope embraced the surcease of drunkenness. Existence in the Choctaw country had dissolved into confusion and anarchy. The birth pangs of Indian removal were occasioning pains worse than physical. They were mean and sordid and without any consoling prospect that the anguish might be rewarded by any fulfillment.

Denied the last chance of a stay by the Senate's ratification of the treaty, by the summer of 1831 some two thirds of the Choctaw had dejectedly admitted their willingness to move west. During the 18 months from the fall of 1831 to the spring of 1832 some 13,000 Choctaw undertook the dreaded journey. The story of the frontier had for the last two generations been largely a story of the movement of people from place to place. It was commonly said at the time that no more was being demanded of the Indians than had been demanded of white settlers in their historic westward surge. But the Choctaw migration represented a sudden dislocation of population of a magnitude without parallel in the frontier's former experience. In the first 15 years of Kentucky's career the area had increased in population at the rate of less than 5,000 a year. Tennessee's first 10 years had been at the rate of less than 4,000, as had Ohio's first 12. Those white pioneers had undertaken their great adventure of their own volition, had had time to make personal preparations they had considered sufficient, had encountered their difficulties in independent, self-reliant family groups, had en route been buoyed up by the anticipation that they were improving their lot and had been sustained by the confidence that they were moving to a land all of whose aspects had been made familiar to them by their former experience. The Choctaw, on the other hand, had been committed against their will in greater numbers in a sudden convulsive eruption to a longer journey to a totally different land with a totally different climate. Marshaled by guards, hustled by agents, harried by contractors, they were being herded on the way to an unknown and unwelcome destination like a flock of sick sheep. Theirs was a very far remove indeed from the high hope and heroic resolve that had marked most other unfoldings of the American frontier story.

Congressional critics of the Removal Bill had charged that the federal government had made no preparations for the conduct of so complex an operation. This accusation was from the outset proved tragically justified. The administration's great effort had been concentrated on maneuvering the Choctaw into a position where they could no longer demur. Little thought had been given to even the minimum means that must be furnished the undertaking were masses of Indians suddenly to give their consent. In December, 1830, Jackson directed the army to consider itself responsible for the supervision and organization of the march.

This seemed a sensible exercise of administrative judgment. The army had had long professional experience with the supply and movement of large groups. It had as long served as the principal agent of the war department in the peaceful as well as the belligerent handling of Indians. But, measured by the dimensions of the sudden need, the army's capacity was fantastically insufficient. Its physical facilities for transport and supply were already strained to maintain its own establishment. This numbered in 1830 less than 6,000 men, somewhat less than a third of the number of Choctaw men, women and children for whose maintenance it had suddenly been made responsible. Moreover, its units were widely scattered in eastern arsenals, coast defense forts and along thousands of miles of northern and western frontier. The most that could be contributed to the overwhelming task was the assignment of a small group of junior officers to act as advisors and supervisors. Nevertheless, the few bright pages in the record of Indian removal were lighted by the devotion of these few professional soldiers to their harrowing duty. They jeopardized their careers by the vigor of their protests to superiors, they emptied their pockets to relieve the sufferings of their charges, they drove themselves to exhaustion in carrying their share of the intolerable burden which weighed upon everyone associated with the project.

The lack of foresight and preparation had made the mechanics of migration appear simple on paper. As fast as the Indians assembled in groups of a thousand or more they were to be started marching to the Mississippi, usually at Vicksburg. For those without the means to provide their own transportation trains of ox wagons were to be furnished for the conveyance of personal property, the sick, young children, and others unable to walk. Those Choctaw who had horses were to ride them. All others were to keep up on foot. Their herds of stock were to be driven with the wagon trains. At the Mississippi some of the migrating groups were to be ferried across to resume their overland journey. Others were to be taken aboard steamboats to be deposited at the head of navigation on the Red or the Arkansas and there to march on to their destination west of Fort Smith.

This casually sketched plan failed in every respect to cope with the suddenly rearing wave of requirements. Indians had scarcely begun to gather at their designated departure points before all who had not been able to bring their own stocks of food began to go hungry. The army having had no equipment or supplies available, responsibility for the transport and support of the Indians en route had had to be farmed out to private contractors. Profit was naturally dependent upon charging the government as much as possible while furnishing the Indians as little.[2] Political influence was actively employed to widen this gap. Delays in furnishing transport were manipulated to lengthen the period in which rations must be furnished. Food deliveries were withheld until those few Indians able to pay had exhausted their remaining resources in buying on the open market. Congress had voted an ample appropriation but a mingling of bureaucratic inefficiency and calculated connivance kept funds unavailable until after months of delay. The steamboats were procured only after other delays and were so few that dangerous overcrowding was practiced. A number broke down in passage and others were without warning withdrawn from the operation after dumping their Indian passengers on the nearest shore. There were instances in which Indian contingents were rescued from starvation only by the charitable contributions of sympathetic white communities en route. Much of the movement was through unsettled country where no volunteer relief was possible.

These were some of the distressing circumstances under which the first general Indian migration contemplated by the Removal Act was conducted. The long somber columns of groaning ox wagons, driven herds and straggling crowds on foot inched on westward through swamps and forests, across rivers and over hills, in their crawling struggle from the lush lowlands of the Gulf to the arid plains of the west. In a kind of death spasm one of the last vestiges of the original Indian world was being dismembered and its collapsing remnants jammed bodily into an alien new world.

Upon this pattern of suffering produced by human mismanagement was superimposed the equal mercilessness of nature. The first winter of the Choctaw migration was the coldest in living memory. A people accustomed to the usual warmth of their deep south homeland, insufficiently provided with clothing and blankets, was benumbed in shelterless camps on frozen ground. Pul-

---

[2] A number of the contractors were wealthy Choctaw who proved as avaricious as their white counterparts.

monary disorders to which Indians were constitutionally susceptible took a fearful toll. The second winter of the migration was
excessively wet. Roads became impassable, swamps became bottom-
less, lowlands became inundated and all but the smallest streams
became unfordable. The inevitable added delays prolonged by
months the period in which the migrants were exposed to sickness
and hunger. The intervening summer was darkened by an even
more grievous natural disaster. The entire region of the lower
Mississippi through which the migrants were passing was afflicted
by a major cholera epidemic. In their crowded and unsanitary
temporary camps the Choctaw died by hundreds.

This first essay at conducting the general removal of an entire
Indian nation had been a shock to their sympathizers in the north,
a disgrace to the federal government and a catastrophe to the Indians. Instead of inducing the other southern nations to follow the
Choctaw example, as the administration had hoped, the spectacle
had fired their resistance. The 7,000 Choctaw still awaiting travel
arrangements in Mississippi had been so horrified by the experience of their fellow citizens that they stubbornly refused to stir
from their homes. In this recalcitrance they received some unexpected support from local white merchants and officials who had
become belatedly concerned over the loss of so many customers
and clients. The expulsion agitation presently died down and no
later serious efforts were made to dislodge them. Most of the 7,000
obdurate Choctaw remained in Mississippi where their descendants constitute a noticeable proportion of the state's present population.

11

The Choctaw migration, although the disastrous first attempt to conduct the removal of an entire Indian nation, was to most observers no more than a kind of dismal sideshow. The main event was occupying the center of the arena where was being staged the Georgia-Cherokee confrontation. It was upon this dramatic conflict that the attention of the nation was fixed. Both antagonists had long foreseen this ultimate collision and both had armed themselves through long considered plans and preparations for the ordeal.

The Cherokee had during the ten years preceding 1830 so successfully strengthened and organized their political institutions that they had been able to impose a discipline upon their people such as no Indian nation had ever before attempted. Most realized as well as did their leaders that this coherence was absolutely imperative were they to stand any chance whatever of holding their ground. Since the Cherokee were committed of necessity to an altogether non-violent resistance there had to be certainty that their people, in obedience to the will of the majority as expressed by the acts of their elected government, would continue to accept patiently all the indignities, insults, deprivations, outrages and other stresses that could be visited upon them. In this endeavor they were astonishingly successful. During the next eight years in which these stresses became daily more oppressive only a very small minority of the nation took the easier course of yielding to

the constant pressures exerted by the state and federal governments. More than 90 percent of the nation continued to stand in
unwavering ranks behind their president, John Ross, and his fellow councilors.

After the discipline with which they were able to maintain their
non-violent resistance the strongest Cherokee weapon was their
opportunity to appeal to the nation's conscience. This appeal had
failed in practice in the instance of the narrow margin by which
Congress had voted the Removal Bill but there remained hope
that the congressional verdict might be reversed. There seemed
every reason to feel that many of the northern votes for the bill
had been less responsive to members' convictions and constituents
than to the demands of party strategy. The dissemination of Cherokee propaganda therefore continued unabated. Their Council
drafted memorials detailing Cherokee grievances which though
ignored by the administration excited debate in Congress and discussion in northern newspapers. Cherokee delegations journeyed
to Washington and when rebuffed by the White House argued the
Cherokee case in every other forum. Cherokee leaders made tours
of the north addressing church organizations and mass meetings.
The presentation of Cherokee aspirations and current developments in their struggle for survival published weekly in the
Phoenix was widely reprinted not only in the press of the country
but in the press of the world. Possibly the most effective of all
Cherokee propaganda devices was the fervor of their white missionaries. All were ardent advocates of Cherokee freedom and all
found in their associations with northern religious bodies a ready-
made avenue for the countrywide circulation of their views. The
sympathetic support elicited by these Cherokee appeals was largely
sectional, a condition which added appreciably to the energy of
the response. It was strongest in Ohio and New England, particularly in religious and intellectual circles, and among the more
devoted political opponents of the administration. As the distant
conflict in the south became more violent this northern sympathy
became more vociferous and emotional.

Georgia's preparations for the contest presented less diversity
but were stamped with an equal ingenuity. The state's dislodgment campaign was devoted simply and directly to rendering conditions surrounding continued Cherokee occupancy so offensive

that the victims must become only too happy to clear out. Georgia's major anti-Cherokee legislation was incorporated in an omnibus act passed by the legislature December 19, 1829. The effective date was delayed until June 1, 1830 in order to reduce the risk that the act's rigor might cost votes in Congress which was then considering the Removal Bill. After the bill's passage, Governor George Gilmer on July 3, 1830 proclaimed the act in force. Among its principal provisions were:[1]

1. Confiscation by the state of Cherokee land for the purpose of its erection into counties and early distribution among white owners. (The distribution was presently effected by the institution of a land lottery.)

2. Abolition of the authority of the Cherokee government, the nullification of all Cherokee laws and the exclusive subjection of all Cherokee residents to state jurisdiction.

3. Prohibition of the meetings of the Cherokee Council and of all other gatherings of Cherokee for any purpose, including religious.

4. Punishment by imprisonment of all Cherokee who advised other Cherokee to refuse to migrate.

5. Abrogation of all contracts between Indians and whites unless they had been witnessed by two whites.

6. Denial of the right of any Cherokee to testify in court against any white.

7. Specific denial of Cherokee right to dig for gold in the recently discovered Cherokee gold fields.

Georgia authorities did not make precipitate use of these extraordinary new powers. It was felt that given a little time to consider the enormity of the threat the Cherokee must realize that they had no other recourse than compliance with Georgia's wishes. In one area, however, the state found no latitude for discretion or delay. Gold had been discovered near Dahlonega in the heart of the Cherokee country and the excitement drew hordes of white gold-seekers who were presently supported by detachments of Georgia militia. They preempted Cherokee diggings, seized or destroyed tools and machinery, and confiscated or burned adjacent property and homes. Federal troops were introduced to restore order in an

---

[1] For text of basic Georgia act and other pertinent documents see Filler, Louis and Guttman, Allen, eds., *The Removal of the Cherokee Nation*. Boston, 1962.

area for which under federal law federal authority was responsible but upon Georgia's indignant protest Jackson hastily withdrew them. Bands of whites, ostensibly en route to and from the gold fields, wandered widely through the Cherokee country. The inhabitants had no defense against their trespasses and outrages since under the new laws no Cherokee could make a legal complaint against any white. Georgia's program of deliberately calculated pressures to be steadily intensified until the Cherokee yielded was in relentless progress.

Meanwhile, the administration was bringing to bear in support of Georgia's campaign pressures upon the Cherokee of its own. The annuities payable to the Cherokee in compensation for land cessions under the terms of former and still presumably valid treaties were withheld. Federal restraints on the introduction of liquor, long a basic feature of the federal government's determination to maintain order in Indian communities, were suspended. Secret funds were made available for the bribery of Cherokee leaders. Complaisant Cherokee were recruited as secret agents to spread rumors and alarms and to betray the proceedings of Cherokee councils. The few Cherokee who consented to migrate were rewarded by exceptionally generous issues of clothing, equipment and supplies and provided with studiedly comfortable transport. While Georgia wielded the stick of compulsion the federal government was extending the carrot of subversion.

The organized maintenance of Cherokee resistance had been sorely handicapped by the bankruptcy of the nation's exchequer. The Council's three principal sources of income, the authority to tax Cherokee citizens, federal annuities guaranteed by existing treaties and the opportune returns from the Cherokee gold fields, had been cut off by Georgia legislation and federal policy. In the continuing emergency the Council's functioning was kept in being by voluntary contributions from Cherokee able to make them. Despite the many other demands such as the maintenance of education, the Council scraped together the money to continue to dispatch official delegations to Washington with representations reciting Cherokee grievances and petitions appealing for their redress.

The 1828 delegation had been given no hearing by the retiring and disconsolate Adams administration. The reply received April

18, 1829 from the Indian affairs spokesman of the new Jackson administration, Secretary of War Eaton,[2] had been outwardly mild in tone, inasmuch as consideration of the Removal Bill was still pending in Congress, but offered no alternative to migration:

If you will go to the setting sun there you will be happy; there you can remain in peace and quietness; so long as the waters run and the oaks grow that country shall be guaranteed to you and no white man shall be permitted to settle near you.

These fervent assurances rang somewhat hollowly in Cherokee ears. They were much more impressed by the knowledge that at that very moment the West Cherokee were being driven from their so recently guaranteed "permanent home" in the lower Arkansas to a new "permanent home" on the plains. Despite Eaton's discouraging advice, the delegates, having during their long wait in Washington discovered northern friends of the Cherokee to be so much more spirited and voluble than were their opponents, returned home with the report that there was genuine hope that the new Congress would support the Cherokee position.

This hope was proved an illusion by the categorical nature of Jackson's first message, December 8, 1829, and the enactment of the Removal Bill by the new Congress, May 26, 1830. Even more clearly than before, the Cherokee appeared left with no other recourse than the right of petition. But the 1830 delegation, arriving in Washington to protest Georgia's recent confiscations, was stripped of this privilege as well. Secretary Eaton refused to consider them the legal representatives of the Cherokee nation until and unless they were authorized to approach him for the sole purpose of discussing a treaty of removal. An indirect reply to the Cherokee appeal was forced from the administration by the intervention of the Senate. A number of senators who had voted with the majority for the Removal Bill on the theory that its provisions were merely permissive, as affirmed by its proponents, had had second thoughts after the act had proved to be one that could be and was being used for compulsive purposes. The Senate February 15, 1831 adopted a resolution calling upon the president to inform the Senate whether he was or was not complying with the provisions of duly negotiated and ratified Indian treaties and, if he was

---

[2] More commonly noticed in American history for his reluctantly gallant espousal of Peggy O'Neill at Jackson's dictation.

not, to give reasons for his failure to enforce them. This passing impulse of the Senate to nourish its co-authority in treaty-making gained nothing either for the Senate or the Cherokee. In his response to the resolution, Jackson's special message of February 22, 1831 was even more brusque than had been his first on the subject. He declared he was in full support of Georgia's removal policy and asserted he had no intention of attempting to enforce any Indian treaty that conflicted in any way with the laws of any state.

Having failed in their appeals to the political authority of the federal government there remained to the Cherokee the possibly more effective appeal to the higher authority of American public opinion. After the crushing impacts of the Removal Bill and Georgia's punitive legislation had begun to register, the Cherokee nation addressed July 17, 1830 a public appeal to the American people:

. . . pleading . . . that the solemn engagements between their fathers and our fathers may be preserved. . . . More than a year ago we were officially given to understand by the secretary of war, that the president could not protect us against the laws of Georgia. . . . Finding that relief could not be obtained from the chief magistrate, and not doubting that our claim to protection was just, we made an application to congress. . . . But, just at the close of the session, an act was passed, by which an half million of dollars was appropriated towards effecting a removal of Indians. . . . Thus have we realized, with heavy hearts, that our supplication has not been heard; that the protection heretofore experienced is now to be withheld; that the guaranty, in consequence of which our fathers laid aside their arms and ceded the best portions of their country, means nothing; and that we must either emigrate to an unknown region and leave the pleasant land to which we have the strongest attachment, or submit to the legislation of a state, which has already made our people outlaws. . . . But in the midst of our sorrows, we do not forget our obligations to our friends and benefactors. It was with sensations of inexpressible joy that we have learned that the voice of thousands, in many parts of the United States, has been raised in our behalf, and numerous memorials offered in our favor, in both houses of congress. To those numerous friends, who have thus sympathized with us in our low estate, we tender our grateful acknowledgements. In pleading our cause, they have pleaded the cause of the poor and defenceless throughout the world. . . . The people of the United States will have the fairness to reflect, that all the treaties between them and the Cherokee were made, at the solicitation, and for the benefit, of the whites; that valuable considerations were given for every stipulation, on the part of the United States; that it is impossible to reinstate the parties in their former situation, that there are now hundreds of thousands of citizens of the United States residing upon lands ceded by the Cherokee in these very treaties; and that our people have trusted their country to the guaranty of the United States. If this guaranty fails them, in what can they trust, and where can they look for protection? . . . We wish to remain on the land of our fathers. We have a perfect and original right to remain without interruption or molestation. The treaties with us, and laws of the United States made in pursuance of treaties, guaranty our residence and our privileges, and secure us against intruders. Our only request is, that these treaties may be fulfilled, and these laws executed. . . . It is under a sense of the most pungent feelings that we make this, perhaps our last appeal to the good people of the United States. It cannot be that the community we are addressing, remarkable for its intelligence and religious sensibilities, and preeminent for its devotion to the rights of man, will lay aside this appeal.

Of all the attempts to appeal the Cherokee case to public opinion none aroused such Georgia animosity as the attention sought by the northern missionaries. They were regarded as malevolent interlopers whose interference in a regional problem of no concern to them was as great a disservice to the Cherokee as to Georgia. A deeper and fiercer resentment was born of the feeling that they were white men who were preferring another race to their own. Georgia's mounting displeasure led to the passage by the legislature December 22, 1830 of an act providing that after the following March 1 no white person might reside in the Cherokee country without a license from the governor which was in turn dependent upon an oath of allegiance to Georgia. In the face of these threats 12 of the principal missionaries to the Cherokee stood up to be counted. Meeting at New Echota December 29, 1830 they unanimously adopted resolutions for publication in the Phoenix which made the declaration of their sentiments equivalent to publication in the press of the world:

Resolved, That we view the Indian Question, at present so much agitated in the United States, as being not merely of a political, but of a moral nature—inasmuch as it involves the maintenance or violation of the faith of our country—and as demanding, therefore, the most serious consideration of all American citizens, not only as patriots, but as Christians. *Resolved,* That we regard the present crisis of affairs, relating to the Cherokee nation, as calling for the sympathies, and prayers, and aid, of all benevolent people throughout the United States.

Their resolutions were accompanied by an extensive statement reciting their conservative estimate, based on their personal knowledge, of the recent progress of the Cherokee in education and religion, which they candidly stated had been less than they had hoped but which they asserted had nevertheless been more than sufficient to compel consideration of the Cherokee as a civilized people. The missionaries' pronunciamento came to the conclusion:

To us it appears that the Cherokee are in course of improvement, which promises, if uninterrupted, to place them, at no distant period, nearly on a level with their white brethren. Laboring, as we are, to aid them in their progress, we cannot do otherwise than earnestly deprecate any measure which threatens to arrest it. In this light we view the attempt to remove them from their inheritance, or subject them, against their will, to the dominion of others. Our sympathies are with them—our prayers have often ascended, and shall still ascend in their behalf—and we earnestly invite the prayers of all our fellow Christians, that HE who rules the destinies of nations will deliver them out of their afflictions, and establish them in the land which he has given them.

The missionaries' memorial roused Georgia to punitive action under the terms of the new residence law. A detachment of militia March 12, 1831 arrested Samuel Worcester, Isaac Proctor and John Thompson, three of the signers. They were released, however, by the Georgia county court in which they were arraigned on the judge's ruling that their association with missions partially supported by federal funds rendered them in effect federal employees and as such not subject to Georgia law. This unexpected obstacle was speedily removed by Secretary Eaton who officially informed Georgia authorities that the administration considered only Worcester a federal employee and he only because of his service as a postmaster. Upon Governor Gilmer's protest to President Jackson, Worcester was thereupon relieved of this post. After the missionaries had again been warned to leave the Cherokee country the militia returned July 7, 1831 to arrest ten of them, together with John Wheeler, the white printer of the Phoenix. The prisoners were treated with a deliberate brutality calculated to demonstrate to the north Georgia's scorn of outside disapproval and to the Cherokee the utter hopelessness of their cause. They were beaten, reviled, loaded with chains and forced to plod at the tailgate of a wagon 35 miles a day, including Sunday, to the county jail at Lawrenceville.[3] There was further evidence of the intensity of Georgia's resentment of the influence exercised by the missionaries upon the Cherokee in the response to the prisoners' request that they be permitted to hold services on their first Sunday in jail. Colonel C. H. Nelson, the militia commander who had arrested them, replied:

We view the within request as an impertinent one. If your conduct be evidence of your character and the doctrines you wish to promulgate, we are sufficiently enlightened as to both. Our object is to restrain, not to facilitate, their promulgation. If your object is true piety, you can enjoy it where you are. Were we hearers, we would not be benefited, devoid as we are of confidence in your honesty.

The defendants were tried September 15, 1831, charged with violation of Georgia's law subjecting white residents in the Cherokee country to the test of an oath of allegiance, and found guilty by the jury. Nine of them gave up the unequal contest and upon taking the oath were released. The other two, Samuel Worcester and Elizur Butler, continued to refuse as a matter of principle based on their conception that their acquiescence would have implied an acknowledgment of Georgia's Cherokee repression laws which they considered unjust and unconstitutional. The next day they were sentenced to four years at hard labor. They were removed to the penitentiary at Milledgeville where during the earlier months of their confinement they were treated with continued rigor and denied all privileges or visitors.

The American Board of Commissioners for Foreign Missions addressed, November 3, 1831, a memorial to President Jackson asserting that the Cherokee missions had been established at the solicitation of and in coordination with the United States government and declaring Georgia's acts of coercion to be in violation of

[3] For detail on this episode and others in the story of the Cherokee missions see Walker, Robert Sparks, *Torchlights to the Cherokee*. New York, 1931.

the Constitution. Jackson's November 14, 1831 reply, delivered by his new Secretary of War, Lewis Cass, took the familiar administration position that the president "has no authority to interfere, under the circumstances stated in the Memorial" with the operation of state laws.

The arrest, conviction and mistreatment of the missionaries had caused a tremendous stir in the north. In Georgia as well there had been some revulsion of public opinion. But the Cherokee had meanwhile ceased to place their sole reliance upon appeals to the American conscience. The previous summer the Cherokee Council, meeting in defiance of Georgia's new laws, had determined to undertake a more direct and formal appeal to American justice. Denied the protection of the state government, of Congress and of the administration they had initiated legal processes by which they were now seeking a justification of their constitutional position in federal courts.

12

The Cherokee appeal was more than a cry for justice from a help-less victim. It was an examining probe thrust into the deepest foundations upon which had been erected the constitutional struc-ture of the republic. The politically inspired founders, two of the most eminent of whom, Thomas Jefferson and John Adams, had died the same July 4th just four years before, had based their hopes for the nation's permanence on two great principles: a natural division of authority between states and the union and a workable balance of power among the three branches of the union's central government. The Cherokee pleadings subjected both of these fundamental doctrines to a protracted and exigent testing.

In seeking counsel to brief and present the Cherokee case Ross was guided by eminent advisors, including Jeremiah Evarts and Daniel Webster. For necessary appearances in state courts the Georgia firm of Underwood and Harris was retained. For the more critical argument of the Cherokee cause in the Supreme Court of the United States the services of William Wirt were volunteered. Wirt had been attorney general in the Monroe and Adams ad-ministrations and had been recognized as one of the country's leading attorneys since he had served as President Jefferson's spe-cial prosecutor at the sensational trial for treason of Aaron Burr in 1807. Also volunteering was John Sergeant, a Pennsylvania attor-ney with a national reputation as speaker and humanitarian who had served repeated terms in the House since 1815. Representation by counsel so distinguished assured the Cherokee of commanding not only the absorbed attention of the court but of the American people.

The Supreme Court in 1830 was perhaps the most memorable of any in all the institution's long history. Virginia, which had supplied the nation four of its first six presidents had likewise from the same apparently inexhaustible reservoir of talent and prestige supplied the Chief Justice, John Marshall, who had presided since 1801. His monumental interpretations of the Constitution had shaped the government of the United States by his successive prescriptions and definitions of its functions and powers. The originality of his reasoning and the independence of his judgment had incensed other presidents before they came into conflict with Jackson's will.

The Cherokee controversy had now drawn into its vortex every major manifestation of power in the country: the President, Congress, the Supreme Court, political parties, the religious community and the press. Clergymen, editors, educators, lecturers, writers, party managers and candidates for any office were as obliged to take some position as had already been senators, congressmen and federal administrators.

An obscure murder trial in Georgia offered Wirt his immediate opportunity to bring the Cherokee case to the attention of the Supreme Court. Corn Tassel, a Cherokee accused of killing another Cherokee, had been condemned to death in Carrol County Superior Court, a Georgia court which the Cherokee nation did not admit could have jurisdiction over its citizens. Unable to speak English, the accused had been unable to understand the charge or to testify in his own defense. Upon Wirt's plea, the Supreme Court December 12, 1830 cited the State of Georgia to appear to show cause why a writ of error should not issue. Georgia was infuriated by this attempted intervention by a federal court which could so clearly lead to a questioning of the validity of the state's new anti-Indian laws. The Supreme Court's order was ignored. With the governor's approval the local authorities proceeded as though there had been no federal interposition. The indignant trial judge attended the execution to make sure that it was promptly conducted. Governor Lumpkin wrote Jackson, "The Supreme Court has as much right to grant a citation to cite the King of Great Britain for any assignable cause as to cite the government of Georgia for the manner in which the state chooses to exercise her jurisdiction."

Georgia's scorn of the court's citation in the Tassel case appeared to Wirt to have opened the way to urging the main Cherokee case upon the court's consideration. As the legal representative of the Cherokee nation he moved in March, 1831, for an injunction against Georgia arguing that the state's recent anti-Cherokee legislation was in violation of treaties of the United States, of laws of the United States and of the Constitution. The court's position on the motion turned on the constitutional status of the Cherokee community. Was it constitutionally eligible to sue a state in the Supreme Court of the United States? Marshall in delivering, March 5, 1831, the opinion of the majority, ruled:[1]

If courts were permitted to indulge their sympathies, a case better calculated to excite them can scarcely be imagined. A people once numerous, powerful, and truly independent, found by our ancestors in the quiet and uncontrolled possession of an ample domain, gradually sinking beneath our superior policy, our arts and our arms, have yielded their lands by successive treaties, each of which contains a solemn guarantee of the residue, until they retain no more of their formerly extensive territory than is deemed necessary to their comfortable subsistence. To preserve this remnant, the present application is made. Before we can look into the merits of the case, a preliminary inquiry presents itself. Has this court jurisdiction of the cause? . . . Is the Cherokee nation a foreign state in the sense which that term is used in the constitution? . . . Though the Indians are acknowledged to have an unquestionable, and, heretofore, unquestioned right to the lands they occupy, until that right shall be extinguished by a voluntary cession to our government; yet it may well be doubted whether those tribes which reside within the acknowledged boundaries of the United States can, with strict accuracy, be denominated foreign nations . . . They look to our government for protection; rely upon its kindness and its power; appeal to it for relief of their wants; and address the president as their great father. They and their country are considered by foreign nations, as well as by ourselves, as being so completely under the sovereignty and dominion of the United States, that any attempt to acquire their lands, or to form a political con-

[1] That spring he was mourning the recent death of his wife, the mother of his ten children, to whom during 48 years of marriage he had been deeply devoted.

nexion with them, would be considered by all as an invasion of our territory, and an act of hostility . . . The court has bestowed its best attention on this question, and, after mature deliberation, the majority is of opinion that an Indian tribe or nation within the United States is not a foreign state in the sense of the constitution, and cannot maintain an action in the courts of the United States. . . . If it be true that the Cherokee nation have rights, this is not the tribunal in which those rights are to be asserted. If it be true that wrongs have been inflicted, and that still greater are to be apprehended, this is not the tribunal which can redress the past or prevent the future. The motion for an injunction is denied.

Justices Joseph Story, Marshall's closest associate on the court and almost as highly regarded as a constitutional authority, and Smith Thompson, an anti-Jackson Democrat who had formerly served on the New York Supreme Court and as Secretary of the Navy in Monroe's Cabinet, dissented from the majority in a minority opinion written by Thompson:

If we look to the whole course of treatment by this country of the Indians, from the year 1775, to the present day, when dealing with them in their aggregate capacity as nations or tribes, and regarding the mode and manner in which all negotiations have been carried on and concluded with them; the conclusion appears to me irresistible, that they have been regarded, by the executive and legislative branches of the government, not only as sovereign and independent, but as foreign nations or tribes, not within the jurisdiction nor under the government of the states wthin which they were located. . . . The injuries complained of are violations committed and threatened upon the property of the complainants, secured to them by the laws and treaties of the United States. Under the constitution, the judicial power of the United States extends expressly to all cases in law and equity, arising under the laws of the United States, and treaties made or which shall be made, under the authority of the same. . . . That the Cherokee nation of Indians have, by virtue of these treaties, an exclusive right of occupancy of the lands in question, and that the United States are bound under their guarantee, to protect the nation in the enjoyment of such occupancy, cannot, in my judgment, admit of a doubt: and that some of the laws of Georgia set out in the bill are in violation of, and in conflict with those treaties and the act of 1802, is to my mind equally clear. . . . These treaties and this law, are declared by the constitution to be the supreme law of the land: it follows, as a matter of course, that the laws of Georgia, so far as they are repugnant to them, must be void and inoperative.

The majority opinion of the court, however, had held against the Cherokee and appeared to have deprived them of their last hope of legal redress. It was Georgia's intemperate proceedings against the missionaries, following within a week upon the announcement of the court's decision, that gave Wirt a new opening. There could be no question that Samuel Worcester was a citizen of the United States and as a consequence there could equally be no question that if his constitutional rights had been violated the Supreme Court must consider an appeal on his behalf. Appearing in this instance not as legal counsel for the Cherokee nation but for the individual, Samuel Worcester, Wirt filed the suit that became famous as *Worcester v. The State of Georgia*. He argued that Worcester had taken residence in the Cherokee country at the invitation of the Cherokee nation, that the Cherokee had been empowered to extend this invitation by valid treaties with the United States and that therefore the laws of Georgia under which Worcester had been arrested and condemned were in violation of the laws and Constitution of the United States. It was an astute legal maneuver for in reviewing the constitutional rights of the citizen, Worcester, the court must be obliged to rule upon the fundamental nature of the relationships involving the Cherokee nation, the State of Georgia and the United States. In again delivering, February 28, 1832, the majority opinion of the court, Marshall ruled:

The plaintiff is a citizen of the state of Vermont, condemned to hard labour for four years in the penitentiary of Georgia; under colour of an act which he alleges to be repugnant to the Constitution, laws and treaties of the United States. The legislative power of a state, the controlling power of the Constitution and laws of the United States, the rights, if they have any, the political existence of a once numerous and powerful people, the personal liberty of a citizen, are all involved in the subject now to be considered. . . . It is, then, we think, too clear for controversy, that the act of Congress, by which this court is constituted, has given it the power, and of course imposed on it the duty, of exercising jurisdiction in this case. This duty, however unpleasant, cannot be avoided. Those who fill the judicial department have no discretion in selecting the subjects to be brought before them.

We must examine the defence set up in this plea. We must inquire and decide whether the act of the legislature of Georgia, under which the plaintiff in error has been prosecuted and condemned, be consistent with, or repugnant to, the constitution, laws and treaties of the United States. . . . The constitution, by declaring treaties already made, as well as those to be made, to be the supreme law of the land, has adopted and sanctioned the previous treaties with Indian nations, and consequently admits their rank among those powers who are capable of making treaties. The words "treaty" and "nation" are words of our own language, selected in our diplomatic and legislative proceedings, by ourselves, having each a definite and well understood meaning. We have applied them to Indians, as we have applied them to the other nations of the earth. They are applied to all in the same sense. . . . If the review which has been taken be correct and we think it is, the acts of Georgia are repugnant to the constitution, laws and treaties of the United States. They interfere forcibly with the relations established between the United States and the Cherokee nation, the regulation of which, according to the settled principles of our constitution, are committed exclusively to the Government of the union. They are in direct hostility with treaties, repeated in a succession of years, which mark out the boundary that separates the Cherokee country from Georgia; guaranty to them all the land within their boundary; solemnly pledge the faith of the United States to restrain their citizens from trespassing on it; and recognize the pre-existing power of the nation to govern itself. They are in equal hostility with the acts of congress for regulating this intercourse, and giving effect to the treaties. The forcible seizure and abduction of the plaintiff in error, who was residing in the nation with its permission, and by authority of the president of the United States, is also a violation of the acts which authorize the chief magistrate to exercise his authority. Will these powerful considerations avail the plaintiff in error? We think they will. He was seized, and forcibly carried away, while under the guardianship of treaties guarantying the country in which he resided, and taking it under the protection of the United States. He was seized while performing, under the sanction of the chief magistrate of the union, those duties which the humane policy adopted by congress had recommended. . . . It is the opinion of this court that the judgment of the superior court for the county of Gwinnett, in the state of Georgia, condemning Samuel A. Worcester to hard labour, in the penitentiary of the state of Georgia, for four years, was pronounced by that court under colour of a law which is void, as being repugnant to the constitution, treaties, and laws of the United States, and ought, therefore, to be reversed and annulled.

The Supreme Court filed its citation March 3, 1832 with the Georgia trial court ordering the release of Worcester. The sweeping decision had seemed a total victory for the Cherokee cause. When news of it reached their country the Cherokee were stirred to a tumult of rejoicing. Federal preparations for the transportation westward of the few families who had that spring consented to migrate were thrown into disarray. All Cherokee were convinced that they had been saved by this momentous determination of their rights by the highest court in the land. Their disillusionment when presently they were forced to realize that their great victory was no more than a legal mirage was consequently the more bitter.

The Supreme Court had declared the law of the land but it possessed no means to command obedience to that law. This was an obligation that devolved upon the executive. President Jackson disapproved of the decision and the intensity of his disapproval had been forecast by his every word and act since entering public life. The Senate's February 15, 1831 resolution of tacit remonstrance with his Indian policy had been voted just after Wirt had brought the Cherokee question to the attention of the Supreme Court. Jackson's February 22 reply to the Senate had therefore been intended to impress upon the Supreme Court as well as upon Congress the inflexibility of his views:

. . . The Indians thus situated cannot be regarded in any other light than as members of a foreign government or of that of the State within whose chartered limits they reside. If in the former, the ordinary legislation of Congress in relation to them is not warranted by the Constitution, which was established for the benefit of our own, not of a foreign people. If in the latter, then, like other citizens or people resident within the limits of the States, they are subject to their jurisdiction and control. To maintain a contrary doctrine and to require the Executive to enforce it by the employment of a military force would be to place in his hands a power to make war upon the rights of the States and the liberties of the country—a power which should be placed in the hands of no individual. . . . Toward this race of people I entertain the kindest feelings, and am not sensible that the views which I have taken of their true interests are less favorable to them than those which oppose their emigration to the West. Years since I stated to them my belief that if the States chose to extend their laws over them it would not be in the power of the Federal Government to prevent it. My opinion remains the same, and I can see no alternative for them but that of their removal to the West or a quiet submission to the State laws. . . . Either course promises them peace and happiness, whilst an obstinate perseverance in the effort to maintain their possessions independent of the State authority can not fail to render their condition still more helpless and miserable. Such an effort ought, therefore, to be discountenanced by all who sincerely sympathize in the fortunes of this peculiar people, and especially by the political bodies of the Union, as calculated to disturb the harmony of the two Governments and to endanger the safety of the many blessings which they enable us to enjoy.[2]

Having delivered a final warning that was so direct and explicit, Jackson was bound to regard the Supreme Court's contrary judgment as a challenge. It was one he could accept with grim relish. He had no slightest intention of giving the Court's decision effect or of permitting it in any way to influence the Indian policy of his administration. He was reported to have privately remarked, "John Marshall has rendered his decision, now let him enforce it."[3]

Georgia had likewise no slightest intention of complying with the Supreme Court's decision. Like the President, Georgia had given ample advance warning of an equal inflexibility. When the Supreme Court had cited Georgia to appear as defendant in the Worcester suit Governor Lumpkin had emphasized the state's stand in his November 25, 1831 message to the legislature:

I submit to the general assembly, for its consideration, copies of two communications received yesterday, purporting to be signed by Henry Baldwin, esq. one of the justices of the supreme court of the United States, and to be citations to the state of Georgia, to appear in the supreme court, on the second Monday in January next. . . . The obvious object of the proceedings to which this notice and these citations relate, is to call in question, and attempt to overthrow, that essential jurisdiction of the state, in criminal cases, which has been vested by our constitution, in the superior courts of the several counties of the state. . . . Any attempt to infringe the evident right of a state to govern the entire population within its territorial limits, and to punish all offences committed against its laws, within those limits,

[2] Vol. 2, p. 1099, Richardson, James D., *Messages and Papers of the President.* Washington, 1897.

[3] There had long been personal ill feeling between Jackson and Marshall. In 1828 Marshall had taken the unprecedented step, while continuing to hold his presumably nonpolitical post on the court, of campaigning against Jackson.

(due regard being had to the cases expressly excepted by the constitution of the United States), would be the usurpation of a power never granted by the states. Such an attempt, whenever made, will challenge the most determined resistance; and if persevered in, will inevitably eventuate in the annihilation of our beloved union.[4]

Having announced in advance its scorn of the authority of the Supreme Court, Georgia did not shrink from the confrontation when the actual decision was handed down. The order for Worcester's release was ignored. Voice was given Georgia's defiance by the state's highest officials. Georgia's United States Senator, George M. Troup, in an open letter of March 5, 1832 to the *Georgia Journal,* pointedly reminded Georgians that if they yielded on this Indian question they were inviting similar federal dictation on the slavery question:

Dear Sirs: The people of Georgia will receive with indignant feelings, as they ought, the recent decision of the supreme court, so flagrantly violative of their sovereign rights. . . . The jurisdiction claimed over one portion of our population may very soon be exerted over *another;* and in both cases they will be sustained by the fanatics of the north. Very soon, therefore, things must come to their worst; and if in the last resort we need defenders, we will find them everywhere among the honest men of the country; whom a just and wise conduct will rally to our banner—for the rest we care nothing.

In his message to the next session of the Georgia legislature Governor Lumpkin defined the state's position:

These extraordinary proceedings of the Supreme Court have not been submitted to me officially, nor have they been brought before me in any manner which called for my official action. I have, however, been prepared to meet this usurpation of Federal power with the most prompt and determined resistance, in whatever form its enforcement might have been attempted by any branch of the Federal Government. It has afforded me great satisfaction to find that our whole people, as with the voice of one man, have manifested a calm, but firm and determined resolution to sustain the authorities and sovereignty of their State against this unjust and unconstitutional encroachment of the Federal judiciary. The ingenuity of man might be challenged to show a single sentence of the Constitution of the United States giving power, either direct or implied, to the general government, or any of

4 *Niles Register,* December 24, 1831.

its departments, to nullify the laws of a State. . . . I, however, deem it unnecessary for me, at this time, to animadvert on this decision of the Supreme Court. Its fallacy, its inconsistency with former decisions, and its obvious tendency to intermeddle with the political rights of the States, and to change our Federal system into one consolidated mass, has been so often exposed by the most able jurists and statesmen that a large majority of the people of this Union are confirmed in the conviction of the fallibility, infirmities, and errors of this Supreme tribunal. This branch of the general Government must henceforth stand where it always ought to have stood in public estimation, as being liable to all the frailties and weaknesses of erring men.

Georgia's actions more than matched Georgia's words. Month after month passed with Georgia authorities continuing to hold the imprisoned missionaries in violation of the Supreme Court's order for their release. Then, their punishment having served its purpose of demonstrating Georgia's determination to exercise full sovereignty, they were again offered a pardon. They again refused on the grounds that to accept a pardon was a tacit admission that they had committed a crime. More months passed. The prisoners finally became convinced that their legal situation promised no further hope and that their sacrifice was ceasing to serve the Cherokee cause. They informed the governor that they were withdrawing their suit, still pending in the Supreme Court, because of "apprehension that the further prosecution of the controversy, under existing circumstances, might be attended with consequences injurious to our beloved country." Lumpkin termed this disrespectful. They modified the wording of their plea and after some further delay to mollify Georgia opinion they were pardoned and released January 14, 1833. Their long martyrdom had proved a useless gesture which had not assisted the Cherokee and had served instead to dramatize Georgia's successful defiance of the Supreme Court.

The court's order demanding the release of the missionaries had been only a part of its much broader pronouncement that Georgia's anti-Cherokee laws were unconstitutional and therefore null and void. Georgia's challenge to this basic exercise of the Supreme Court's authority was even more deliberate and devastating than in the case of the missionaries. During the months immediately following the delivery of the court's decision the state's surveys of

the Cherokee country were pressed. The machinery for the operation of the land lottery was set up and in December the drawings
commenced. By means of the lottery all land was being taken from
its former Cherokee owners for delivery to new white owners
selected by chance. For the ostensible purpose of protecting the
surveyors and other state officials against molestation by the distracted Cherokee, large detachments of Georgia militia were quartered in the Cherokee country with general orders to stand on the
alert to crush in its inception the slightest indication of Cherokee
resistance. The premeditated brutality of the militia's daily conduct suggested their commanders' hope of provoking a Cherokee
reaction which might provide an excuse for their immediate
physical expulsion. The carefully disciplined Cherokee instead
patiently submitted even when the provocations extended to the
burning of their homes, the confiscation of their property, the
mistreatment of their women, the closing of their schools, and the
sale of liquor in their churches. The Cherokee country was still an
area in which formerly recognized law had placed all responsibility for the maintenance of peace and order on the federal government. Georgia's invasion could have exhibited a no more striking scorn of federal authority had it been an accompaniment of an
armed insurrection.

That the issue did not develop into armed conflict was entirely
due to Jackson's determination that in this instance the duties of
his office did not require him to accept the Supreme Court's definition of the law. Instead of using his executive authority to restrain acts of Georgia ruled illegal by the court or to protect Cherokee rights ruled valid by the court he directed his administration's agents in the Cherokee country to redouble their efforts, in
coordination with Georgia's more overt efforts, to persuade the
Cherokee to migrate as the sole possible escape from their tribulations.

The President's contempt for the authority of the Supreme
Court was saved from development into a greater constitutional
crisis by the extraordinary contrast between his impulse to weaken
federal authority in this instance and his determination to
strengthen it in all others. His northern critics could not justify
their accusations that as a southern President his magnification of
states' rights represented a premeditated depreciation of the union.

For at the very moment that he was delivering his sensational blow at the prestige of the Supreme Court he was giving even stronger indications of his utter devotion to the union. Though as a westerner he had all his life been a confirmed and ruthless expansionist and as a southerner he accepted and defended slavery, he was continuing to withhold active support from the American settlers in Texas because of his concern lest the addition of so large a slave territory would destroy the carefully maintained north-south balance in Congress and hence could threaten the union. During this same 1832 that he was condoning Georgia's trespasses on the federal government's Indian wards he was in the nullification controversy condemning South Carolina's attempt to question the authority of the federal government.

This anomaly in Jackson's Presidential attitudes led the Cherokee and their more ardent sympathizers to a conclusion which increased their disquiet. If Jackson was as devoted a believer in the republic and in those constitutional powers which permitted its government to function as most of his actions indicated then the obvious explanation for the glaring inconsistency of his Indian policy must be his instinctive conception that the laws of the republic had been instituted to guard the freedom of white men only. This subject of racial inequalities had developed in the north a peculiar sensitivity. Negro slavery could be regarded as an incubus that the country had inherited and which might eventually be shaken off but the nation's continued toleration of its existence caused many to feel a greater sense of secret guilt and public outrage that still another race should be singled out for penalization.

This seemed to present an issue that the Cherokee, many of their friends, and many of Jackson's political opponents could welcome as offering a certain appeal in the country's north and east where major centers of population were concentrated and discontent with slavery was becoming increasingly evident. It was an issue that Jackson himself had thrust into the spotlight of public attention by his humiliation of the Supreme Court. It was also one of special concern in those religious, intellectual, and humanitarian circles which by their nature could command public attention and arouse emotional excitement. Meanwhile, that public's verdict need not be long delayed. 1832 was a presidential election year.

By proclamation of President Ross, the 19th of July, 1832, was appointed a day of Cherokee fasting and prayer. The Cherokee had some reason for another revival of hope. In the hotly contested campaign Jackson's many enemies were lending much strident support to the arguments of his organized opposition. That opposition appeared formidable in its own right. There could be no question that it was also committed to the Cherokee cause. The Cherokee's most notable advocate, Henry Clay, was Jackson's principal opponent as Presidential candidate of the National Republicans. His Vice Presidential candidate was John Sergeant, associate Cherokee counsel in the Supreme Court suit. Their chief counsel, William Wirt, was Presidential candidate of the Anti-Masonic party, a new group in which religious and political interests were allied and which had taken over much of the National Republican organization in the north and east.[5] It was felt that Wirt might capture much of Jackson's vote in the east while Clay was cutting into his totals in the west.

The National Republicans, meeting to nominate Clay at Baltimore, December 12–14, 1831, in the first national convention to be held by a party, announced their views on the issues to be decided in the coming campaign. In an Address to the People of the United States, a forerunner of what was presently to become that quadrennial statement of a party's principles known as its platform, they centered their fire on Jackson's Indian policy:

The last point which we shall notice in the conduct of the administration . . . perhaps the most important of all, as far as concerns the principles involved, is that of our relations with the Indian tribes, and particularly that portion of the Cherokees situated within the territorial limits of Georgia. A series of solemn treaties concluded successively by all the administrations of the general government since the period of its establishment, guaranteed to these Indians the possession of their lands without interference or intrusion from any quarter, their right of governing themselves according to their own laws within those

5 There had been a continuous evolution in the names of political parties during the preceding 30 years. Jefferson's party had been known as Republicans and that of Hamilton and John Adams as Federalists. Monroe's supporters called themselves National Republicans. Jackson had been elected in 1828 by previously unorganized supporters popularly known as "Jackson men" or "Jackson Democrats" who presently became known simply as Democrats.

limits, and their character of sovereign states. An act of congress passed in the year 1802, authorized and required the president to protect the Indians in the rights guaranteed to them by those treaties, if necessary, by the employment of military force. In open violation to all these solemn engagements the state of Georgia has extended her jurisdiction, over the territory and persons of the Cherokee situated within her limits, interrupted them in the possession of their dwellings and plantations, and attempted to deprive them of the character of distinct communities; while the president, instead of protecting the Indians against these acts of wholly unauthorized violence, has openly countenanced the pretentions of Georgia, and instead of employing the armed force of the United States, in their defence, has actually withdrawn that force at the instance of the offending party, from the scene of action, and left the unoffending natives entirely at the mercy of their enemies. The recent inhuman and unconstitutional outrages committed under the authority of Georgia upon the persons of several unoffending citizens heretofore residing as missionaries within the territory of the Cherokees, constitutes, perhaps, the most unjustifiable portion of these proceedings. They have received, like the rest, the countenance and approbation of the general executive. Few examples can be found, even in the history of barbarous communities, in which the sacred character of a minister of religion has furnished so slight a protection against disrespect and violence.[6]

Fort Sumter was still 30 years away but the Indian removal controversy, with its overtones of racial and religious prejudices, had already generated north-south antipathies which had moved a national political party meeting in national convention to demand the employment of the Army of the United States to compel the submission of a recalcitrant state to the national will. As the campaign gathered momentum the Supreme Court decision sharpened the political issue and offered a new focus to the moral misgivings of Jackson's northern critics. Friends of the Cherokee and opponents of Jackson found common ground in making as much political capital as possible of Jackson's attack on the Supreme Court and the violent denunciation of the court by his southern supporters. The Young Men's National Republican Convention, May 11, 1832, resolved:

that the Supreme Court of the United States is the only tribunal recognized by the constitution for deciding, in the last resort, all ques-

6 *Niles Register,* December 24, 1831.

tions arising under the constitution and laws of the United States and that upon the preservation of the authority and jurisdiction of that court inviolate, depends the existence of the union.

Jackson's partisans evidenced no reluctance to pick up the gage and the repute of the Supreme Court became a political football throughout the campaign. Northern newspapers supporting Jackson had as little hesitation in castigating the Supreme Court as had the most fervent states' rights journals in the south. Among examples:

Onondaga (NY) Standard: In regard to the intimation of judge McLean, that upon the enforcement of this decision depends the resolution of the court ever to convene again, we have only to say that we trust in heaven they will adhere to their determination. We should rejoice in the event.

Boston Statesman: . . . this last decree of the supreme court on the Georgia question is the boldest, though of all opinions heretofore given, this is surely the least creditable to the intellectual character of the court; there is not a constitutional lawyer in the United States who will not be shocked by the heresies which it contains.

New Hampshire Patriot: Previous to the decision of the supreme court, upon the Indian question, was there not a caucus comprised of judges Marshall, Thompson and Story and Messrs Clay, Sergeant, Webster, Everett and some few others? Did not Messrs Clay, &c, urge upon the *judges* the necessity of their sustaining them on the Indian question, solely on political grounds?[7]

In the ultimate submission of the issue to the judgment of the American people Jackson proved to have estimated their temper far more astutely than had his critics. The practical aspects of such issues as the national bank, the tariff, and internal improvements were more readily grasped by the average voter than the ethics of Indian removal or the sanctity of the judiciary. Concern for the rights of a remote racial minority did not impinge on his emotions as deeply as did concern for his own economic welfare. The image of Jackson as the fearless champion of the democratic interests of the common people who had not hesitated to challenge the vested interests of the moneyed class carried overwhelming weight with the mass of voters, both north and south. Jackson's popular vote

[7] For contemporary detail on 1832 campaign see *Niles Register*, Vol 42.

was 707,000 compared to Clay's 329,000 and Wirt's 255,000. He swept the electoral college with 219 to Clay's 49 and Wirt's 7.

The Cherokee cause had been staggered by the blows of Jackson's 1828 election and the 1830 enactment of the Removal Bill by Congress. The considered verdict of the American people in 1832 had been a yet more stunning blow. From it there appeared no appeal for there could be no higher tribunal. Georgia was pressing on relentlessly with the confiscation and redistribution of Cherokee land. Still the Cherokee would not yield. Families forced from their homes took up their abode in forest encampments. Another delegation, headed by Ross, himself, was dispatched to Washington to renew the demand that the President enforce federal law and to remind Jackson that the Cherokee would never, under any circumstances, consent to removal. The trend of Cherokee opinion at the end of 1832 was recorded by a leading article in the *Phoenix:*

The state of Georgia is about to perpetrate one of the most shameless and atrocious depredations, that was ever committed in times of peace, upon any nation or people. Without awaiting the extinguishment of the Indian title, as pledged by the general government to that state, without regard to the most solemn treaties, guaranteeing forever to the Cherokee the occupancy of their lands, her governor has fixed upon the 22nd instant, as the day, when she will commence drawing for our lands and gold mines by a lottery system. . . . While we have submitted to one calamity, another and another, like the billows of an angry sea, has rolled upon us. Still our position has not been moved, nor not even by the appointment of that day when Georgian honor was to be run through a sporting wheel to enable her to seize our lands. We have looked forward to the crisis, when the President of the United States would be moved by public opinion to the execution of our treaties and would restore to us the rights affirmed to us by the supreme court. But the president continues to withhold his fostering care of these rights, and refuses to fulfill in good faith our treaties with him.

Removal of the southern Indians had been decreed by two of the three branches of the national government and by the national electorate after a campaign in which it had been a major issue. But removal had still to be accomplished. The controversy was still in its earlier, more rational and least violent stages. The task was to generate increasing misery, shame, suffering and sectional recrimination through each of the next seven years. Aside from the 18,000 eastern Cherokee, there were 22,000 Creek, mostly in Alabama, 7,000 Choctaw in Mississippi, 5,000 Chickasaw, also in Mississippi, and 5,000 Seminole in Florida. All were desperately unwilling to migrate and remained determined to cling to their homes until driven from them at the bayonet's point. Indian removal was to become a problem progressively more complex while every attempt at any solution was to become more murderously difficult. Any satisfactory resolution was with each passing year to be made less possible by the ominous circumstance that removal was being demanded by one section of the country with a determination as furious as was the sense of outrage provoked in another.

In the closing words of his 1832 message to his legislature, Governor Lumpkin of Georgia described the prospect with a pungency more prophetic than he knew:

Finally, fellow citizens, let us strive to be of one mind—let our measures be founded in wisdom, justice and moderation—constantly bearing in mind the sacred truth, that a Nation or State "divided against itself, cannot stand."

13

No Indian nation north of Mexico had had a longer and more dramatic history than the Creek. Measured even in the terms of that portion of it recorded by white men, in 1832 the Creek nation had had a place on the pages of history for 304 years, compared to the 57 years that had elapsed since the name of the United States had first been entered upon them. They had been the first Indians within the present area of the United States to engage in war with white men. In 1528 they had routed the army of Panfilo Narvaez, even though the Spanish invaders, the first white men the Creek had ever seen, had descended upon them equipped with such mysterious and terrifying paraphernalia as ships, horses, armor, steel weapons, cannon and firearms. Thereafter for three tumultuous centuries the Creek had continued successfully to resist the perpetually recurring attempts of Spaniards, Englishmen, Frenchmen and Americans to seize possession of their country.

The final years of Creek independence had been shaped by the devotion to their survival of two remarkable men, one a Creek and the other an American. Alexander McGillivray, the last great principal chief of the Creek, coming to power during the Revolution, had marshaled Creek defenses with such perspicacity that during his lifetime he was able to stem the advance of the most menacing of all the Creek people's long succession of white adversaries, the American settler. Born of a Creek-French-Scotch family more renowned for the beauty of its women than the vigor of its men, he suffered ill health throughout his life and yet summoned the energies to conduct an astounding series of military and diplomatic maneuvers which so successfully maintained Creek autonomy that his alliance was earnestly sought by Spain and the United States. The masterly timing and phrasing of his notes, messages and pronouncements clothed his policy with a standing in international affairs which led to his being received with obsequious honors as a visiting chief of state in both Spanish and American capitals. When he died in 1793 he had long been receiving tribute from both powers. The Creek decline expected after his death was delayed for another generation by the efforts of Benjamin Hawkins, a former United States Senator from North Carolina. Visiting the Creek country as a treaty commissioner, he became so absorbed in their problems that he accepted the post of United States Agent to the Creek and dedicated the next 20 years of his career to their welfare. His efforts centered upon the promotion among them of farming, stock-raising, spinning, weaving and other civilized arts and crafts which if practiced in time might maintain their standard of living after the inevitable collapse of their hunting culture. A substantial majority of the Creek people, particularly of the women who controlled most family property, responded with such interest that there appeared some reason to believe that, like the Cherokee, they might before too late bridge the gap between their old way of life and the new from which there was clearly no longer the possibility of escape. These mounting hopes were so painfully crushed by the Jackson invasion that Hawkins resigned in despair December 17, 1814

But in 1832 their centuries-old struggle, prolonged in the afterglow of hope produced by the services of McGillivray and Hawkins, came to an end. The rush of recent events had foreshadowed the certainty of the outcome. On every side loomed threats which could no longer be averted by any Creek exertion. Jackson's corridor had separated them from their former neighbors, the Choctaw, Chickasaw and Seminole. Their one-time patron and ally, Spain, had likewise ceased to be a neighbor with the 1820 cession of Spanish Florida to the United States. Their remaining neighbor, the Cherokee, were being dispossessed by Georgia's land lottery. The Creek had four years before themselves being expelled from Georgia. Their homeland which once had stretched from the

Tennessee to the Gulf and east to Atlantic tidewater had been reduced by successive enforced cessions to a beleaguered strip in eastern Alabama which represented a diminishment to less than a fifth of the area they had held as recently as 1813. Passage by Congress of the Removal Act and the repudiation by the administration of the Supreme Court decision had become new portents offering even less prospect that the terrible pressures upon them might ever relent. Most menacing of all threats was the overwhelming increase in numbers of their immediate white assailants. From 1820 to 1830 the population of Alabama had increased from 127,901 to 309,527. There appeared no means by which Alabama's adamant insistence upon their removal west, supported by the administration's endlessly repeated injunctions, could longer be resisted.

Creek delegations had kept journeying to Washington to plead for some redress of the grievances occasioned by Alabama's increasingly exacting demands and oppressions. The administration's perpetual reply had been the unsympathetic reiteration of its advice that the one certain escape from their troubles lay in their abandonment of their country. Then, in the spring of 1832, federal authorities revealed an apparent change of heart. In response to a sudden spate of promises so much more favorable than any Creek expectation, the bewildered Creek delegates signed the Treaty of Washington, March 24, 1832. By it the Creek nation ceded to the United States all of its remaining land east of the Mississippi. But in consideration for this long sought cession the United States engaged to sequester from the some 5,000,000 ceded acres more than 2,000,000 acres to be allotted in plantation or farm-size plots to Creek chiefs and heads of family. The individual Creek who was thus to become owner of his personal share of land, title to which formerly had been held by his nation, was to be free to hold it as long as he chose or to sell it in the event he elected to move west with the federal government's assistance. Whichever course he elected, the treaty stipulated that he was to be guaranteed in the interim protection of all his rights, property and civil, by the United States. Had the terms of the treaty been observed the Creek people would have been offered a more equable solution to their problems than any of them had imagined could be in the offing.

The interminable history of diplomatic relations between Indians and white men had before 1832 recorded no single instance
of a treaty which had not been presently broken by the white
parties to it. Many of these breaches of faith could be excused by
the circumstances that subsequent acts of war by some Indians
could be construed to constitute a relinquishment by all Indians
of their rights under the treaty that applied. Other breaches could
be mitigated by the frequent willingness of Indian minorities to
negotiate a new treaty which could be presumed to have superseded the old. Still others could be rationalized by the perpetual
advance of the white frontier which continued to alter conditions
with which earlier treaties had dealt. In every event, there had
never been an Indian treaty, however solemnly embellished with
such terms as "permanent," "forever," "for all time," "so long as
the sun shall rise," that had not, usually sooner than later, been
unilaterally nullified by the refusal of its white signers to abide
by its terms. But no agreement between white men and Indians
had ever been so soon abrogated as the 1832 Treaty of Washington. Within days the promises made in it on behalf of the United
States had been broken. Its sole effect had been a transfer of Creek
title to the United States for which the Creek received nothing in
return.

The moment word of the treaty's signing reached Alabama
hordes of white adventurers, looters and land seekers swarmed into
the Creek country. Some had come to preempt land, certain that
they could presently secure state validation of title to land upon
which they had fixed after frightening the Indian occupants into
withdrawing. Others came equipped with spurious claims calculated to take advantage of the federal allotment of $100,000
which, under one of the terms of the treaty, had been advanced
the Creek to pay the debts of those disposed to migrate. Others
came with contracts, bills of sale and promissory notes which
Indians unable to read could be persuaded to sign and which
could be sustained in state courts in which Indians, under state
law, were denied the right to testify. Others came with wagon
loads of whisky, aware that Indians befuddled by drink could the
more readily be victimized in whatever way seemed at the moment
most profitable. The most of the intruders came in armed bands,
roaming capriciously, stealing Indian stock and property and

committing nameless depredations. The terrified Creek could only submit since they realized that any resistance could precipitate an immediate invasion by state militia kept standing by ready for such a hoped for contingency. State authorities regarded these occurrences with detached approval, on the theory that every worsening of the Indian situation could be expected to hasten Indian readiness to migrate. Within months of the signing of the treaty thousands of the Creek had been driven from their homes to become starving refugees in adjacent forests and swamps.[1]

Secretary of War Lewis Cass had instructed United States Marshal, Robert L. Crawford, to guard the Indians against all molestations and intrusions and to remove intruders by force when necessary. But the directive was hedged about with so many cautions and reservations, so many admonitions to consider the sensibilities of the people and government of Alabama, so many warnings against resort to provocative measures, that federal officials and officers on the scene were given no impression that their superiors in Washington were in earnest. They hesitated to take actions which when protested by Alabama might be disowned by those superiors. The Indians feared to ask for federal assistance since this served only to excite their tormentors. Only the most cursory protection was afforded the Indians.

Feeble as was federal disposition to meet federal obligations under the treaty, the few efforts that were made encountered instant and indignant resistance from white citizens and state authorities. Federal marshals were defied and intimidated. Soldiers were derided and insulted. The few trespassers who were evicted returned at once accompanied by armed bands of their friends and accomplices. Indians who complained to federal officers were whipped and despoiled. Always detachments of state militia stood ready to enforce the local supremacy of state authority. The marshals were helpless except when supported by federal troops and this support was withheld, except under the most extreme circumstances, in conformance with the administration's anxiety to appease Alabama.

The essence of the situation was another confrontation between federal and state authority. The United States was generally obli-

[1] For exhaustive detail on this campaign of terrorism see *U.S. Senate Document 512*, 23rd Congress, 1st session, particularly volumes II, III and IV.

gated under laws and precedents recognized since the foundation of the republic to maintain the peace and security of its Indian wards and specifically obligated by the guarantees included in the recent Treaty of Washington to protect the Creek on the land which they had ceded not to Alabama but to the United States. The state of Alabama on the other hand had taken the position that it alone was responsible for the maintenance of order within its borders. Its legislature had already divided the Creek country into counties, and state authorities held that if Indians had complaints they should be presented to state courts, in which they could not testify, or to state officials, whose invariable response was the reminder that the supplicants could escape their difficulties by migrating.

In the constitutional crisis projected by this confrontation the governing impulse of the administration was not to assert federal power but to cast about for grounds upon which an assertion could be avoided. General Enoch Parsons and Colonel John J. Abert were commissioned May 2, 1833 to negotiate a new treaty with the Creek. Under this proposed revision of the Treaty of Washington the Creek were to be permitted to manage their own immediate migration west, with the cost underwritten by the federal government, while the United States would assume responsibility for collecting compensation from the eventual sale of their evacuated lands. It was hoped that the proposed freedom of movement and assurance against losses from swindlers might so strongly appeal to the Creek that they would save the United States and Alabama further trouble by promptly migrating. After an investigation of local conditions Abert candidly reported that in his opinion this alternative could not provide a possible escape hatch for the government. The Creek, he said:

. . . are incapable of such an effort and of the arrangements and foresight which it requires. Nor have they confidence in themselves to undertake it. They fear starvation on the route; and can it be otherwise, when many of them are nearly starving now, without the embarrassment of a long journey on their hands. . . . You cannot have an adequate idea of the deterioration which these Indians have undergone during the last two or three years, from a general state of comparative plenty to that of unqualified wretchedness and want. The free egress into the nation by the whites; encroachments upon their lands, even upon their cultivated fields; abuses of their person; hosts of traders, who, like locusts, have devoured their substance and inundated their homes with whiskey, have destroyed what little disposition to cultivation the Indians may once have had. . . . They are brow beat, and cowed, and imposed upon, and depressed with the feeling that they have no adequate protection in the United States, and no capacity of self-protection in themselves. They dare not enforce their own laws to preserve order, for fear of the laws of the whites. In consequence, more murders of each other have been committed in the last six months than for as many previous years; and the whites will not bring the offender to justice, for he, like Iago, no matter which kills, sees in it his gain.[2]

The attempt to negotiate a new treaty providing for the immediate migration of the Creek encountered such violent opposition from Alabama and Georgia whites who had accumulated claims to individual Creek land holdings that the Indians became further alarmed and the project was abandoned. The conflict between federal and state authority had become much less a test of their relative powers than between the relative seriousness of their respective intentions. On this score there could be no faintest doubt. The federal government was perpetually ready to retreat. The state was as perpetually taking the initiative, seeking new opportunities to force the issue. These contrasting attitudes were strikingly revealed by the Owen affair.

Hardimand Owen was a white man who had established a residence in the Creek country after beating and robbing the former Indian occupants he had dispossessed. It was a trespass so flagrant that a deputy U.S. marshal, Jeremiah Austill, felt compelled to intervene. The enraged Owen mined his house in which he had proposed that the marshal meet him. The house was blown to bits just after Owen had left by the back door but the approaching Austill escaped death when he was warned at the last moment by observing Indians. Pursuing soldiers shot Owen when he raised his rifle to fire upon them. Alabama flamed with outrage at what was termed this tyrannical exercise of illegal and unwarranted authority by federal marshals and troops. The state eagerly grasped the opportunity to establish, beyond any shadow of any doubt, the supremacy of local government over national government.

[2] *U.S. Senate Document 512,* 23rd Congress, 1st session, Vol. IV, p. 423.

An Alabama county grand jury indicted James Emmerson, the soldier supposed to have shot Owen, for murder. The other soldiers and officers involved, along with the marshal, Austill, were indicted as accessories. Austill was arrested and the commandant at Fort Mitchell, Major James S. McIntosh, was cited for contempt of court when he refused to deliver up Emmerson. County authorities called for Alabama militia to enforce the county court's decrees. Bands of armed citizens assembled to prepare for an assault on the fort. McIntosh was compelled to refuse marshals' requests for military protection on the plea that if he diminished his garrison he feared he might not be able to hold his post against the attack he expected. The federal government's stand had thus degenerated into an admission that, far from being able to protect Indians, it was unable even to protect its own officers.

President Jackson, still blazing with the fervor with which he had defended the union in the nullification controversy, was not so deeply moved by this new challenge to its dignity, even though Alabama's defiance had been so much more direct and peremptory than had been South Carolina's. Meanwhile no new storm of protest was sweeping the north. Public opinion had been profoundly impressed by the overwhelming nature of Jackson's election victory. Religious sympathizers with the Indian cause had been somewhat mollified by Georgia's recent release of the imprisoned missionaries. The injustices which Indians were suffering, the arrogance of southern state authorities and Jackson's repudiation of the Supreme Court decision, all of which had so strongly aroused northern indignation, had been discussed and debated so long that people were tending to weary of the subject. This relaxation in northern opinion was perfectly illustrated by the major address delivered in Pittsburgh, July 8, 1833, by that outstanding champion of the union and critic of the president, Daniel Webster:

Gentlemen, it is but a few short months, since. . . . A new and perilous crisis was upon us. Dangers, novel in their character, and fearful in their aspect, menaced both the peace of the country and integrity of the constitution . . . a time had come, when the authority of law was opposed by authority of law—when the power of the general government was resisted by the arms of state government . . . every intelligent friend of human society throughout the world, looked, with amazement, at the spectacle we exhibited . . . it was at this moment that we showed ourselves to the whole civilized world, as being, apparently, on the eve of disunion and anarchy—at the very point of dissolving, once and forever, that union, which had made us so prosperous and so great.

He was not referring to Georgia's rejection of the judgment of the United States Supreme Court or to Alabama's rejection of the autonomy of the United States Army or to the categorical refusal of both to countenance the exercise of federal authority within their borders. He was alluding to South Carolina's disinclination to accept a congressional tariff act. He overlooked Jackson's repudiation of the Supreme Court and his acquiescence in the intimidation of U.S. marshals and soldiers but for the vigor with which Jackson had defended the union in the nullification crisis he had unstinted praise:

Gentlemen, the president of the United States was, as it seemed to me, at this eventful crisis, true to his duty. He comprehended and understood the case, and met it, as it was proper to meet it. . . . The issuing of the proclamation of the 10th of December, inspired me, I confess, with new hopes for the duration of the republic . . . its great and leading doctrines I regard as the true and only true doctrines of the constitution. They constitute the sole ground on which dismemberment can be resisted. Nothing else, in my opinion, can hold us together. While these opinions are maintained, the union will last; when they shall be generally rejected and abandoned, that union will be at the mercy of a temporary majority in any one of the states.

Webster continued, with his characteristic eloquence, to suggest the immense dangers to the nation inherent in an overzealous insistence upon states rights. But at no point in his long address, devoted almost in its entirety to an impassioned defense of the union, did he so much as mention the role of the federal judiciary in defining the powers granted to the union by the constitution. Still less was there any reference to the question of Indian rights which was at the moment so perilously inflaming relations between state and federal governments in Georgia and Alabama. It could not escape notice that even in the discerning mind of the renowned senator from Massachusetts, hailed as the nation's foremost exponent of progressive political principles, there was a clear distinction in the relative need to defend the constitutional rights of citizens measured by the distinction between races.[3]

Having once more correctly estimated the temper of the majority of his countrymen, Jackson's response to the murder charges against representatives of federal authority was a search for convenient compromise. He recruited the services of the nationally revered patriot, Francis Scott Key, to conduct a personal investigation on the infinitely troubled scene in Alabama. Key's preliminary report, as candid as had been Colonel Abert's, suggested that had federal protection been at the outset afforded the Indians, as guaranteed by the treaty, the ensuing crisis might never have developed. It was now too late, he feared, to reassert federal authority except by an exercise of armed force which would threaten a civil war. Meanwhile most local whites regarded him as a northern interloper who might much better have remained at home to busy himself with the north's own affairs. County authorities refused to cooperate with him or even to permit him to examine the indictments and he was disturbed by much continuing wild talk of designs to mount a mob attack on Fort Mitchell for the purpose of seizing and lynching the accused. But after many conferences with state officials and legislators calmer counsels prevailed and the general outlines of a compromise with which both parties could live began to take shape. The federal government agreed to refrain from further attempts to evict trespassers, except in the most obnoxious instances in which the suppression might be approved by state and local opinion, and to overlook the presence of the some 10,000 white intruders who had already gained lodgment on Indian lands. The state for its part undertook to make more earnest efforts to maintain law and order and to prevent personal excesses against Indians. The murder charges were dropped. The principal result of the compromise was to remove any last lingering Indian hope that any of their grievances might ever be redressed by federal action.

The survey of Indian lands was completed in November 1833 while the compromise was reducing federal-state tensions. As a result each individual Creek allotment, unless it had already been

[3] For text of address and an account of the circumstances surrounding its delivery see *Niles Register*, October 12, 1833. In the same issue is a detailed report of the assault by a street mob on an abolitionist meeting in New York casting further light on northern racial attitudes.

preempted by a white squatter, could be described and reserved for the designated Indian owner's use or sale. The process by which this was achieved involved an identification of the Indian in relation to his plot of land and then a certification to Washington so that the conveyance to him could become official and final and thus enable him, if he chose, to offer it for sale to a prospective buyer.

There developed an immediately flourishing trade in these certifications which offered a quasi-legal source of profit to replace that from the overt outrages against Indian persons and property which the state was now making some effort to suppress. Since the earlier steps in the legal process and the later transfer of title in the event of an ostensible sale were under state supervision and jurisdiction the opportunities to defraud the Indian claimants were innumerable. Indians who could not read or write and were in constant terror of white neighbors, officials and courts could be persuaded to scrawl their X on any sheet of paper thrust upon them. Homeless Indians could be bribed for trifling sums to impersonate Indian proprietors. Records in county offices could be altered. Other devices for gaining title to Indian allotments for little or nothing included plying them with liquor, threatening them with arrest, inveigling them into gambling games. One of the most lucrative of all sources of profit depended upon the circumstances that so many heads of Creek families were very old and had died since the signing of the treaty. The nearest county court was authorized under state law to assume administration of the estate, including land, stock and all property, and to appoint a white custodian who was responsible not to the family and heirs of the deceased but to the court. Almost the sole interference with these various frauds was the fierce competition among the several rival land companies whose staffs of agents were employed in gaining title to Indian land allotments. This unbridled and undisguised swindling operation continued through 1834 and 1835 and only diminished when the last parcels of Indian land had passed into the possession of speculators.

The number of landless and homeless Indians, subsisting on what they could find in forests and swamps, had during the two years multiplied by many thousands. Efforts to organize any substantial migration of Creek had meanwhile failed. Those who had already lost their property felt that they lacked the resources to undertake so long a journey to so dubious a destination. Those who still had property had been given ample reason to fear that preparations to leave would prove a signal bringing down upon them an extemporaneous shower of claims and demands which would strip them of what they had left. The basic Creek objection to migration was not easy to answer. They argued that the treaty had assured them of remuneration for the property they were obliged to leave behind, that they should not be expected to accept the risks and expenses of the move until they had received that compensation, and that this had been made impossible by the so nearly universal practice of fraud in the administration of certifications and conveyances. Their reluctance to leave was covertly abetted by the swarm of speculators battening upon them who were equally reluctant to see them go while any of them still possessed anything of value of which they might still be dispossessed. But beyond all these considerations, the basic impulse strangling their inclination to migrate was a nostalgic attachment to the land of their birth. Miserable as had become the condition of most, they could not bring themselves to cut the last tie with their ancient country. In any event, during 1834 and 1835 only a few hundreds struck out for the west.

But as 1836 dawned both state and federal authorities had come to the conclusion that the time had come when the Creek must go. If there was not a tacit conspiracy the concatenation of successive events could have been no more striking had there been one. For months Georgia and Alabama officials had been proclaiming strident warnings of the imminence of a Creek uprising. It was maintained that among so many wandering and starving Indians a spirit of desperation was bound to develop. There was undoubtedly some basis for a supposition that among a one-time warlike people now deprived of hope there must be some who instead of supinely awaiting death might feel moved to strike one last blow against their oppressors. When the long prophesied "war" did come, the first shots were fired by Georgia militia upon a party of Creek refugees seeking sanctuary among the Georgia Cherokee. Fed by rumors, the fears of white settlers in and along the edges of the Creek country continued to grow, especially in those sections near the Georgia border. Garbled reports of great Indian successes in the current Seminole war in Florida added to public apprehension. In May the so well advertised Creek uprising did occur. There was much evidence, some of which was later acknowledged by Governor Clement C. Clay of Alabama, that the outbreak had been incited by white adventurers who foresaw new profits if an Indian war could be precipitated. At any rate, several small bands of a primitive branch of the Lower Creek, occupying an area near the Georgia-Alabama line where they had been particularly subject to white oppression, began killing settlers and attacking traffic on the Federal Road west of Columbus, Georgia. The alarm spread to adjoining settlements. The former crowds of wandering Indian refugees were replaced by streams of white refugees.

The outbreak died down as suddenly as it had flared up. Alabama militia commanders in the field reported that there was not nor had been a serious emergency. The *Montgomery Advertiser* termed the Creek War "a humbug" and declared it "a base and diabolical scheme, devised by interested men, to keep an ignorant race of people from maintaining their just rights." But to the administration in Washington the incident presented a providential opportunity to dispose of the Creek problem. Having embarked upon an armed rebellion, on however nominal a scale, the Creek nation could be considered to have forfeited its rights under the Treaty of Washington and without further ado be compelled to migrate. Congress, still chary of the use of outright force in Indian removal, could now be assured that the Creek by their defiance of the United States had by their own acts obliged the United States to resort to force. In response to the prodding of Congress, an incipient federal project to undertake new investigations and rectifications of the recent wholesale defrauding of the Creek had been announced. It was canceled. Secretary Cass instead ordered Brigadier General Thomas S. Jesup, May 19, 1836, to take the field in Alabama with a federal army to suppress the rebellion, pacify the Creek and remove them forthwith to the west.

Major General Winfield Scott, called from his absorption in the army's Seminole troubles, had already arrived in Alabama to study the situation and plan the campaign. Somewhat less than a hundred Creek had been actually engaged in the depredations but more than a thousand of their immediate Creek neighbors, realizing that they too might be held responsible, had fled from their homes to hide in the woods from the impending white invasion. Other thousands flocked to Fort Mitchell to establish their innocence by their public subjection to white authority. Scott's first endeavor was to establish a military cordon across southern Alabama to prevent the flight of either hostile or frightened Creek to join the Seminole in Florida. Jesup arrived to take field command of an army of 11,000, the organization of which had been made difficult by monumental supply deficiencies and the unreadiness of the militia and volunteer contingents of which it was principally composed. The majority of Creek had been appalled and infuriated by the damage to their cause provoked by the outbreak and 1800 warriors were contributed to Jesup's army.

Irritated by the defeats in the Seminole War and the delays in getting the Creek campaign under way, Jackson recalled Scott to face a court of inquiry. The general's defense statement to the court revealingly reflected the furious impatience of the man in the White House to expedite the expulsion of the southern Indians:

. . . unable, as I am, to remember one blunder in my recent operations, or a single duty neglected, I may say, that to find myself in the presence of this honorable court, while the army I but recently commanded is still in pursuit of the enemy, fills me with equal grief and astonishment. And whence this great and humiliating transition? It is, sir, by the fiat of one, who, from his exalted station, and yet more from his unequalled popularity, has never, with his high displeasure, struck a functionary of this government, no matter what the office of the individual, humble or elevated, who was not from the moment withered in the general confidence of the American people. Yes, sir, it is my misfortune to lie under the displeasure of that most distinguished personage. The President of the United States has said, "Let General Scott be recalled from the command of the army in the field, and submit his conduct in the Seminole and Creek campaigns to a court for investigation." And lo! I stand here to vindicate that conduct, which must again be judged in the last resort, by him who first condemned it without trial or inquiry.[4]

4 For detail on court proceedings see Mansfield, Edward D., *Life and Services of General Winfield Scott*. New York, 1852, pp. 274–86 and *American State Papers*, Military Affairs, Vol. VII. The president's displeasure notwithstanding, Scott was acquitted by the court, he returned to active service, and at the conclusion of Jackson's terms of office continued his rise to the highest rank. In 1841 he became commanding general of the United States Army, a post which he held during the Mexican War and into the early months of the Civil War.

In July Jesup's army began to converge upon the area of forest and swamp in which the terrified Creek refugees had hidden. No shots were fired. All except a handful who had contrived to escape to Florida surrendered without resistance. Some 1,600 Creek who were presumed to have been engaged in the spring hostilities, or to have sympathized with those who had, were assembled. The men were manacled and linked together with chains for the march westward under military guard. Their women and children trailed after them. Another 900 Creek who had inhabited adjacent villages were herded along with the doleful column.

Other military detachments descended upon the other Creek communities inhabited by families who had no conceivable connection with the uprising and whose guilt by association could only be asserted on the grounds that they were members of the Creek nation. They were driven to assembly points and in batches of two or three thousand marched westward under military escort. Any remaining chance of compensation for land and property left behind had vanished. Supply was dependent on the same private contract system which had failed so miserably in the Choctaw removal and which failed as miserably again. There were the same delays, the same lack of shelter, food, clothing, blankets, the same want of medical attention, even the same decrepit and over-crowded steamboats and ferries. A people so dispirited had little resistance to fatigue, hunger, exposure or sickness. The mildest illnesses tended to become fatal. By midwinter the interminable, stumbling procession of more than 15,000 Creek stretched from border to border across Arkansas. Starving Indians were accused of stealing food en route and bands of armed settlers gathered to accelerate their passage. The sick were left untended and the dead unburied. The passage of the exiles could be distinguished from afar by the howling of trailing wolf packs and the circling flocks of buzzards.

It might have appeared that the Creek had suffered from the prejudice and avarice of their white neighbors and the indifference and perfidy of the federal government about as much as a people could suffer. They had been robbed not only of their homes and possessions but of their pride as a nation and their identity as human beings. After years of an oppression under which they could only beg unavailingly for mercy they had been driven into exile over a road of horror along which they had left hundreds of their dead. But a grosser outrage was still in store for them.

In the summer of 1836 while the enforced migration was gathering momentum, Creek spokesmen begged for an advance on the federal annuity due the following year. This was imperative, they pointed out, since they had been deprived of so much of their personal property and it had been made obvious by the Choctaw experience that the military escort and the private contractors could not be relied upon to provide all the essentials for survival en route. At the direction of the President, Jesup offered to make this advance if the Creek would furnish a corps of warriors to serve in the Seminole War with which the American army was currently finding so little success. For the sake of gaining the desperately needed annuity advance upon which the fate of the nation appeared to depend some 800 Creek volunteered. They were promised that their families would be left unmolested in their Alabama homes under federal protection until the warriors returned. The volunteers set off for Florida where at a cost of many of their lives they contributed with spirit if not dignity to that extraordinarily difficult campaign.

They had kept the bargain but nobody else did. Whites coveted the volunteers' land and property as fiercely as that of any other Creek. Federal protection arrangements were as inadequate as always. Bands of armed whites, masquerading under the name of militia, descended upon the absent warriors' families. They were driven from their homes, robbed of horses, cattle, food and even trinkets, their boys and old men confined in compounds, their women ravished. Federal authorities had made no preparations to defend them. On the plea that there was no other way to assure their safety the army removed them altogether from the Creek country to a concentration camp on Mobile Bay where hundreds died from malnutrition and epidemics.[5]

The volunteers, returning the following summer from hunting their Seminole cousins through Florida swamps, were understandably embittered by the realization that their service to the United States had instead of securing any advantage to their families sub-

[5] For detail on this episode see *American State Papers*, Military Affairs, Vol. VII, pp. 867–70.

jected them to worse privations than had they accompanied the main Creek migration. And for them, too, the terrible road west was still to be traveled. The harsh months spent by the warriors in the field and their families in detention camps had left all less able to endure it. This last major contingent of Creek migrants was hustled through New Orleans, then suffering from another yellow fever plague, and on westward to a midwinter arrival on the plains. As a macabre footnote to this last spasm of Creek removal, the overage and overcrowded steamer, *Monmouth,* foundered in the Mississippi with a loss of 311 of its 611 Indian passengers. Among the dead were four of the children of the Indian commander of the Creek volunteers.

The expulsion of the Creek, like that of the Choctaw, had proved a more appalling assault upon a helpless minority which the United States was morally, legally and constitutionally bound to protect than the sharpest congressional critics of the administration's Indian policy could have foreseen during the 1830 removal debate. It had provided a spectacle peculiarly abhorrent in a democracy dedicated since its inception to respect for the rights of man. The Indians had been so flagrantly oppressed that even the white inhabitants of the border area that had suffered most from the brief spring uprising addressed to Congress a memorial protesting the mistreatment of their Creek neighbors. Gusts of passionate disapproval swept certain religious and intellectual circles in the north. But there was no upsurge of public opinion. There was every opportunity for the expression of a popular rebuke for 1836 was a Presidential election year. It was a campaign more violent and virulent than most. Every sort of charge and counter-charge was exchanged. Yet there was no evidence that the Indian removal scandal was considered a significant issue by any of the hundreds of office-seeking orators speaking from the hustings throughout the country during those same months the Creek people were being shepherded across Arkansas by wolves and vultures.

14

Of the five southern Indian nations the Seminole were in 1830 the most primitive and in many respects the most colorful. Their name signified fugitive or separate. They had become a people by a coalescence of remnants of the ancient Apalachee, Yuchi and Yamassee nations which in the early 18th century had been dispossessed and scattered by their several enemies, the Cherokee, the Shawnee and the English Carolina colonists. These original fugitives had from time to time been joined by stray groups of Creek who preferred the comparative calm of the Seminole country to their own often troubled area. The Seminole owed the peace and quiet they enjoyed through the late 18th century to the circumstance that their habitat in northern Florida was under the dominion of Spain and was therefore not yet subject to the threat of American settler aggression which hung so heavily over every other Indian nation east of the Mississippi. The naturalist, William Bartram, who visited them in 1776 has left an idyllic vignette of the Seminole way of life in those last years that white men left them undisturbed:

The Siminoles are but a weak people with respect to numbers. . . . Yet . . . they enjoy a superabundance of the necessaries and conveniences of life, with the security of person and property, the two greatest concerns of mankind. . . . They seem to be free from want or desires. No cruel enemy to dread; nothing to give them disquietude. . . . Thus contented and undisturbed, they appear as blithe and free as the birds of the air, and like them as volatile and active, tuneful and vociferous. The visage, action, and deportment of the Siminoles, form the most striking picture of happiness in this life; joy, contentment, love, and friendship, without guile or affectation, seem inherent in them, or predominant in their vital principle, for it leaves them but with the last breath of life . . . not even the debility and decrepitude of extreme old age, is sufficient to erase from their visages this youthful, joyous simplicity; but, like the gray even of a serene and calm day, a gladdening, cheering blush remains on the Western horizon after the sun is set.

But the same Spanish border which for so long represented Seminole security from American intrusion became itself the agent of their destruction. Negro slaves who fled their American masters customarily sought sanctuary among Indians. Among these possible Indian sanctuaries none was so inviting as the Seminole. It provided the double advantage of its situation in a foreign country and of its offer of a special welcome. Prosperous Seminole had from the earliest times procured Negro slaves by purchase. The simplicities of the Seminole social and economic structure permitted slaves to own cattle and horses, to cultivate their own parcels of land, and eventually to intermarry. The descendants of these earlier slaves tended to merge with the Seminole community. With these long established interracial sympathies the Seminole had become a society in which fleeing blacks could find acceptance as well as refuge.

As the population along the southern frontier of the United States increased the number of escaping slaves likewise mounted. The Spanish border extending across southern Georgia represented the same goal in their flight that came to be assumed by the Ohio River in the later days of the underground celebrated in *Uncle Tom's Cabin*. The American south flamed with indignation. The general public shared the fury of the plantation owners. The impulse to continue pursuit across the line became irresistible. The Spanish military establishment was too weak to control passage of the border by either pursued or pursuers. Parties of armed Americans began disregarding the international boundary, pressing their man hunts deep into the Seminole country and seizing any black they could find. The Seminole were forced to resist and to arm many of their own Negroes who fought with a resolution inspirited by the knowledge that they were defending their freedom which many had learned to consider more important than their lives. A species of guerrilla warfare, with Negroes of every category as the spoils, developed along the border. Outrage bred outrage. The dangers in the Florida situation were aggravated by the sudden new influx of Creek fleeing from Jackson's 1813 invasion of their country. Some of the Creek refugees were proprietors who brought their own slaves. It became less and less possible to establish legitimate identification of Negroes living in Seminole towns. In a Georgia or Alabama court, for example, a claim to ownership of an abducted Seminole Negro could be successfully based on the assertion that the Negro was the grandson of a slave who had once escaped from the claimant's grandfather. The trans-border trade in seized blacks became steadily more profitable. Local officials, sheriffs, judges, militia officers and even army officers became as involved in it as professional slave traders and kidnappers. As an instance of the ramifications of this contraband traffic, the young hero of Horseshoe Bend, Lieutenant Sam Houston, resigned from the army in protest against the accusation of Secretary of War Calhoun that he had been participating in it.

The loss of slaves by flight over the border had become so intolerable to the American south that in 1816 the War Department reluctantly authorized an official punitive expedition to penalize Seminole welcome of the fugitives. A detachment of the U.S. Army, assisted by some Creek auxiliaries, crossed the border, penetrated 60 miles into Spanish territory, laid waste intervening Indian fields and villages, and laid siege to a stockade on the lower Apalachicola in which more than 300 Negroes and Seminole, with their families, had sought refuge. Cannon fire set off the magazine and most of the inmates were blown to bits in the resulting explosion. The Seminole retaliated by attacking settlements on the American side of the border. In one of these counterattacks 40 white men, women and children were killed in a flatboat on the river. The fugitive slave scandal had manifestly mushroomed into what amounted to a frontier war.

The United States government in 1818 authorized Andrew Jackson to undertake another punitive expedition, this one to be on a scale calculated to put an end to Indian intransigence. An army of 3,000 regulars, militia, volunteers and Indian auxiliaries was assembled. Drawing upon the military prestige he had won at Horseshoe Bend and New Orleans and fully aware of the opportunity to advance the south's territorial designs upon Florida, Jackson moved with that ruthless vigor of which no one was more capable. He not only ranged far and wide through Spanish territory, destroying Seminole towns and capturing as many Negroes as could be caught, he also forced the capitulation of the Spanish garrisons of Pensacola and St. Marks and seized two resident traders, Alexander Arbuthnot and Robert Ambrister, who were British citizens. He shot the two Englishmen on the charge that they had been conspiring with Indians and Negroes.

The Monroe administration hastily disavowed Jackson's actions and earnestly sought to soothe Spanish and British indignation. But Jackson's impetuous truculence had served his purpose. Spain's inability to defend Florida against American aggression had been abundantly demonstrated. His campaign accelerated the pending negotiation of the Spanish-American treaty, signed February 22, 1819, by which Spain ceded Florida to the United States in return for American recognition of Spain's permanent title to the plains approach to the southern Rockies and the entire far west and southwest below the 42nd parallel, an area which included the present states of Texas, Colorado, New Mexico, Utah, Arizona, Nevada and California.

Elimination of the boundary between Florida and the United States left the dismayed Seminole and their Negro associates helplessly exposed to the application of American power. The boundary had not proved a certain shield against slave raiders and punitive expeditions but it had served to discourage the advance of American settlement. This deterrent had now been dissipated. American landseekers began at once flooding into Florida. The areas most attractive to white settlement were the belt of fertile land extending across north Florida from St. Augustine to Pensacola, which was adjacent to Georgia and Alabama but occupied by the Seminole, and the coastal perimeter where initial settlement could be fostered by seaborne access. To Florida's new possessors it became obviously imperative to dislodge the Indian occupants from these more attractive areas with the least possible delay. This process was initiated with extraordinary energy and dispatch.

Establishment of Florida as a territory in 1822 made effective the authority of local legislators and administrators dedicated to the need to replace Indian occupants with white settlers wherever the latter appeared to demand land. Federal administrators were meanwhile impressing upon the Seminole the necessity of their prompt withdrawal from their ancestral homeland. Enough signatures to the September 18,1823 Treaty of Camp Moultrie to give an appearance of binding the Seminole nation were gained by the easy expedient of offering the chiefs who signed large personal landholdings in north Florida. All of the Seminole other than these few prominent signers were bound by the treaty to abandon their homes in the north and withdraw into the south-central interior of the peninsula. By the dictate of this remarkable treaty all of the Indians of Florida were required to withdraw not only from the north but from every seacoast, thereby relinquishing at one startling stroke every portion of Florida so far coveted by the newly arrived Americans.

The central Florida area north of Lake Okeechobee to which the Seminole had been forced to resort was then a wasteland of shallow lakes, sluggish rivers and undrained swamps incapable of productive cultivation. It was a region so handicapped by nature that it was not even able to support appreciable quantities of wild game. The formerly prosperous Seminole, accustomed to the agricultural fertility of northern Florida, were not equipped by experience to cope with such a marginal existence. To their despairing appeals for relief federal administrators gave the traditional reply that the one escape from their troubles was their consent to withdraw altogether from Florida by removing to the west. After Jackson's accession to the Presidency these federal pressures were intensified.

At a May 9, 1832 conference at Payne's Landing a group of Seminole chiefs agreed to undertake a journey to the western plains in order to inspect the country to which they were being urged to move. The United States later maintained that this agreement implied a Seminole commitment to removal but the Seminole had not had that understanding at the time. Most of the inspecting chiefs were offended by the arrogance of the federal agents in charge of their tour and others were disturbed by the war then in progress between eastern Indian colonists and the wilder Indians of the plains but some professed to be satisfied by what they had seen. Upon their return delegates representing the Seminole nation were again assembled at Payne's Landing in the spring of 1834. United States Agent to the Seminole, Wiley Thompson, angrily lectured his charges, assuring them that they had no other recourse than to remove, and declaring that the only purpose of the conference was to agree upon methods of disposal of their cattle and property and upon the selection of modes of transportation. Excerpts from the replies of some of the spokesmen for the Seminole cast a revealing light on the infinitely troubled Indian state of mind:

We were all made by the same Great Father, and are all alike His Children. We all came from the same Mother, and were suckled at the same breast. Therefore, we are brothers, and as brothers, should treat together in an amicable way.

Your talk is a good one, but my people cannot say they will go. We are not willing to do so. If their tongues say yes, their hearts cry no, and call them liars.

When a man has a country in which he was born, and has there his house and home, where his children have always played about his yard, it becomes sacred to his heart, and it is hard to leave it . . . my people are around me, and they feel that while they remain here, they can be happy with each other. They are not hungry for other lands.

If suddenly we tear our hearts from the homes around which they are twined, our heart-strings will snap. . . . When a man calls another his friend, let him be poor or mean as he may, he ought to yield to him his rights, and not say *he* will judge for that other, and compel him to do as *he* pleases. Yet while you say you are our friend, you tell us we *shall* go to the West.[1]

Though the Seminole were clearly not yet ready to migrate Thompson had contrived to round up 15 chiefs and subchiefs who could be persuaded to sign a stipulation purporting to represent Seminole consent to removal at the first Payne's Landing conference. This disputed instrument was promptly ratified by the Senate as though it were a bona fide treaty. It committed the Seminole to removal within three years from the date of the tentative discussion in 1832. The War Department began chartering

[1] For contemporary detail on this conference and ensuing events see Cohen, M. M., *Notices of Florida and the Campaigns,* Charleston, 1836. For further contemporary detail see Drake, Samuel G., *The Book of the Indians,* Book IV. Boston, 1841.

vessels, contracting for supplies, assigning military escorts, and making other preparations for the migration. One contingent of emigrants under the leadership of a chief who had been made amenable by impressive personal rewards actually sailed from Tampa Bay but among most Seminole there was increasing evidence of reluctance and among some of a disposition to resist.

Had the United States insisted upon removal immediately after the 1821 annexation when the Seminole were still peaceful agriculturists in north Florida there could have been no more difficulty in requiring them to take the road west than in the case of the Choctaw and Creek. But in the 12-year interim of their residence in the central Florida swamps they had been so hardened by adversities that they had reverted to a wilder and more primitive state. They had become suspicious and refractory savages with whom it was to prove as hard for white men to deal as when Narváez had first encountered their like on these same coasts three centuries before. As the impulse to resist began to stir among the Seminole, a major influence in the ferment was exerted by a young chief of little former importance. Like his great predecessor among Indian rebels, Pontiac, until the moment of crisis he had been relatively unknown. But the name and fame of Osceola were soon to capture the imagination of the American public which followed every incident of his brief, violent career with absorbed, fascinated and even sympathetic attention. Two of Agent Thompson's many mistakes had precipitated Osceola's resolve. Thompson had subjected Osceola to disciplinary confinement in irons and had delivered into slavery the younger and more beautiful of his two wives.

During the summer of 1835 there were premonitory tremors of the coming storm. On June 19 a party of white hunters assaulted a party of Indian hunters, beating and whipping them and finally shooting two. Though the whites had been the aggressors, Thompson ordered the Seminole to deliver the surviving Indian hunters for trial. On August 11 a military courier carrying mail was killed on the road to Fort King, headquarters of Brigadier General D. L. Clinch at the northern edge of the Indian country and at the junction, a few miles south of Lake Orange, of the military roads connecting the fort with Tampa Bay and St. Augustine. The supposition was that the victim had been attacked by revenge-seeking relatives of the slain hunters. On November 26 Charley Emathla, most important and influential of the chiefs advocating removal, was killed by fellow Seminole as a warning to any who might be disposed to yield to white wishes. Some said it was by the hand of Osceola and in any event it must have been by his direction, for it represented the last bound in his sudden rise to power.

More significant than these isolated acts of violence was the day-to-day behavior of the Indians. Their women and children had disappeared. The men who appeared for consultation with Thompson and army officers on removal preparations were sullenly evasive. Osceola and his immediate followers were openly defiant. Nevertheless Thompson directed that all Seminole assemble in the first week of December to dispose of their stock and property and hold themselves in readiness for embarkation. None came.

By now the white inhabitants of Florida were seized by alarm. Each succeeding rumor of the impending danger was more disturbing than the last. The American population of Florida had already increased to an estimated 35,000, six times the Indian total. But it was indicative of its many defense problems that more than half were slaves. This new kind of American settler did not live in a rude cabin which could be abandoned at a moment's notice and as quickly rebuilt when destroyed. His more likely holding included plantation house, slave barracks and a sugar mill. He might as readily as any squatter save his life by timely flight but this was not a recourse that could save him a commercially crushing property loss. In former frontier wars a principal Indian objective had been the capture of horses. In this one it would be the capture of so much more valuable slaves. Among the many defense disadvantages to which the American inhabitants were subject, one was unique and irreparable. Their scattered settlements extended in an immense arc across northern Florida and down the eastern seacoast to the tip of the peninsula. They were thus exposed to attack at any point by Indians able to emerge at will from their secret strongholds in the interior wasteland. Painfully aware of these rapidly mounting dangers the territorial government mustered Florida's militia for frontier defense and dispatched one regiment, 650 strong, to reinforce Clinch's regulars at Fort King.

The spontaneity of the Indian outbreak in late December, 1835, evidenced how thoroughly premeditated had been Indian plans and preparations. Bands of Seminole raiders emerged simultaneously from the central wilderness to attack settlements so widely separated that defense forces were hopelessly distracted. The assaults struck all along the white perimeter from Cape Florida in the far south north to St. Augustine and west to the Suwannee. Everywhere the raids were devoted to the murder of white families, the recruitment or capture of slaves and the destruction of property. Soon white settlers had been forced to abandon the whole east coast from St. Augustine to the vicinity of the present Miami. Ruined refugees thronged St. Augustine. Indians were observed in the city's environs. For weeks St. Augustine itself expected attack. For the next five years the white inhabitants of Florida could expect assured security only in fortified places.

Osceola made his own pounce December 28, 1835. He had selected as his prey Agent Thompson, regarded by Osceola as his personal antagonist and by most Seminole as their nation's principal enemy. Thompson and a companion, Lieutenant Constantine Smith, were surprised and shot down while walking within gunshot of Fort King. Three other Americans were killed in a sutler's house as insultingly near the fort. All whites without the walls were forced to flee for their cover. During those same hours of that humiliating day a greater disaster was developing.

Additional regular troops had been transported from Key West to Fort Brooke on Tampa Bay to strengthen the military forces assigned to maintain order and compel Indian compliance during the Seminole migration which federal authorities believed about to get under way. Major Francis L. Dade was directed to proceed with a column numbering 102 soldiers and 8 officers north from Fort Brooke along the military road to conduct supply and reinforcement to Fort King. Shortly after crossing the Withlacoochee River the column was overcome by a surprise Seminole attack from which only three soldiers escaped. What had happened could not have been more vividly described than in the eyewitness account of Rawson Clarke, one of these survivors:

It was 8 o'clock. Suddenly I heard a rifle shot in the direction of the advance guard, and this was immediately followed by a musket shot from that quarter. Captain Fraser had rode by me a moment before in that direction. I never saw him afterwards. I had not time to think of the meaning of these shots, before a volley, as if from a thousand rifles, was poured in upon us from the front, and all along our left flank. I looked around me, and it seemed as if I were the only one left standing in the right wing. Neither could I, until several other vollies had been fired on us, see an enemy—and when I did, I could only see their heads and arms peering out from the long grass, far and near, and from behind the pine trees. . . . Our men were by degrees all cut down. . . . Lieut. B. was the only officer left alive, and he severely wounded. He told me as the Indians approached to lay down and feign myself dead. I looked through the logs, and saw the savages approaching in great numbers.

Dade's disaster had presented the tragic reenactment of a long familiar pattern. In this last flareup of Indian belligerency east of the Mississippi the first pitched battle of the war was lost by the impact of the classic Indian surprise tactic that had decided so many earlier battles in the long and bloody annals of frontier warfare. Always the debacle had sprung from the same set of circumstances. Always there had been the column of regular troops, impeded by supply trains and artillery, pushing on into the mazes of the wilderness, unaware whether there were Indians within a hundred miles or a hundred yards. Always there had been the sudden burst of gunfire at the head of the column and then upon its recoil the greater blast along its flanks. Always regular soldiers with their instinctive discipline had attempted to maintain their formation and had thereby become a mass target, as vulnerable as a stupefied flock of sheep, to the continuing gunfire from a surrounding enemy still invisible. Dade's dying moments may well have been haunted by a military textbook recollection of Washington's famous parting advice to St. Clair: "General St. Clair, in three words, beware of surprise . . . again and again, General, *beware of surprise.*" He could as well have been warned by the ghosts of the long succession of earlier commanders who had been assailed by that same terrifying shock: Braddock at Turtle Creek; Aubry at Niagara; Dalyell at Detroit; Grant at Fort Duquesne; Bouquet at Bushy Run; Herkimer at Oriskany; Dennison at Wyoming; Crawford at Sandusky; Winchester at Raisin River. Dade's ordeal had had two distinctions. His was the smallest regular force to be subjected to such a trial and his was the highest casualty rate. Of 110 men he lost 107.

After the assassination of Thompson but before he had learned of Dade's fate, Clinch attempted a reconnaissance in force in the direction of the Withlacoochee River where numbers of Indians had been reported assembling. His December 31, 1835 attempted crossing was opposed by Osceola with such vigor that after a loss of 4 killed and 52 wounded Clinch retreated to his base. In his official report he ascribed his defeat to the fanatical determination with which Osceola appeared to have inspired his followers and to the misbehavior of the Florida volunteers who shrank from following his regulars across the river under fire. The Florida regiment's brief enlistment period was expiring and though the war was just commencing its members returned to their homes. The regulars left in the area along the northern border of the Seminole country were too few to patrol or maintain communications or to hope to attempt more than the holding of their isolated posts.

Detailed news of the travail in Florida was slow in reaching the north and the administration was even slower in extending Congress an attempted explanation of the sensational collapse of its Seminole removal program. It was necessary, however, to apply to Congress for money to conduct the expanded military effort that had become so suddenly required. To disarm criticism the first request sent to the capitol was for a modest $80,000. A Congress that had since 1830 been so narrowly divided on the removal question was in no mood to welcome this administration admission that the policy had encountered some of the catastrophic difficulties so many members had prophesied. When the appropriation bill came up in the House, January 6, 1836, Representative Vinton, of Ohio, always one of the more determined critics of removal, demanded to be given "information as to the cause of the war, or who commenced it?" New York's Churchill Cambreling of the Ways and Means Committee which had reported the bill was obliged to rely on the time-honored retort which has represented every administration's refuge in any sudden foreign emergency and with which no Congress had ever been able to deal:

The war was progressing. Fifteen hundred Indians were in the field, and they were opposed by only two hundred troops. Unless speedily repressed, they would probably make inroads upon the State of Georgia. If the gentleman from Ohio desired to raise a question or a debate upon the treaty, he could select another opportunity, without embarrassing the present measure.

By the time the appropriation had reached the Senate the explosively expanding demands of the war had required an increase to $500,000. Clay gave voice to the helpless indignation of those who were politically opposed to the Jackson administration or opposed to the Indian removal policy, or both, and who yet were now obliged to come to the rescue:

. . . it was a condition, altogether without precedent, in which the country was now placed. A war was raging with the most rancorous violence within our borders; congress has been in session nearly two months, during which time this conflict was raging; yet of the causes of the war, how it was produced, if the fault was on one side or on both sides, in short, what had lighted up the torch, congress was altogether uninformed.

Webster, certainly no champion of either the administration or removal, was in floor charge of the Finance Committee's report of the bill. The circumstances of the emergency required him most uncomfortably to reply:

It was as much of a surprise to him, as to any one, that no official communication had been made to congress on the causes of the war. All he knew on the subject he had gathered from the gazettes. . . . The view taken by the gentleman from Kentucky was undoubtedly the true one. But the war rages, the enemy is in force, and the accounts of their ravages are disastrous. The executive government has asked for the means of suppressing these hostilities, and it was entirely proper that the bill should pass.[2]

These first appropriations were passed without dissent and Congress, with the remorseful reluctance of many of its members, continued to provide funds for the increasingly unpopular war while the total mounted to millions and then tens of millions. As the news from Florida gathered volume and detail in late January the dismal nature of the unexpected war became fully apparent. Far from proving capable of a swift punishment of the Indians who had massacred Dade's column, the military forces of the United States in the area remained pinned down and ineffective. No white inhabitant south of Georgia was unthreatened. Settlements stretching along 500 miles of Florida's frontier had been abandoned. The whole border was in flames. The loss of property had been immense and the loss of life distressing. Under circumstances

[2] For further detail on this frustrated debate see *Niles Register*, January 30, 1836.

so grim Congress had no other recourse than to continue to provide the administration with the means needed to prosecute the
war. Not only those members who had in 1830 voted for the
Removal Bill only on the assurance that force would never be used
but those as well who had passionately proclaimed the basic injustice of the whole removal policy were now alike compelled to
accept the bayonet as the sole arbiter of every contention.

The administration had need of the sympathy and support of
both Congress and the public. In those early months of 1836 other
threats than those emanating from the Florida swamps were loom-
ing as suddenly on other horizons. The brief uprising among the
lower Creek had raised the possibility that the flames of the Seminole War might spread to a greater conflagration among the more
numerous Creek. The flight of Creek refugees to the Cherokee
country suggested the possibility of a further spread. Santa Anna's
whirlwind invasion of Texas and the fall of the Alamo had swept
that anti-American conflict to the American doorstep. Confronted
by the apparent likelihood that it was about to be required to
furnish troops for coincidental campaigns in the Creek Country,
in the Cherokee country, and on the Texas-Louisiana border as
well as in Florida, the tiny regular army of less than 7,000 men was
obviously inadequate to cope with the multiple emergency.

The old warrior in the White House responded to the crisis
with a vigor reminiscent of his famous days as a field commander.
A torrent of his incisive orders and directives issued from the War
Department. The garrisons of northern posts and coastal forts
were stripped to furnish reinforcements for field operations.
Troops were assigned or earmarked for service in the Creek and
Cherokee country and on the Texas and Florida frontiers. The
governors of Florida, Georgia, South Carolina, Alabama, Mississippi, Louisiana and Tennessee were urgently requested to furnish
contingents of militia and volunteers. Major General E. P. Gaines
was assigned command of the regular army in Florida and Major
General Winfield Scott given over all command of all forces, state
and federal, being mobilized there.

The Creek and Texas threats appeared at the time potentially
far more menacing but it was only in Florida that an actual war
was already under way and it was here that the impromptu national effort first reached the stage of military action. The south-

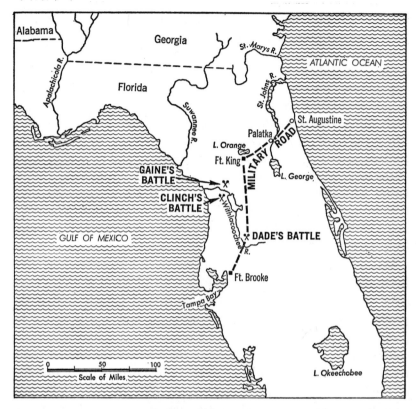

At the outbreak of the Seminole War, Indian depredations threatened every settlement in every quarter of Florida and caused apprehension in adjoining areas of Georgia and Alabama.

ern states responded with their customary military ardor to the calls for aid, though in some instances the availability of their troops was delayed by organization, transportation and supply problems. But before the end of January a regiment of Louisiana volunteers had joined Gaines and the first shipload of South Carolina volunteers had appeared to reinforce St. Augustine which had been expecting momentary attack.

Gaines, who had formerly been stationed at Memphis, Tennessee, arrived by sea at Tampa Bay February 9, 1836 with 435 regulars and 700 Louisiana troops. With this impressive force he undertook a passage of Dade's route north, visited Dade's battleground, buried the dead, and continued to Fort King. At this beleaguered post he found insufficient supplies to maintain his army and was obliged to head back at once for Tampa Bay. The Seminole had been content with his march north but felt no such complacency about his return south. At the Withlacoochee he was opposed by Osceola with several hundred warriors who succeeded in preventing his crossing for ten days during which his increasingly hungry men ate their horses. Osceola then proposed a truce which the hard-pressed Gaines was glad to accept. By its terms the Indians agreed to cease attacking the frontier and to remain south of the river while the army agreed to cease pursuing them, a stipulation which was equivalent to an official acquiescence in their remaining in Florida instead of removing to the west. The truce saved Gaines but soon became inoperative as neither side abided by its terms.

When Scott arrived to assume the responsibilities of commander-in-chief he signalized his appearance with blasts of scathing criticism of the conduct of generals Gaines and Clinch and of the people of Florida. As a demonstration of how much better he proposed to manage, he mounted a textbook campaign with three columns driving southward through the heart of the Indian country to a projected convergence near Tampa Bay. After a number of hitches due to transport and supply difficulties, military and volunteer inefficiencies, and disputes among commanding officers, the three columns got under way. In areas where the exchange of couriers was not feasible on account of Indian command of the intervening wilderness they kept one another informed of their respective locations by the periodic firing of cannons as signals. This method served also to keep the Indians informed. The Seminole had three times successfully opposed the march of American armies but this new concentration of force was so overwhelmingly greater than any they could muster that they were obliged to adopt other tactics. Each day, as the columns plowed southward, there were always Indians in evidence but they were always in small groups hovering to cut off stragglers or isolated snipers keeping the marches the target of their distant fire. Sometimes a few ranged close enough to deliver a punishing volley. But no responding charge of cavalry or infantry ever succeeded in bringing on an engagement. Whenever approached the Indians invariably faded into the background of swamp and grass. Occasionally whole regiments were deployed to surround an area in which Indians had been seen to take cover but always when the net had closed there was nothing in it.

The columns trudged on, impeded by mud, rivers, swamps, heat, sickness, and, eventually, by hunger, as supply arrangements proved inadequate. They met as planned after having marched at will through the Seminole heartland but Scott's success had come no nearer winning the war than had Dade's disaster or Clinch's repulse or Gaines' frustration. He had instead merely demonstrated to the Seminole more clearly than ever that they had no occasion to fear the cumbersome movements of an organized army tethered to its reliance upon supply, shelter and roads. They had found it easy to evade its monstrous lunges. It was safe for them to beard and tantalize it as gadflies might infuriate a bull. Their women and children could remain hidden in secret villages no white man had been able to locate. Their war parties were still emerging at will from the central marshland to torment the settlers' frontier. So far the Seminole could feel that if they were not winning the war they certainly were not losing it.

The ravages of tropical disease had indicated that white soldiery could not keep the field in Florida during the heat of summer. When Scott's operation ended in its meaningless success, his volunteers and militia were returned to their states, his regulars gathered in their fortified camps and posts and most of central Florida left to the Seminole. An irate Jackson ordered Scott to Washington for investigation of his failure both to conclude the Seminole War and to commence the Creek War and when he was twice acquitted each time angrily directed the court martial to reconsider.

Meanwhile the administration had been relieved of its other apprehensions. Neither the Creek nor the Cherokee had essayed the slightest resistance. Sam Houston had won his miraculous victory at San Jacinto, the Republic of Texas had come into being and the threat of hostilities with Mexico had been indefinitely postponed. But the Seminole War was only beginning and it was likewise beginning to become apparent how much more difficult it was likely to become. The army already understood. No soldier who had been there had failed to learn to abhor service in Florida.

It was not a good war. It was not even a dangerous war, or a fighting war. It was a miserable war, an embarrassing war. Men who had experienced its miseries and indignities, suffered in a cause for which no one had heart, wanted no more of it. During 1836, 103 commissioned officers resigned from the regular establishment. At the end of the year there were only 46 officers left to be allocated to the 40 companies of the midget army. The harassed and hunted Seminole could accept their ordeal with more spirit. Men who are defending their freedom can endure much.

The discovery had often before been made that it was much more difficult to stop a war than it had been to start it. There was no conceivable way to stop this one, no matter how unpopular it had become. Florida could not very well be given back to the Indians and the only alternative was to get the Indians out of Florida. The United States therefore got on with the war that by now nobody wanted. Furnished ample funds by an unhappy Congress and prodded by a determined President, the War Department prepared for a greatly expanded effort. When Major General Thomas S. Jesup took the field for the spring campaign of 1837 he commanded an army of 4,637 regulars, 4,078 volunteers, 100 seamen and 978 Indian auxiliaries. He achieved no more than had his predecessors. The Seminole were not susceptible to mastery by large armies. They faded from the view of advancing soldiers into the vast natural wasteland of which they were a part and only emerged again when able to strike at some unwary sentry, straggler, stock tender, supply convoy or settler who had returned too soon to his ruined farmstead. The inaccessible collections of grass huts in which they hid their women and children were likewise beyond any military grasp for they could at a moment's warning be made to flit from place to place through mutations as mysterious as the disappearances and reappearances of their warriors.

The war staggered on, year after year. New plans were laid, new armies organized, new generals appointed, new millions spent. The basic inability of uniformed, disciplined white men burdened with equipment to run naked Seminole to earth in the labyrinthine depths of Florida's swamps stultified every effort. There ensued a frantic casting about for various devices which might reduce this fatal disadvantage. Indians were recruited to hunt down their fellow Indians. When the first Creek auxiliaries failed to seem sufficiently at home in the swamps it was assumed they might have been deterred by some lurking sympathies for their Seminole cousins. At much greater expense northern and western Indians were enlisted, transported, schooled, armed and introduced to the swamp country. They were no more successful than had been the Creek. The adaptation of the Seminole to his environment was to be matched only by the crane or the alligator. In the hope of reducing Seminole capacity to resist special efforts were made to capture their horses, cattle and Negroes. Indian auxiliaries were paid head money for each Negro they succeeded in bringing in. To procure funds for these rewards the Army established what amounted to slave markets. The difficulty of identifying captured blacks, many of whom had been born in the Seminole community, or of determining the legitimacy of the assertions of ownership pressed by competing white claimants, committed the Army to the role of slave trader. As a final desperate expedient, some dozens of bloodhounds, trained as manhunters, were imported from Cuba. This provoked a great outcry in Congress and in some moralistic circles in the north but the protest was wasted. As it turned out, the prevalence of water upon the trails they were expected to follow made the bloodhounds useless.

The one device that eventually did achieve the downfall of the Seminole was one in which neither the army, the administration, Congress nor any American could take pride. For the Seminole the war offered no future. They were hungry, constantly hunted like wild animals, and their families subjected to unremitting danger. The war seemed to them so witless, so unproductive of gain for anyone concerned, that they could not bring themselves to believe that their assailants were not as anxious as they to bring it to a close. They were therefore perpetually willing to treat. Some were by now willing to discuss terms under which they might after all remove west, others were willing to discuss a possible agreement to withdraw within narrower confines deeper into south-central Florida, but all were desperately eager to discuss any proposition that might lead to the termination of a war in which both sides were losing so much. At the end of each inconclusive campaign the frustrated Army fretfully agreed to a truce to permit such discussions.

The first such general truce came at the end of Jesup's 1837 campaign. Nearly 3,000 Seminole emerged from their wild haunts to camp in sight of their recent white antagonists. A number of their leaders professed readiness to discuss removal and 24 transports were in waiting in Tampa Bay. An essential premise of the truce had been Jesup's promise that Seminole Negroes would receive the same consideration as other Seminole. He failed, however, to prevent an invasion of the Seminole camp by white slave traders who began seizing Negroes with the assertion that they were identifiable as runaway slaves or the descendants of such runaways. The alarmed and angered Seminole broke camp in the night and disappeared into the wild background from which they had emerged.

Later truces were even more disturbed and controversial. It became a standard practice in American military policy to concoct allegations of Indian misconduct under which Indian negotiators could be arrested and held without regard for the flag of truce under which they had appeared. To Indians, who had since the most primitive days of intertribal warfare preserved a traditional regard for the sanctity of ambassadors and safe conducts, this seemed an incredible disgrace. But American commanders whose prestige had been undermined by the frustrations of a just completed campaign in that Florida graveyard of military reputations were not disposed to be so finicky. It appeared an opportunity too attractive to be neglected. If Seminole chieftains who had successfully evaded capture for months and years had now come within arm's length some sufficient excuse could surely be contrived to seize and hold them. The treachery could be considered clothed with a species of respectability inasmuch as it served to save Seminole as well as American lives. What had at first been a temptation soon became an established procedure. The Seminole continued to come in to negotiate. Even after repeated deceptions they appeared unable to believe that the next safe conduct would not be honored. It could have been that the victims felt a secret wish to submit and had found a way to save face in this subjection to American chicanery. The arrest of each additional chief prepared the ground for persuading his immediate followers to surrender. It was true that a considerable number of the Seminole had so tired of the war that they were ready for any alternative, even removal. In any event, as the months and years rolled on, the intermittent seizure of negotiating chiefs resulted in a steady trickle of Seminole who could be thrust aboard transports and shipped westward. Most of these involuntary migrants suffered more en route than during the years they had been hunted by soldiers through the Florida swamps. Meanwhile, some thousands of their still intransigent fellow Seminole were still being hunted.

The Seminole War and its companion piece, the psuedo-war in the Creek country, had proved of enormous service to the administration's removal program. Under cover of the military emergency unstinted force could be applied to compel the removal of the Creek and Seminole and preparations proceed for a similarly compulsive removal of the Cherokee. Congressional critics had been confused. Congress had on the contrary been obliged to appropriate vast sums to expedite the administration's favorite projects. The wars' effect on public opinion was even more injurious to the Indian cause. During the crises of 1830 and 1832 the presumed injustices being visited upon Indians had aroused great indignation in the north. But the same injustices which can stir emotion one year cannot continue to stir an equal emotion year after year. This tendency of public opinion to tire of a cause was accelerated by the Seminole War. Large segments of a public which had warmly sympathized with Indians began to feel that if Indians were actually killing white people then everybody concerned would probably be better off, and everybody else relieved of further anxiety, if the Indians were in fact all packed off to the west. The ineptitude with which the war was conducted added to the public's growing impatience and disgust. The ability of the Seminole to prolong the war was actually a disservice to the Indian cause. People were getting sick of the whole Indian question and tired of struggling to determine the relative rights and wrongs involved.

15

When John Ross, Cherokee president, arrived in Washington January 8, 1833 to reiterate in the nation's forum his people's demands for consideration there would have been every justification had he betrayed evidences of discouragement. During the past year the Cherokee cause had suffered crushing reverses from which no one but Ross could have detected much hope of recovery. First, the President's refusal to recognize the authority of the Supreme Court's decision affirming the constitutional rights of the Cherokee had encouraged Georgia to proceed with its inexorable program of dispossession which could only lead to Cherokee expulsion or extinction. Then, this executive dictate had been upheld by the American people through their overwhelming preference, in the Presidential election of 1832, of Andrew Jackson, chief enemy of the Cherokee, to Henry Clay, William Wirt and John Sergeant, their most eminent champions. But an even more crippling blow had fallen, with an effect not at first fully appreciated, which was to prove final and fatal. In a letter to the Cherokee of April 17, 1832 Secretary of War Lewis Cass had summarized with many explicit details the federal government's proposals and promises bearing on the administration's Cherokee policy:

The president is willing to enter into an arrangement, for your removal west of the Mississippi, upon the following general principles:

194

1. That a country, sufficiently extensive and fertile, shall be distinctly marked out, west of the territory of Arkansas, for you and your brethren, where they now are.

2. That this country shall be conveyed to you by patent, according to the provisions of the act, 1830, and that it shall be forever without the boundaries of any state or territory.

3. That you shall have all the powers of self government so far as may be compatible with that general supervisory authority, which it is necessary congress shall exercise over you.

4. That you shall have the privilege of appointing an agent, who shall reside at Washington, to communicate your claims and wishes to the government, and who shall be paid by the United States.

5. That if congress assent to the measure you shall be allowed a delegate to that body, and shall also, when your improvement and other circumstances will permit, and when congress think proper, be placed in the relation of a territory.

6. That all white persons, unless specially authorized by the laws of the United States, shall be excluded from your territory.

7. That you shall remove to your new country, at the expense of the United States.

After explaining that the Cherokee might select modes of transportation and means of administering the cost, all to be furnished by the United States, the letter detailed further assurances:

That subsistence shall be provided by the United States, for the term of one year, after you reach your destination.

That an annuity, proportionate to the value of the cession you may make, be secured to you.

That all the improvements upon the ceded territory, which add real value to the land, be appraised and paid for.

That ample provision be made for the support of schools and teachers, and of blacksmiths, &c. for the supply of steel and iron, and for the erection of mills, school-houses, Cherokees' council houses, and houses of a few of your principal chiefs.

That a rifle and equipments be given to each male adult; that a quantity of blankets be allowed to your families, together with axes, hoes, wheels, cards and looms.

That your stock be valued and paid for by the United States.

That the annuities due to you by former treaties, be paid to you west of the Mississippi.

That provision be made for your orphan children.

That protection be guaranteed to you against the hostile efforts of any
other Indians.

After all these fervent promises the letter had closed with the
time worn admonition:

I cannot but hope that you will see, in this frank and liberal offer, full
evidence of the desire of the president that the difficulties of your
present situation may be removed, and your future destinies placed
beyond the reach of those causes which have occasioned such misery to
the Indian race. Shut your ears, I entreat you, to bad counsels, if any
such should be offered you. Whatever may be told to you, it is impossible you can remain where you now are and prosper. And if you
persist in the effort, the time of regret will come, I am afraid, after the
most injury to yourselves.

The text of the federal government's offer together with the
August 6, 1832 reply of the Cherokee General Council were published in full September 8, 1832 by the *Cherokee Phoenix*. The
Council found no difficulty rejecting the offer. The promises of
permanent land tenure in the west were regarded as meaningless.
The same promises had been made the Cherokee immigrants in
1807 and 1818 and had been broken the moment white settlers
had appeared on the Arkansas to covet the Cherokee colonists'
land. It was months before most Cherokee began to realize the
significance of the fatal time bomb planted in the Cass letter in the
passing mention at the end of the list of assurances that:

It is the wish of the president that all your people should remove, and
he is therefore unwilling that any reservations of land should be made
in the ceded territory. Still he would not make this an indispensable
condition, but would agree, should it be found necessary, that reservations should be made for a few of your people, in situations and under
circumstances rendering such a measure proper, and within the scope
of his legal authority.

In this superficially innocent passage the federal government
was craftily resorting to the tactic which had brought ruin to so
many Indian nations in the past. By offering special inducements
to a few of a nation's leaders, even though after defection they
could speak for an inconsiderable minority of the people they
presumed to represent, the recipients of this federal bounty could
be led to favor an acquiescence in white demands which could

thereupon be construed to constitute an acquiescence by the entire nation. It was clearly indicative of the inherent weaknesses of the Indian social, economic and political structure, based on the personal freedom of choice which every Indain regarded as the essential proof of his stature as an individual, that such defectors had always been easy to find in every confrontation between white and Indian interests. For the last 15 years the Cherokee had maintained a remarkable unity, unprecedented in Indian history. But the shrewd American thrust in 1832 was at last finding a chink in the Cherokee armor. Implicit in the federal suggestion was Georgia's readiness to reserve from confiscation the property of those more influential Cherokee who ceased to oppose removal.

The division instigated in the Cherokee community, at first scarcely noticed, was of a peculiarly pernicious nature. It tended to set a small propertied class against the less prosperous majority. Most Cherokee had been so poor that they had few material possessions to lose. They had lived in rude dwellings on tiny farms comprehending a corn patch and two or three pigs or cows. When dispossessed by Georgia's militia they retired to a brush hut in the woods or mountains, cultivating half an acre where before they had planted three and relieving the privations of their existence by reliance on their traditional dancing, story telling and ball playing. But the few wealthy Cherokee owned hundreds of acres, plantation houses, slaves, herds of cattle, mills, ferries, stores. They had a great deal to lose and reflection was stirring in them an increasing reluctance to lose it. Most of the larger Cherokee proprietors could feel with some reason that they were an elite quite distinct from the Cherokee masses. They were well above the Cherokee average in education, they sent their children to school and college, they had a wider knowledge of the world, they were acquainted with the intricacies of white commerce, they had traveled, and, above all, they had some grasp of the realities of American politics. It was this last conception that helped them accommodate a devotion to general Cherokee welfare which they continued to claim to a conviction that, since removal was eventually inevitable, the sooner the Cherokee submitted to it the less they would lose and the less, most certainly, the propertied class would lose.

This diminishment in resolution in the Cherokee upper class

was a gradual and for a time a groping development. At first it amounted to no more than a covert exchange among them of whispers flirting with the conceivable advisability of negotiating to learn how favorable might actually prove the terms that could be extracted from the federal government. The near unanimity of Cherokee public opinion had produced an atmosphere which continued to give men of property much reason to remain discreet. But in 1832 the ineffectuality of the Supreme Court's decision, the accelerated progress of Georgia's land seizure program and the provocative inducement proffered in the Cass letter identified for many of them the range of their future prospects. Of the five most prominent Cherokee, John Ross, the two Ridges, Stand Watie and Elias Boudinot, only Ross resisted the temptation to seek an accommodation with superior white power. At the July, 1832, Council meeting there was for the first time revealed evidence of the willingness of some Cherokee to compromise. In August Elias Boudinot resigned as editor of the *Phoenix*, thus relinquishing his post as one of the most eminent leaders of Cherokee resistance. At the October, 1832, Council meeting John Ridge boldly introduced a resolution proposing negotiation. It was overwhelmingly voted down but the seeds of division had been sown. After Jackson's tremendous election victory they began to sprout with fateful vigor.

In Washington Ross was persisting in his long argument with the administration. He did not shrink from the blasts of presidential temper before which so many other men had quailed. Cherokee obstinacy was having one intermediate success. The administration, desperately impatient to escape a dilemma which permitted it to satisfy the south only by a humiliating sacrifice of its prestige in the north, was gradually increasing the amount it was prepared to pay for Cherokee land so that the controversy could be ended by a federal delivery of a quiet title to Georgia and Alabama. Jackson raised his offer to $2,500,000 and then to $3,000,000. Ross held his ground. The gist of his rebuttal was that if the federal government insisted upon its inability to protect Cherokee constitutional rights in Georgia it must prove similarly unable to protect them in the west. To this there could, of course, be no realistic answer.

The Cherokee under Ross's leadership had so far avoided all the mistakes made by their fellow Indians. They had been neither timid, gullible nor belligerent. If they had shunned the dangers of the conference table they had with equal perspicacity shunned the greater dangers of a resort to arms. Their remarkable successes in self-improvement had won them worldwide sympathy. Their social, economic and political achievements had countered the popular conception that, being Indians, they were bound to be either erratic savages who required constraint or helpless ne'er-do-wells who required guardianship. Their absolute refusal to negotiate what they considered their basic rights had deprived state and national governments of the opportunity to insert that entering wedge of subversion which had confounded every other former Indian attempt to resist dispossession. Their appeal to the courts for protection of their constitutional rights had placed their adversaries at an immense moral disadvantage. The studied care with which they had refrained from offering the slightest physical resistance, no matter how cruelly mistreated, had given the state and federal governments no excuse to expel them by force and had compelled the wielders of white power to accept the role of deliberate and heartless aggressors. Every aspect of the Cherokee posture had dramatized the affirmation that their one great reliance was upon the righteousness of their cause and thus rendered less defensible the course taken by their opponents. These attitudes had sufficed for years but were no longer sufficient in the pyramiding crisis. The prospect Ross could offer his followers was becoming with each passing month more bleak and comfortless. He could only counsel them to persist in their attitude of nonviolence, of patient submission to every insult and deprivation, until the awakened conscience of the country had obliged Congress to come to their rescue.

Upon the return of Ross from Washington in the spring of 1833 the formerly secret stirring of oposition to his policy within the Cherokee community began to come into the open. Ridge and his small coterie of fellow proprietors had been infuriated by Ross's refusal to consider Jackson's offer of $3,000,000 for Cherokee land. Evidence, which Ross for long could not bring himself to accept, was accumulating that the Ridge-Boudinot faction had entered into an outright conspiracy to undermine his authority as acknowledged spokesman for the Cherokee as a necessary preamble to making the nation totally subject to the will of Georgia and the United States. Their plans to forward this projected *coup d'etat* had been discussed with state and federal authorities. The leading members of the cabal had been assured of personal rewards in the shape of title and financial preferences as a by-product of removal and had had made available to them funds to give practical effectiveness to their political maneuvers. In spite of this covert collusion with Georgian and federal administrators they could continue to profess with some plausibility a devotion to the long-range best interests of the Cherokee people as patriotic as that claimed by and for Ross. Along with these protestations they ridiculed Ross's assumption of a greater nobility of purpose and decried his visionary obstinacy as certain to lead the nation to ruin.

Meanwhile Georgia was intensifying those confiscation pressures calculated to make Cherokee existence intolerable. By the processes of the land lottery Cherokee property was being turned over at an ever accelerating rate to white claimants who held winning tickets. The confiscations were conducted by Georgia militia commanded by Colonel William Bishop, notorious for his truculence, who was operating under orders which in pursuance of a deliberate policy encouraged him to indulge in behavior which was to the last degree provocative and brutal. Special attention was given to the penalization of every influential Cherokee opposed to removal. Ross and every Council member loyal to him were dispossessed. At the same time care was taken to preserve the property interests of the pro-treaty faction. Their holdings were withheld from the lottery while they were advanced secret funds to finance their agitation. Particular efforts were made to eliminate every center of influence which had been devoted to Cherokee education and improvement. The missionaries, Samuel Worcester and Elizur Butler, only recently released from penitentiary, were driven from their homes. The *Cherokee Phoenix* was suppressed and its plant confiscated. Schools and council houses were occupied. Missions were converted into military headquarters, stables or taverns.[1]

While Georgia was so painfully tightening the screws designed to break Cherokee passive resistance, federal agents, coordinating

[1] For detail on this campaign of terrorism see *Memorial and Protest of the Cherokee Nation to Congress, June 21, 1836.* For recently discovered additional detail on the pro-treaty conspiracy and its operations, see Woodward, Grace Steel, *The Cherokees.* Norman, 1963.

their activities with the state's, were redoubling their efforts to persuade the Cherokee to migrate. In 1834 they proved able to round up nearly 700 who were wearily ready to give up the struggle. Their journey west was marked by the usual suffering from privation, hunger, exposure and disease. The deaths of 81 were reported en route, chiefly from measles and cholera, of which 45 were children under 10. Another epidemic was encountered at their destination from which half of those who had survived to reach it died during their first year in the west. A peculiarly disheartening feature of the 1834 migration was the identity of one of its number. The American Mission Board had long been the Cherokee's greatest benefactor and Samuel Worcester their most dedicated champion. But the Board had abandoned hope of continuing its work under the conditions that had been imposed by Georgia and directed Worcester to accompany the migration so that he might re-establish his mission in the west. The Board's surrender to the proponents of removal struck another agonizing blow to Ross's hopes.

Among all these disappointments and tribulations Ross's resolution remained unshaken. Most of his people had been driven into a precarious existence in the woods and mountains but their attachment to him was as devoted as ever. They had obeyed his injunctions that they maintain their nonviolent attitude in order that they might afford their enemies no provocation. They believed his prophecy that if they continued to endure the justice of their cause must save them by eventually winning the goodwill of the American people. But by now forces were in motion against which endurance or courage or justice could not of themselves prevail. After many discreet exchanges of views with the President of the United States and the Governor of Georgia, the pro-treaty faction met November 27, 1834 in the house of John Ridge at Running Water to organize as a party in preparation for claiming recognition as the legal spokesmen for the Cherokee nation.[2] The Cherokee Council, elected by the Cherokee people, still gave Ross its overwhelming support. He was again dispatched to Washington at the head of the official Cherokee delegation with instructions to

[2] To the pain caused Ross by his abandonment by so many of his one time trusted comrades in the long struggle for Cherokee rights was added a sharper pang when his brother, Andrew, joined the dissidents.

renew his argument of the Cherokee case with the government of the United States and in the hearing of its people.

When he reached Washington in February, 1835, he was confronted by another Cherokee delegation representing the pro-treaty faction and boldly asserting a stronger claim than his to represent the Cherokee nation. His attempts to reason with the administration, to appeal to Congress, and to court the attention of the country were distracted by the necessity of devoting his principal energies to this dispute with his Cherokee rivals who had relieved the administration of the role of his primary opponent. The competition between the two delegations, superficially fierce, had nevertheless already been decided. The president had made it known to the Ridge group before they left the Cherokee country that he would deal with them and only with them. Fishing in these troubled waters, the administration compounded Ross's difficulties by raising the offer for a total Cherokee cession to $3,250,-000, then to $4,500,000 and finally to $5,000,000. To emphasize the absurdity of this attempt to set a sales price on Cherokee rights Ross sardonically offered to sell out for $20,000,000. This bandying of figures tended further to obscure the moral issue.

Sensing the possibility of an imminent break in Cherokee unity, the administration selected a new coordinator of its now climactic effort. John F. Schermerhorn was appointed United States Commissioner with the mission of procuring by whatever means a Cherokee acceptance of a removal treaty. He was a former Dutch Presbyterian minister of Pennsylvania who had more recently found a more congenial calling as Indian agent. In 1833 he had tricked the touring Seminole chiefs at Fort Gibson into the signing of a document which could later be construed to represent a Seminole consent to migrate west, an expedient which presently precipitated the Seminole War. It was now his function to perform a similar service in the Cherokee case. When he departed for the Cherokee country he was armed with a May 25, 1835 letter from Acting Secretary of War C. A. Harris setting forth the president's last word. Though ostensibly intended as a communication for the information of the Cherokee people it was not addressed to Ross or the General Council, the nation's elected representatives, but to W. H. Underwood, the Georgia counsel for the Cherokee during the Supreme Court suit who now served the pro-treaty

faction, and to John Ridge, the faction's principal spokesman. In
the letter Harris wrote:

. . . the president . . . has instructed me to authorize you to an-
nounce publicly to the Cherokees, that no propositions for a treaty
will hereafter be made, more favorable than those now offered to
them. . . . So far from this, he has instructed me to say that the
present is the last proposition he will make to them, while he remains
in office; and they must abide the consequences of its rejection.[3]

Schermerhorn labored mightily with the obdurate Cherokee
through the summer and into the fall. Countless local councils
were assembled at which Indian communities were obliged to
listen to his harangues and to those of his federal associates and pro-
treaty advocates. The sustained effort to persuade the Cherokee to
consent to removal had all the trappings of an exceptionally bitter
election campaign with the added contentiousness that most arguments were accompanied by threats. Schermerhorn was constantly
advised on tactics by the pro-treaty leaders and both were in constant touch with the Georgia governor's mansion and the White
House. No means were spared to convince the Cherokee that their
case was hopeless and their only recourse removal. The few who
professed acquiescence were rewarded by indulgent issues of food
and clothing and the many who did not were denied everything,
including services and support guaranteed them under former
treaties. Most of Ross's leading associates were jailed. Ross himself
was forced to take refuge in Tennessee. The Georgia militia intensified their confiscation and persecution program. Still the frantic
campaign gained few converts. The vast majority of the Cherokee,
including literally all of those most impoverished and ignorant,
persisted in heeding Ross and his appeal to principle.

At the next General Council in October, 1835, held at Red Clay
in the safety of its situation on the Georgia-Tennessee line, before
which Schermerhorn and his allies declaimed long and caustically,
the proposed treaty was rejected by a practically unanimous vote.
So strong was the feeling that even Ridge, Boudinot and their
fellow pro-treaty advocates, fearing assassination, voted against it.
The Council then directed Ross to return to Washington and
there renew his petitioning for a redress of Cherokee grievances.

Schermerhorn had so far failed in his mission but he had by no

[3] *Niles Register,* July 4, 1835.

means shot his bolt. He summoned the Cherokee nation to meet with him in another council, this one not to be held on the neutral ground of Red Clay but at the old Cherokee capital, New Echota, in an area totally dominated by Georgia. To compel the obdurate Cherokee to attend, he ruled that all who did not would be counted as voting for the proposed treaty. The vast majority of the Cherokee continued to hold firm, continued to look only to Ross for guidance. The Cherokee leaders of the pro-treaty party were baffled and incensed by this persistent loyalty of the mass of their people to Ross, even after his policies had reduced them, in every material sense, to so wretched and apparently hopeless a pass. They advised Georgia's governor that the one hope of rendering the Cherokee people more amenable to reason was to deny them the opportunity to continue to listen to Ross. This posed something of a problem, for Ross was conducting his activities in the refuge of his new home in Tennessee to which he had resorted when dispossessed of his former home in Georgia. With the knowledge and the assumed approbation of Schermerhorn and United States Agent to the Cherokee, Benjamin F. Currey, a detachment of Georgia militia, under cover of a heavy rain, crossed the Tennessee line, November 7, 1835, seized Ross and haled him back across the border to confinement in Georgia. This arrogant adventure stirred an immediate and predictable reaction in Georgia's sister southern state, Tennessee. The indignation of Tennesseans was given voice, among many other cries of rage, in the November 18, 1835 issue of the *Tennessee Journal:*

Mob extraordinary. We have been informed that the Georgia guard, who are little better than a lawless banditti, have lately come into the state of Tennessee and arrested John Ross, principal chief of the Cherokee nation, and some strange man who was temporarily at Ross's, and carried them in custody to Spring Place, Georgia. We do not know under what pretence this has been done; but we do know it is an outrage upon the personal rights of Mr. Ross and his guest, and a contumelous insult to the authorities and citizens of Tennessee. . . . We care not what the charge against Mr. Ross may be; he is a citizen of Tennessee, under the protection of our law, and has been lately decided by the supreme court of the state, secured in his rights of person and property by the constitution and laws of the land. If he has been guilty of any offence against the laws of Georgia, why was he not prosecuted in the usual form? Why has he thus been lawlessly seized, without authority, and in violation of the laws of the state, which promised him protection, and carried by force to Spring Place, in the custody of the redoubtable captain Bishop? It was at first rumored that major Currey, the agent of the Cherokees, had procured Mr. Ross's arrest, but upon inquiry, we can find no evidence that he was concerned; and we hope, for the honor of our country, he was not.

It was Georgia's misfortune that the "strange man" taken with Ross turned out to be the celebrated author, John Howard Payne, whose "Home Sweet Home" had captured the affections of millions of Americans. He had been visiting Ross in the course of working upon a contemplated history of the Cherokee people, a project which, as his personal investigation continued, was developing into a recital of Cherokee wrongs with which he hoped to command the attention of the American people. The two prisoners, after much maltreatment en route which Payne later described at indignant and eloquent length, were confined in a log outhouse in Spring Place, site of the original Cherokee mission established by the Moravians in 1801. Among the studied afflictions to which they were subjected during their incarceration was the suspension from the rafters over their heads of the decaying corpse of an earlier Cherokee prisoner. Their private papers, including Ross's official files and Payne's literary notes, had been seized and searched for some evidence of legal culpability. Payne was accused by his captors of being an "abolitionist," which was a very dirty word everywhere in the country in those days, in the apparent hope of rousing the neighborhood to a lynching but happily no such disposition developed. After 13 days without any charges being preferred against them, they were released.

Georgia had been belatedly made aware of the necessity of backing away from the hornet's nest by the nationwide wave of disapproval and, more particularly, by the official protest of the governor of Tennessee to the governor of Georgia containing an implied threat of a counter invasion. The official apology offered Governor Newton Cannon of Tennessee by Governor William Schley included, among other excuses:

The commander of the guard, Colonel Bishop, was in Milledgeville at the time; and the act was done by a subordinate officer, who, I presume was not aware of the possible consequences of such an act. Be assured, sir, that whilst Georgia is tenacious of her own rights of sovereignty, and will always maintain them with becoming dignity, she is also the last state in the union who would knowingly and wilfully trespass on the rights of a sister. The act of which you very justly complain is not the act of Georgia, but of a few men, who, without proper knowledge or reflection, have committed a trespass on the person of Mr. Payne. They had no warrant or authority from any department of the government of Georgia for the act they have done. Their term of service expired within a few days after that act, and they were disbanded.[4]

The attempt to remove Ross from circulation in no way diminished his influence over his people. Upon his release he returned to Washington to renew his protestations. He could not even yet bring himself to believe that the enormity of what was occurring could fail to arouse American public opinion. Those who had instigated his arrest had been mistaken in imagining that his presence among the Cherokee made any difference. In his absence in Washington they remained as mindful as ever of his injunctions. Most declined even to participate in an official census of the nation, which included an enumeration of stock and other property for which compensation was to be paid as one of the considerations for removal. Enraged by their passive resistance many men and women were stripped and beaten by Georgia militia attending the federal census takers. In spite of the most rigorous threats and pressures, when the appointed day for the New Echota conference came fewer than 500 of the more than 17,000 Cherokee appeared.

Schermerhorn delivered an address and a reading of the proposed treaty with as much official solemnity as though this were a legitimate convocation of the Cherokee nation. The major terms of the treaty provided for a Cherokee cession of all their territory east of the Mississippi, a Cherokee agreement to migrate, an allocation of land in the west by the United States for permanent and forever undisturbed Cherokee occupation and eventual payment to the Cherokee nation of $5,000,000 in various forms of compensation, allowances, expenses and annuities. The treaty was accepted by the rump council December 29, 1835. Schermerhorn had at last accomplished his mission. Of the hundred odd Cherokee signatures attached to the document most were those of unim-

4 See *Niles Register*, January 16, 1836 for complete text of this intriguing diplomatic exchange.

portant and even unknown men. The more prominent signers were John Ridge, Major Ridge, Elias Boudinot and Stand Watie. All had once been among the most vigorous battlers for Cherokee rights. All still insisted that they were being moved by the most patriotic consideration for Cherokee welfare.

Ridge and Boudinot headed the delegation which set out for Washington with the treaty. Ross was able to confront their assertions of the instrument's legitimacy with the counter declaration, which no one could attempt to deny, that it represented at most a consent to remove by something less than a twentieth of the Cherokee nation.

Another moment of decision had come, this one clothed with a terrible aspect of finality. Once more the burden of judgment had been laid on the government and people of the United States.

16

The moral perplexities shrouding the Indian question had become steadily more confounding during the six years since Congress had presumably settled it by passage of the Removal Bill in 1830. The removal policy had so far proved an execrable failure, as galling to its proponents as its opponents. Most southerners, immediately concerned on material grounds or as a matter of political principle, were dissatisfied with the rate of progress that had been made in implementing it. Most northerners, sympathizing with varying degrees of sincerity with Indian reluctance, were as dissatisfied with the indecent pressures that had been imposed to hasten removal. Every development had compounded the disappointments of all concerned. The discriminatory and coercive practices inflicted upon Indians by the states of Mississippi, Alabama and Georgia had excited condemnation in the north. Any disposition to interpose federal authority in defense of Indians had provoked denunciation in the south. The physical removal of the Choctaw and Creek had been accompanied by outrageous inhumanities that no one, north or south, could condone. The mismanagement of Seminole relations had precipitated a war which was becoming as damaging to the self-esteem of the United States as to its reputation abroad. The dissensions between the President and the Supreme Court had struck at the very roots of the Constitution. North-south animosities had been stimulated to an intensity threatening the stability of the nation. The whole stumbling, contentious, vituperative effort to solve the Indian problem by removal had served to make any more sensible and equable solution less possible while creating a host of more critical problems. Now that Congress was again confronted by the repugnant issue it was made even more exasperating by having had tacked onto it an even more repugnant aberration.

What was particularly sticking in the congressional craw was this collateral illegitimacy superimposed upon the dubious merits of the removal policy. It raised a point that could not be easily sidestepped by a government and a people with a highly developed regard for the forms of legality. It flaunted a glaring irregularity for which the proponents of removal could not attempt to account, let alone justify. No one could deny that the Schermerhorn treaty was an agreement reached with a small minority of the Cherokee people or that it was frantically opposed by the great majority of them whose dissent was being voiced by a democratically elected government. Yet the administration which had negotiated it was now presenting it for ratification as a legitimate compact between the United States and the Cherokee Nation. There was no slightest way to disguise, nor was any attempt being made to disguise, the unvarnished fact that the United States was expected to become a witting party to a cynical subterfuge solely designed to expedite Cherokee dispossession. Many congressmen who had believed in the advisability of removal or had at least been convinced it was inevitable were now realizing unhappily that there could be no way to view this cold-blooded stratagem other than as a compromise of the good faith of the United States. From the beginning active opponents of removal had been actuated by moral regard for justice, by religious principles, by sectional antipathies, or by a partisan desire to embarrass the president. The margin by which the Removal Bill had been passed had been provided by the votes of less committed members who believed removal instrinsically wrong but who considered the larger interests of the country excused their continued support of the administration. Nowhere in this whole range of opinion, clearly a congressional consensus, was there any other response to the Schermerhorn treaty than contempt and aversion.

The unfriendly atmosphere in Congress awaiting the treaty was made the less hospitable by the circumstance that the Cherokee were the special favorites of the large segment of American public opinion harboring Indian or other racial sympathies. The Creek, Choctaw, Chickasaw and Seminole were by comparison remote and unfamiliar and their troubles had therefore seemed of less moment. But the Cherokee self-improvement experiment had been conducted on the forefront of the national stage where it had been fostered by wide and influential circles of people with many religious and intellectual connections. The Cherokee struggle, made more understandable and appealing by the emergence of such heroes as Sequoyah and Samuel Worcester and John Ross, had long been watched by great numbers of this particularly articulate class which was exceptionally gifted in expressing its views. These were views capable of rousing gusts of public opinion calculated to disturb the peace and comfort of many middle-of-the-road congressmen who had hoped that they had been rid of the supremely vexing removal question in 1830. That it should not only have returned but now have attached to it the redundancy of this diplomatic fraud appeared to them an unrelieved misfortune. None could doubt that to resort to such means to achieve an expulsion of the Cherokee from their homeland must awaken new waves of popular indignation.

Ross, returning to Washington to keep his finger on the pulse of congressional intentions, was greatly encouraged by all he could learn. It was obvious that the treaty had been received as a bitter pill which few members could swallow without the greatest difficulty. He was assured not only by such established Cherokee supporters as the northern and western senatorial giants, Webster and Clay, but by such leading southern senators as Calhoun of South Carolina and White of Tennessee that he need have no fear that it might ever be ratified. The burden of consideration fell more directly on the Senate, clothed by the constitution with co-responsibility with the president in treaty making, but the House was likewise involved, inasmuch as appropriations to implement the treaty must originate there. The debate in the Senate was secret, with the treaty being considered in executive session, but the general congressional debate on the question had actually been commenced at the last session of the former congress, having been precipitated the moment the appearance of the two rival Cherokee delegations in Washington had revealed the administration's new plan to overcome the Cherokee by subversion.

At the very initiation of the great debate a note was struck that was singularly disappointing to Indian hopes. Edward Everett, about to leave the House to become governor of Massachusetts, rose January 19, 1835 to make a sensational revelation. During his five terms in Congress he had gained recognition as one of its most distinguished, eloquent and influential members. He had through the years spoken so often and so vigorously in opposition to re‑ moval that he had come to be regarded as the chief spokesman in the House for the Indian cause. He had taken the floor on this occasion, as he had so often in the past, to present an Indian memorial. But this was not another Indian petition crying out against removal. It was an Indian petition inviting removal. It was the resolution drafted by the Running Water meeting of the Cherokee pro-treaty faction, brought to Washington by John Ridge and Elias Boudinot. In the bitter struggle for recognition between the two rival Cherokee delegations, the success of Ridge and Boudinot in winning Everett's sponsorship represented a tri‑ umph for them and another stunning setback for Ross. In his address to a startled House, Everett made a headlong retreat from the stand he had so long and earnestly maintained:

. . . I certainly never expected to present a memorial in this house in favor of the removal of Indians; but I as little expected to be re‑ quested by Indians to do so. I have performed this duty, at the request of a delegation of three, two at least of whom were among those, most active and influential, among their brethren, at the time the great stand was made on this floor, against the Indian policy of the govern‑ ment. You cannot, sir, have forgotten those discussions; you took a prominent part in them. I have changed no opinion then expressed by me. But it is the lesson of practical wisdom to yield, when it can be no longer helped, to the force of circumstances. I have long since come to the conclusion, in common I believe with all the friends with whom I acted on that occasion, that the best advice I could give to our Indian brethren, was, to yield to the hard necessity of their condition. . . . I am firmly persuaded, that the social, political and moral condition of this interesting tribe, strongly invites them to the west. I fear that swift and certain destruction impends over them, if they much longer delay their removal. I believe that they can now make better terms with the government, than they will be able hereafter to make, and that the longer they remain in their present abode, the more of that, which they most wish to preserve—their national identity, will perish. If congress can do anything (and I believe it can do every thing) to enable them to make their removal in a manner consistent with life, health and comfort; to heal their dissensions, to sooth their feelings, to mitigate their sufferings, and establish them advantageously in their new abodes, I hope it will be done, it ought to be done; for when all is done, I fear a heavy debt will lie against us, in the court of conscience.[1]

Aside from the direct reverberations of this recantation of his former personal convictions, Everett's turnabout was made more discouraging to the Cherokee and their supporters by his having been elected by a New England constituency which prided itself upon its devotion to religious and moral considerations. New England had long been a fountainhead of Indian sympathies, a generous source of contributions and donations to Indian schools and missions, the background which had furnished so many missionaries to the Indians. It came therefore as a more fearful blow to Indian hopes when New England's most influential representative began suddenly to preach unconditional surrender. It was moreover a blow that fell upon a wound still open. It was in this same religious and intellectual atmosphere that the American Mission Board had deliberated while coming to the recent decision to order Samuel Worcester to move his mission west. It was becoming depressingly apparent that many of the supporters upon whom the Cherokee had most relied had been animated by more philanthropy than resolution. Now that the battle was approaching its climax they were edging from the field.

The debate, of course, was only beginning. Two days later that most steadfast of Cherokee champions, Frelinghuysen, the "christian statesman," rose in the Senate to present the rival memorial brought to Washington by Ross. In it Ross had made a considerable concession dealing with that sensitivity to states' rights upon which so much congressional resistance to Cherokee appeals was based. He could have been led to feel safe in making the offer by the certain knowledge that Georgia would reject it but in any event he made it. He sought to make the Cherokee position appear more reasonable by proposing that the United States purchase all land held in common by the Cherokee nation, for delivery to Georgia, that individual Cherokee be guaranteed possession of such private plots as they had cultivated and improved, and that such Cherokee land holders become citizens of Georgia sub-

[1] *Niles Register,* January 24, 1835.

ject to Georgia laws but assured of all the civil rights and privileges of other citizens of Georgia.

The debate came into full flower when Clay rose in the Senate February 4, 1835 to deliver one of the major addresses of his long congressional career. He had chosen as an unheralded occasion his introduction of the Ridge-Boudinot memorial with which he then proceeded to explain at passionate length how thoroughly he disagreed. His was a voice able to attract a national attention only rivaled by that accorded Webster and the president himself. During the more than a quarter of a century that he had been a towering figure on the national scene he had again and again dominated the course of events. The stimulus of his long oposition to Jackson, the fervor of his own presidential aspirations, the sincerity of his personal convictions, lent weight and vigor to his words. In the development of the slavery controversy his pragmatic moderation had won him distinction as The Great Compromiser but in this issue of Indian removal he found no room for compromise.

He opened his address with a dissertation upon the obligation of the United States, defined by treaties which had been designated by the Constitution the supreme law of the land, to recognize and protect the rights of Indians. Indian survival and the good name of the United States, he argued, depended equally on the faithful observance of these treaties. He then went a long step further. Involved in the question, he said, was not only the validity of treaties between the United States and Indians but between the United States and Great Britain. He recalled that in the Treaty of Ghent ending the War of 1812 the United States had promised civil protection to the rights of Indians who had been Great Britain's former wards and allies. In the stormy negotiations leading to that peace, he reminded his hearers, "Great Britain . . . advanced, as a principle from which she would not recede, as a *sine qua non,* again and again" that there be included in the treaty an explicit American guarantee of Indian rights and boundaries. The American negotiators had given such assurances. This was a subject upon which Clay could speak with unchallenged authority. As leader of the "war hawks" in Congress he had precipitated the War of 1812 and as peace commissioner he had been a principal architect of the treaty that had ended the war, achieving a peace that had been unbroken since. He could therefore feel justified in asserting:

. . . if the American commissioners . . . had then stated that any one state of this union who happened to have Indians residing within its limits, possessed the right of extending over them the laws of such state, and of taking their lands, when and how it pleased, that the effect would have been a prolongation of the war. . . . Sir . . . let me ask whether in adopting the new code which now prevails, and by which the rights of the Indians have been trampled on, and the most solemn obligations of treaties have been disregarded, we are not chargeable with having induced that power to conclude a peace with us by suggestions utterly unfounded and erroneous?

Turning from this discussion of the treaty obligations of the United States, Clay entered upon a detailed exposition of the wrongs inflicted upon the Cherokee by the state of Georgia. A lengthy and biting presentation of these details led him to the declaration:

The senate will thus perceive that the whole power of the state of Georgia, military, as well as civil, has been made to bear upon these Indians, without their having any voice in forming, judging upon, or executing the laws under which he is placed, and without even the poor privilege of establishing the injury he may have suffered by Indian evidence: nay, worse still, not even by the evidence of a white man. Because the renunciation of his rights precludes all evidence, white or black, civilized or savage. There then he lies, with his property, his rights and every privilege which makes human existence desirable, at the mercy of the state of Georgia; a state in whose government or laws he has no voice. Sir, it is impossible for the most active imagination to conceive a condition of society more perfectly wretched. Shall I be told that the condition of the African slave is worse? No sir, no sir. It is not worse. The interest of the master makes it at once his duty and his inclination to provide for the comfort and the health of his slave: for without these, he would be unprofitable. Both pride and interest render the master prompt in vindicating the rights of his slave, and protecting him from the oppression of others: and the laws secure to him the amplest means to do so. But who—what human being, stands in the relation of master or any other relation, which makes him interested in the preservation and protection of the poor Indian thus degraded and miserable? Thrust out from human society, without the sympathies of any, and placed without the pale of common justice, who is there to protect him, or defend his rights?

Clay went on to dwell upon the anomalies of the administration position which, in contradiction to the Supreme Court's opinion, had led it to claim the federal government was powerless to fulfill its promises to Indians who had by no act of their own become residents of states, while continuing to claim, as a means of persuading them to migrate, a power to protect them after their removal to the west. He doubted the validity of this distinction:

And then, as to those who desire to remain on this side of the river, I ask again, are we powerless? Can we afford them no redress? Must we sit still, and see the injury they suffer, and extend no hand to relieve them? It were strange, indeed, were such the case. Why have we guaranteed to them the enjoyment of their own laws? Why have we pledged to them protection? Why have we assigned them limits of territory? Why have we declared that they shall enjoy their homes in peace, without molestation from any? If the United States government has contracted these serious obligations, it ought, before the Indians were reduced by our assurances to rely upon our engagement, to have explained to them its want of authority to make the contract. Before we pretend to Great Britain, to Europe, to the civilized world, that such were the rights we would secure to the Indians, we ought to have examined the extent and the grounds of our own rights to do so. But is such, indeed, our situation? No sir. Georgia has shut her courts against these Indians. What is the remedy? *To open ours.* Have we not the right? What says the constitution? "The judicial power shall extend to all cases in law and equity, arising under this constitution, the laws of the United States, and treaties made, or which shall be made, under their authority."

Having returned to this basic issue of the sanctity of treaties, Clay reminded the Senate of the current dispute with France arising out of that nation's failure to abide by a treaty with the United States which was at the moment stirring so much American excitement and indignation:

How should we stand in the eyes of France and of the civilized world, if, in spite of the most solemn treaties which had existed for half a century, and had been recognized in every form, and by every branch of the government, how would they be justified if they suffered these treaties to be trampled under foot, and the rights which they were given to secure trodden into the dust? How would Great Britain, after the solemn undertaking entered into with her at Ghent, feel after such a breach of faith? And how could he, as a commissioner on the nego-

tiation of that treaty, hold up his head before Great Britain, after
having been thus made an instrument of fraud and deception, as
assuredly he would have been, if the rights of the Indians are to be
thus violated, and the treaties by which they were secured violated?

He came then to his dramatic peroration:

How could he hold up his head, after such a violation of rights, and
say that he was proud of his country, of which they all must wish to be
proud? For himself, he rejoiced that he had been spared, and allowed
a suitable opportunity to present his views and opinions on this great
national subject, so interesting to the national character of the country
for justice and equity. He rejoiced that the voice which, without
charge of presumption or arrogance, he might say, was ever raised in
defence of the oppressed of the human species, had been heard in
defence of this most oppressed of all. To him, in that awful hour of
death, to which all must come, and which, with respect to him could
not be very far distant, it would be a source of the highest consolation
that an opportunity had been found by him, on the floor of the senate,
in the discharge of his official duty, to pronounce his views on a course
of policy marked by such wrongs as were calculated to arrest the attention of every one, and that he had raised his humble voice, and pronounced his solemn protest against such wrongs.

When Clay sat down it could hardly longer be said that the
larger portion of the American people must remain unaware or
uninformed on the ethical factors in the removal issue. His words
were to reecho in innumerable newspapers, from countless pul-
pits, in every sort of gathering and meeting.

Senator Alfred Cuthbert of Georgia, rising to reply, complained
that Clay's obviously prepared address had taken him by surprise,
that he and colleagues who shared his views had received no warning of an intention to launch the Senate on so important a discussion. In any event, he asserted, it did not represent an appropriate
subject for senatorial debate:

. . . he did not propose to enter into the discussion of the subject at
this time; or at any time to the extent to which the senator from
Kentucky had gone. It was one which could never be discussed here,
for any useful purpose. Georgia did not plead before this tribunal. He
did not stand here to plead in her behalf. . . . The gentleman from
Kentucky had reminded the senate that there was a final day of judgment at hand, when the state of Georgia would have to answer for her
conduct to these poor Indians. . . . If these Cherokees were to appear
at that day of judgment to urge their wrongs against Georgia, where

were the hosts of shades of all the original red men on this side of the Mississippi? Upon whom were they to seek revenge? It seemed that Georgia alone was to be held up to general odium.

Hugh White of Tennessee rose to press the case for the south. He had recently become involved in an embittered controversy with his fellow Tennessean, Jackson, and was preparing to become a presidential candidate in the coming election in which he would succeed in wresting political control of Tennessee from his great rival. He had no wish to come to Jackson's aid in this matter of his Indian policy with which many Tennesseans had little sympathy. But the discussion had touched the raw nerve of an issue which White, as a southerner, regarded as of infinitely greater importance than any other. He personally favored protection of the Indians, he said, but:

. . . the gentleman from Kentucky had gone into a discussion relative to the merits of the laws of the several states, for the government of the Indians within their limits. He did not think any good was likely to result to the people of the United States, or the Indians themselves, from such discussions. . . . Each state having asserted, and maintained its independence, thought that it had a right to govern any population within the limits of their territories. This right was secured to each of the states, by the articles of confederation, by which it was provided that the general government should never interfere with the bounds of the states, nor with their internal regulations.

White went on, in fearfully sober and measured words, to raise once more the dread specter of civil war which had been so often and insistently raised by southern members since the removal debate had first preempted the attention of Congress in 1827:

The state of Georgia had extended her jurisdiction over the Indians within her limits. Alabama, Tennessee, and Mississippi, have done the same. They say that they are sovereign and independent states, and that you shall not interfere with any portion of their population. Now how are you to get over this? Can you expect these states to repeal their laws? Are you to employ the forces of the federal government to make four independent states yield to your demands? And what will be the consequences if you do? Why, civil strife and bloodshed enough to make any man shudder.

The debate in Congress was necessarily interrupted by the long summer hiatus between the last meeting of the 24th Congress, March 3, and the first of the 25th, December 7. The most resounding reply to Clay came not from the floors of Congress but from the White House after adjournment. Jackson, characteristically unshaken in his determination, addressed, March 16, 1835, a formal letter to "the Cherokee tribe of Indians east of the Mississippi river" which he intended primarily as a recapitulation of his views on the question for the benefit of the people of the United States:

My friends: I have long viewed your condition with great interest. For many years I have been acquainted with your people, and under all variety of circumstances, in peace and war. Your fathers were well known to me, and the regard which I cherished for them has caused me to feel great solicitude for your situation. To these feelings, growing out of former recollections, have been added the sanction of official duty, and the relation in which, by the constitution and laws, I am placed toward you. . . . I have no motive, my friends, to deceive you. I am sincerely desirous to promote your welfare. Listen to me, therefore, while I tell you that you cannot remain where you now are. Circumstances that cannot be controlled, and which are beyond the reach of human laws, render it impossible that you can flourish in the midst of a civilized community. You have but one remedy within your reach. And that is, to remove to the west and join your countrymen, who are already established there. . . . The choice is now before you. May the Great Spirit teach you how to choose. The fate of your women and children, the fate of your people to the remotest generation, depend upon the issue. Deceive yourselves no longer. Do not cherish the belief that you can ever resume your former political situation, while you continue in your present residence. As certain as the sun shines to guide you in your path, so certain is it that you cannot drive back the laws of Georgia from among you. . . . Think then of all these things. Shut your ears to bad counsels. Look at your condition as it now is, and then consider what it will be if you follow the advice I give you. Your friend.

Andrew Jackson[2]

During the summer and fall of 1835 while Congress was in adjournment Schermerhorn was engaged in his manipulations of factionalism in the Cherokee country that led to the controversial treaty. When Congress reassembled there were new and more strident expressions of those sectional animosities which, increasing in

[2] For text of the January-February debate and Jackson's March letter see *Niles Register,* April 4, 1835.

intensity, so much impeded reasonable consideration of the removal question or any other issue upon which there were north-south differences. Waddy Thompson of Georgia, speaking in the House December 21, 1835 on a bill affecting slavery in the District of Columbia, was referring to every northern attempt to pronounce moral judgments on the south:

As to discussing this subject before any human tribunal, I will not. I will not condescend to vindicate to this House or elsewhere, this or any other of our domestic institutions. It is no affair of yours; you have no right to touch it, still less to demand a reason of us for its continuance. . . . Who is it at the North that we are to conciliate? The fanatics? Fanatics, did I say, sir? Never before was so vile a band dignified with that name. They are murderers, foul murderers, accessories before the fact, and they know it, of murder, robbery, rape, infanticide.[3]

By January of 1836, Ridge and Boudinot were journeying northward to Washington. In their custody was the Schermerhorn treaty, providing for the cession of the Cherokee homeland and the removal of the Cherokee people within two years. There was general public awareness of the significance of their burden. Their progress northward was noted with interest by the press in anticipation of the congressional controversy certain to be generated by their arrival. But news of even more sensational portent was traveling northward that same January. Disclosure of the outbreak of the Seminole War came as a rankling shock to an incredulous nation which had by now largely forgotten the realities of Indian wars. Each day the newspapers blazed with new and more appalling reports. These were capped by accounts of other and apparently graver threats to the safety of Georgia, Alabama and Louisiana as well as of Florida.

Therefore when the administration laid the Cherokee treaty before the Senate Congress was distracted by wars and rumors of wars. Much of Florida had been devastated. The forces of the United States engaged there had suffered humiliating mortifications and blood-drenched defeats. There appeared reason to fear an extension of this Indian war to the Creek and Cherokee country. An even more portentous foreign threat had as suddenly loomed. Santa Anna's all conquering Mexican army was plunging

[3] ADC, House. December, 1835.

northward across Texas, laying waste its American settlements and driving toward the Louisiana border. The President had called upon every southern state for volunteers. Thousands of other volunteers were rallying on their own initiative to rush to the aid of their fellow Americans in Texas. Congress was being bombarded by Presidential requests for additional military appropriations. All these tocsins sounded alarms of apparently greater concern than the legitimacy of the Cherokee treaty.

It had been one of the paradoxes in the functioning of the American democracy that Congress had in every crisis proved instinctively and impulsively chauvinistic. This had not been foreseen by the founders. As a means of restraining the feared adventuresomeness of the executive, the Constitution had with great care vested in Congress the sole authority to declare war. In practice it had instead always been the President who had been obliged to restrain Congress. The first three Presidents, Washington, Adams and Jefferson had been compelled again and again to resort to every sort of precaution and pressure to control outbursts of congressional belligerency. The fourth President, Madison, had been less resourceful and had failed to deter Congress from launching an unready country into the War of 1812. The rule had remained unshaken. From the foundation of the republic it had been the President who had striven to preserve the peace and Congress which had clamored for an appeal to arms. This congress was no exception. It reacted in a fever of excitement to the war news. The guilt of the Seminole in resisting white armies and killing white settlers tended to become a guilt attached as well to their neighbors. This Congress was as quick as had been its predecessors to respond to provocation with retaliation. Each chamber rang with angry demands for the suppression and expulsion of all Indians as an invited and therefore legitimate act of war. Every administration request for military appropriations was granted without delay or dissent. Unstinting provision was made for the conduct of the actual Seminole War and as well for the raising of thousands of troops to prosecute the mythical Creek and Cherokee wars. The result was to give the president a free hand. Jackson used it by declining, in consonance with his profound devotion to the union, to move to the aid of the American revolutionists in Texas. But he also took advantage of it to satisfy his long cherished determination to assure Indian removal before the end of his term.

The developing political situation interfered with any objective consideration of the Cherokee treaty perhaps even more vitally than did the war fever. This was the year of another presidential election. The aging Jackson, with his enormous and proven vote-getting capacity, would not again be the Democratic standard bearer. Instead, he had arbitrarily selected a northerner, the relatively colorless Martin Van Buren, as his successor. Van Buren was not popular in the south, which had been Jackson's stronghold, and there was every likelihood that any general southern defection would sweep the Democrats from power. In this party emergency northern Democratic senators were implored by party managers not to offend the south by voting against their own administration on the Indian issue.

In the face of these extraneous twin pressures of war and politics liberal senators sturdily marshaled their forces. During the week-long executive session they continued to argue that the treaty posed a fundamental moral issue to which neither of these other considerations was relevant. Uneasily aware of what was expected of them by their constituents, a number of northern Democrats resisted the temptation to flee the field and waveringly stood their ground. As the Senate reluctantly approached a vote, a count of noses by anti-treaty leaders satisfied them that ratification would be rejected by a majority of one. But over night a senator formerly pledged to vote against the treaty abruptly changed sides. Word seeped from the secret session that the last-minute switch was that of Robert Goldsborough of Maryland. Another rumor made it Hugh White of Tennessee. At any rate, with the treaty now assured of ratification by a majority of one, a number of sweating northern senators felt free to scurry back to the fold of party loyalty. The recorded vote thus became 31 to 15 for ratification. Unlike the former votes on the Indian removal issue this final and decisive roll call was not sectional. The division was wholly political. More northern than southern senators voted for ratification, including both from Maine, New Hampshire, New York, Pennsylvania, Indiana and Illinois.

This total rout of the liberal forces in Congress resulted in a defeatist attitude from which they never recovered, as was exemplified by Webster's May 12, 1838 letter to Hiram Ketchum nearly two years later:

Dear Sir: This Cherokee subject is difficult and delicate. The public sympathies are aroused *too late*. The Whig members of Congress, who have taken an interest in seeing justice done to the Indians, are worn out and exhausted. An Administration man, come from where he will, has no concern for Indian rights, so far as I can perceive. We shall endeavor to do something or say something. We are all willing. You think that I ought to do some act to clear myself from the shame and sin of this treaty. My dear sir, I fought it a week in the Senate, on the question of ratification. . . . On all occasions, public and private, I pronounce the treaty a base fraud on the Cherokee Indians. What can I do more?[4]

4 Curtis, George Ticknor, *Life of Webster*, Vol. I, p. 576.

17

The Senate ratified the New Echota Treaty May 18, 1836 and the President proclaimed it effective May 23. Jackson could now feel that the effort upon which he had embarked before the turn of the century had been crowned finally with success. The Cherokee, the last of the southern Indian nations to evade diplomatic entrapment, had now been entangled in the meshes of a treaty which provided the United States with a legal excuse to use military force to compel their removal.

Ross hurried home to explain to his people this last in so long a series of disasters. By a succession of local councils and meetings he sought to revive their hopes and spirits. He exhorted them to persist in their nonviolent resistance. He assured them that all was not yet lost. He continued to forecast the eventual awakening of the American conscience. Most of them were by now homeless and hungry but they continued to give the same devoted heed to his counsel that they had in the past. He was not consciously misleading them. On his every northern excursion, not only to Washington but to other cities, he had received everywhere overwhelming testimony to how committed were northern sympathies, at least in the circles among which he moved, to the Cherokee cause. He was aware of the storm of northern indignation stirred by the Senate's cynical ratification of the obviously fraudulent treaty. He had himself so high a regard for principle that he could never cease believing that principle must in the end prevail.

To Georgia the President's proclamation came, on the other hand, as a signal that triumph was in sight and as a fresh spur to the state's program of calculated harassment. There was the possibility that if the Cherokee were sufficiently plagued large numbers might elect to migrate without waiting for the two-year limit set by the treaty. There was the further incentive that haste must be made if possession were to be taken of such property as was still held by any Cherokee before they contrived to take it west with them. This impulse chiefly endangered the wealthier members of the pro-treaty faction who had formerly enjoyed protection but who now began to find themselves sharing the vicissitudes of their poorer brethren. John Ridge, for whose services Georgia now had less need, was already repenting his part in promoting the treaty. He got off an indignant letter, June 30, 1836, to the President, whose eager instrument he had been:

Even the Georgia laws, which deny us our oaths, are thrown aside. Notwithstanding the cries of our people, and protestations of our peace and innocence, the lowest classes of the whites are flogging the Cherokees with cowhides, hickories, and clubs. We are not safe in our homes. Our people are assailed day and night by the rabble. Even justices of the peace and constables are concerned in this business. This barbarous treatment is not confined to the men, but the women are stripped also, and whipped without law or mercy. Send regular troops to protect us from these lawless assaults, and to protect our people as they depart for the West.

He then came to the heart of his protest:

If this is not done, we shall carry off nothing but the scars of the lash on our backs, and our oppressors will get all our money, and we shall be compelled to leave our country as beggars and in want. We speak plainly, as chiefs having property and life in danger, and we appeal to you for protection.[1]

The administration's principal concern was that the Cherokee were being so harshly oppressed that they might be driven to armed resistance, as had the Seminole and a few of the Creek. The flight of many Creek to the Cherokee country appeared to lend substance to this fear while at the same time giving the Georgians an excuse to practice new severities. To deal with this threat, Sec-

1 Mooney, *Myths of the Cherokee*, 127.

retary of War Cass directed Brigadier General John Ellis Wool, June 30, 1836, to assume federal command in the Cherokee country for the purpose of maintaining order. No regular troops being available, due to the more pressing requirements of other fronts, a brigade of East Tennessee Volunteers under the command of Brigadier General R. G. Dunlap was assigned to him. He was also authorized to call Georgia militia into the federal service if that proved necessary. The Cass directive centered around the instruction to Wool:

. . . Should the conduct of the Cherokee require the application of force you will proceed to subdue them. . . . Should a portion of the Cherokee remain friendly you will still require them to deliver up their arms.[2]

Upon his arrival in the Cherokee country Wool was unable to detect any signs of incipient revolt. He had been led to believe all more responsible Cherokee favored the treaty and was astonished to discover how nearly universal was Indian repudiation of it. Personal acquaintance with the oppression to which the Indian population was being subjected by Georgia authorities and citizens caused him concern. He was soon providing another striking illustration of the independence of judgment so frequently manifested by the higher officers of the United States Army of his time. His official attitude and conduct began to prove a great disappointment to his civil superiors in Washington, from whom he made no attempt to conceal his budding Cherokee sympathies and to whom he did not hesitate persistently to report instances of white brutality. In his initial order to Dunlap and his Tennessee brigade Wool instructed him to:

. . . proceed without delay to New Echota and such other parts of the Cherokee nation within the limits of Georgia as may be necessary to give protection both to the Cherokees and the white inhabitants residing in that section of the country. You will allow no encroachments upon either side. . . . You will also prevent any interference on the part of the Georgia troops with the Cherokees.[3]

There followed further instructions to Dunlap to expel from the Cherokee country any detachments of Georgia, Alabama, Ten-

[2] *American State Papers*, Military Affairs, Vol. VII, p. 549.
[3] *Ibid.* p. 550.

nessee, or North Carolina militia who were not under Wool's direct command. Wool's unforeseen and unprecedented disposition to regulate the conduct of whites as well as Indians provoked angry protests in Georgia and Alabama. It also brought down upon his head a series of remonstrances and reprimands from the Secretary of War and the President. Wool remained unbending in his determination to perform his duty as he saw it and to deal evenhandedly with both races. He continued as candidly as ever to report his views to Washington. As late as March 31, 1837 he was writing Joel R. Poinsett, Secretary of War in the Van Buren administration:

Recent occurrences, which are but repetitions of those which have heretofore taken place, show plainly that it is vain to appeal to the civil authorities of the country to repress the disposition of the whites to oppress this people and trample on their rights. In illustration, I would refer to a case of an aggravated cast which occurred a few days since within a few miles of this place. An Indian at his home was shot down and basely murdered by a party of white men, who had not the semblance of provocation, unless an attempt to escape from their barbarity be so considered. These men were arrested by my order, and immediately turned over to the civil authority to be dealt with according to their deserts; but so strongly have the prejudices of the people, stimulated by avarice, been excited against the Indians, that it is exceedingly doubtful if justice can be done in the case. With these people it really seems to be no crime to kill an Indian.[4]

Wool's Cherokee sympathies were presently shared by Dunlap and his Tennesseans. They had upon arrival in the Cherokee country undertaken the construction of prison stockades for the confinement of captured warriors of the Cherokee whom they had been told might be expected momentarily to revolt. They soon realized how unfounded had been these fears and that instead the Cherokee under Ross's leadership were totally committed to nonviolence. As their personal contacts with their charges developed the Tennesseans became the increasingly friendly and willing guardians of Cherokee rights. Upon the mustering out of the brigade in March, 1837 Dunlap stated:

I gave the Cherokees all the protection in my power (the whites needed none). My course has excited the hatred of a few of the lawless

[4] *Ibid.* p. 563.

rabble in Georgia who have long played the part of unfeeling petty tyrants, to the disgrace of the proud character of gallant soldiers and good citizens. I had determined that I would never dishonor the Tennessee arms in a servile service by aiding to carry into execution at the point of the bayonet a treaty made by a lean minority against the will and authority of the Cherokee people. I soon discovered that the Cherokees had not the most distant thought of war with the United States, notwithstanding the common rights of humanity and justice had been denied them.[5]

The principal spokesman for Georgia's dissatisfaction with the conduct of Wool and Dunlap was Wilson Lumpkin, who, upon being succeeded as governor by William Schley in 1835, had been appointed United States Commissioner to supervise the execution of the removal treaty. His primary functions were to facilitate the departure preparations of those Cherokee immediately willing to migrate, most of whom were of the propertied pro-treaty faction, and to strive to convince all others that they could not hope to escape joining the migration within the two-year limit set by the treaty. As a representative of Georgia's interests who had been congressman and governor and was about to become United States senator he was as devoted to a prompt and strict execution of the treaty as he was jealous of Georgia's reputation which had been so often assailed by Cherokee sympathizers. He was understandably incensed by Ross's encouragement of the Cherokee majority's passive resistance and presently became almost as exercised by the inclination of Wool and Dunlap to protect the Indians from white molestation. He gave vent to his displeasure in an extensive and protracted correspondence with the President, the Secretary of War, the Commissioner of Indian Affairs and the governors of Tennessee and Georgia which casts much light on the southern attitudes toward federal intervention during those troubled months following the treaty's ratification. He was writing Jackson September 24, 1836:

Through General Wool, and other channels of information, you are fully apprised of the mischievous efforts of John Ross and his white associates to prevent a speedy and faithful execution of the late Treaty. This man Ross, sir, has already been the instrument in the hands of bad men to bring more than enough evil upon this unfortu-

[5] Royce, C. C., *The Cherokee Nation of Indians*, p. 286.

nate race—*the Cherokees.* I cannot believe the Federal Government so destitute of power as to permit a single individual to thwart and overturn its treaties, involve the Nation in war, blood and massacre, and produce a state of things which must eventuate in the certain destruction of a remnant tribe of the aboriginal race, to whom the United States stand pledged by every consideration of honor and duty arising under the strongest and most explicit treaty stipulations. If the laws of the United States do not provide for the arrest and punishment of such men as Osceola, John Ross, &c., it is the solemn duty of the approaching Congress to take the subject under serious consideration.

Lumpkin had been intensely irritated by the unexpected behavior of Georgia's southern neighbors, Dunlap and his Tennesseans, of whom he said in the same letter:

When I entered the Cherokee country of Georgia I assure you I felt some alarm at the excited state of feeling amongst many of the Georgians, on account of prejudice which they had imbibed against General Dunlap, of Tennessee, and some of his subordinates in command. Without expressing an opinion as to who was wrong or right, be assured that *stationary volunteers* from one State should not be quartered in another State. . . . I should be reluctant to attempt to discharge the duties of Commissioner assigned to me in the Cherokee country, encountering the daring and cunning opposition of Ross, and have no force or protection at my command but men and officers believed to be more friendly to the schemes of Ross than they are to the objects of my mission, or that of the Government and administration under which I am acting. . . . If we have to rely upon subordinate officers of the Federal Government for our rule of action, this Treaty will never be brought to a happy issue.

This complaint struck a responsive chord in Jackson who was beginning to become irascibly aware that his home state, whose idol he so long had been, was showing signs of deserting his standard to vote Whig in the approaching election. Lumpkin had refrained for a time from quarreling with Wool but in his December 1, 1836 letter to Jackson he made no further attempt to conceal his opinion or to disguise the warning he felt necessary:

My confidence in the General's judgment . . . has been greatly weakened, ever since he suffered himself to be the organ through which Mr. John Ross communicated the insulting result of his mischievous Council to the Government of the United States. Notwithstanding your instructions through the War Department of the 17th of October last to the Commissioners, as well as to General Wool, you will perceive from the copy of the General's letter herewith submitted, that he still reserved to himself the right of judging whether the *requests* of the Commissioners will be acquiesced in or not. Now, sir, if the General continues to assume *this right,* contrary to your instructions of the 17th of October, I assure you that the stipulations of the Treaty will never be executed.

Lumpkin had succeeded in organizing two minor migrations. Some 600 relatively prosperous pro-treaty Cherokee set off overland January 1, 1837. They were able to take with them Negro slaves, saddle horses, droves of cattle, wagon loads of furniture and ample provisions on their journey through Kentucky, Illinois, Missouri and Arkansas. Another party of 466 less well equipped Cherokee, setting out March 3, 1837 by flatboat down the Tennessee, had a far less comfortable experience. They suffered from disease and privation and the many other hardships made familiar by former migrations.[6]

Much of Lumpkin's attention was necessarily devoted to the examination of creditors' claims against the Cherokee which under the terms of the treaty were to be paid by federal funds which he was authorized to disburse. He proved a diligent guardian of the public purse and resisted payments that appeared clearly unjustified. As one example, claims for legal services rendered the Cherokee, chiefly from Georgia firms which had provided local representation during the Supreme Court litigation, totalled $153,372. He ordered this pared to $31,000. But his irritation at every interposition of federal authority to maintain order continued to seethe. He wrote Commissioner of Indian Affairs C. A. Harris January 30, 1837:

. . . let it be distinctly understood that the officers and agents of the Government referred to are not to be permitted to treat with insult and contempt our official efforts to discharge duties with which we have been charged by the President of the United States. . . . We are by no means singular in not being able to cooperate with Gen'l Wool, as it is well known here that he has constantly complained of every officer and agent of the Government here, since he entered this coun-

[6] See Foreman, *Indian Removal* for detailed study of the composition and experiences of successive Indian migrations.

try, from the President down, who has had the misfortune to have to advise or instruct him in his operations.

But it was Ross who remained the paramount object of Lumpkin's dissatisfaction. Ross had spent much of the winter in Washington vainly attempting to win political support for a revocation of the treaty before returning to urge his people to continue to stand fast. Lumpkin wrote Harris June 5, 1837:

We would still hope this Treaty may be carried out without the effusion of human blood; but we are compelled to say since the return of Ross we consider the issue much more doubtful than before. The military force in this country has not had the slightest effect in maintaining the quiet and good order of the Indians. . . . Indeed, we fear that the ignorant Indians construe the kind protection extended to them by the civil and military officers of the Government—shielding their rights, property and persons—as indications of a want of power to carry out the late Treaty without the consent of Ross. Ross is at the foundation of all this mischief, and we apprehend his ambition may lead him to destroy his people, rather than let it be said that he had yielded in the least to the most powerful government on earth.

Jackson had come to the end of his second term March 3rd. In the new Democratic President, the New Yorker, Martin Van Buren, the south had not the same confidence. He was reported perilously close to having an open mind on the question of the treaty's legitimacy. Lumpkin undertook to offer him possibly needed counsel in his letter of June 19, 1837:

After much reflection, we have considered it our duty to address you directly, on the subject of our present relations with the Cherokee Indians. You may consider the communication either private or official, as your judgment may determine best. It is made from a sense of duty to the country, and from a desire to render you every aid in our power which may in any degree promote the success of your administration . . . the military stationed here to secure the peace of the country have been worse than useless. The Commissioners and other authority have been disregarded, if not contemned. . . . Nothing was done by the military which we advised to be done. In the meantime, Ross, who is the soul and spirit of all opposition to the Treaty, repaired to Washington, and, although faithfully informed by the Government that the Treaty would be scrupulously and faithfully executed, he seems nevertheless to have gained strength and confidence amongst his adherents, from the respectful and kind treatment which he received at Washington and elsewhere. He has returned home with increased weight of character. . . . He, Ross, feels secure in the courtesy and respect which he receives from every officer of your administration, and the kind feelings entertained for him, in a special manner, by the Army agents. Sir, under this state of things, the Cherokees will not emigrate under this Treaty, except by force of arms, and when that is applied the result may be war. . . . In conclusion, we assure you that this man Ross is sporting with the lives of thousands of human beings. Has not the Government power to prevent such a catastrophe? We think it has.[7]

Lumpkin was a sufficient spokesman for Georgia's point of view but Alabama, within the northeastern border of which a portion of the Cherokee resided, was equally dissatisfied by Wool's conception of his peace-keeping duty. The Alabama legislature resolved June 30, 1837, "That the stationing of an armed force in any portion of our State . . . is . . . a wanton interference with the powers and authorities of our courts." The governor was directed to lodge a demand with the Secretary of War that all forces under federal command be withdrawn from Alabama.

Wool had meanwhile tired of the unrewarding struggle and had requested that he be relieved. He was succeeded July 1, 1837 by Colonel William Lindsay who was instructed to place Ross under arrest if he continued his public agitation against Cherokee conformance with the treaty. As a consequence of the Georgia and Alabama accusations Wool demanded a court-martial so that he might have an opportunity to clear himself of charges which were based specifically on instances in which he had interfered with the mistreatment of Indians by whites. The court assembled at Knoxville, Tennessee, under the presidency of Major General Scott who had so recently survived the ordeal of a similar inquiry. As further evidence of the spirit of independence permeating the commissioned ranks of the army, Wool was not only acquitted but commended by the September 4, 1837 verdict.[8]

Ross was well aware of the extent to which American vexation with the inglorious Seminole War had hardened the American attitude toward all Indians. He was, moreover, himself dedicated to nonviolence as the only policy affording Indians any hope what-

[7] For text of this July 8, 1836–September 12, 1837 correspondence see Lumpkin, *Removal of the Cherokee Indians from Georgia*, Vol. II, pp. 36–178.

[8] For text of proceedings see *American State Papers*, Military Affairs, Vol. VII, p. 582.

ever of gaining consideration. He was therefore receptive to a government appeal that he offer to mediate, in the name of the Cherokee, between the Seminole and the United States with a view to bringing the Florida war to an end. He wrote an earnest letter to the Seminole reminding them that in his considered opinion their one sensible course was to submit to such terms as might be secured by reasonable negotiation with a power against which they could never expect to prevail. The government which had been refusing to recognize Ross as still the principal chief of the Cherokee nation was now happy to accept him as spokesman for the Cherokee in order to gain the advantage of his intercession with the Seminole. It was the same government which was urging other more distant Indian leaders to intercede with the Seminole while at the same time recruiting hundreds of Indian warriors from the same remote nations to assist in the conquest of the Seminole. Ross, convinced that he was engaging in a worthy cause, appointed a delegation of distinguished Cherokee to deliver his peace message to the beleaguered rebels.[9]

The Cherokee delegation's arrival in Florida was greeted by the disconcerting news that Osceola, the young Indian hero of the rebellion, had been captured under circumstances most unlikely to promote Seminole faith in negotiation. At the conclusion of the spring campaign season another uneasy armistice had been agreed upon by the opposing forces. Osceola had approached the American lines October 18, 1837 under a flag of truce to discuss certain terms of this armistice upon which dispute had developed. By order of Major General Jesup, commander of the American forces in Florida, Osceola and his fellow envoys were suddenly encircled by a cordon of American troops, seized, disarmed and hustled off to the military prison in St. Augustine to join other Seminole prisoners, most of whom had been taken by similar tactics. The earlier instances had attracted little general attention but the romantic fame of Osceola excited countrywide criticism of the deceit producing his capture. Jesup's defense of the stratagem was based on the argument that since the Seminole frequently broke their engagements there appeared to him no reason Americans

9 One of the delegates, Jesse Bushyhead, owed his family name to the shock of red hair of the progenitor of his line, the famous British administrator, John Stuart, who had married a three-quarter white Cherokee girl, Susannah Emory, during the French and Indian War at Fort Loudon, the first English military post to be founded west of the Appalachians.

should feel obliged to feel bound by theirs, and on the more cogent consideration that by such seizures, though admittedly breaches of faith, many lives, Indian as well as white, might be saved. To put his case more bluntly, he had been convinced by long and bitter experience that the Seminole were to be subdued by no other means. Osceola was ill when captured; his condition, as was usually the case with Indians when confined, grew worse in prison and after transfer to captivity in Fort Moultrie he died January 30, 1838. During his last days his portrait was painted by the eminent specialist in Indian picturization, George Catlin.

The Cherokee delegates, mindful of the instructions they had received from Ross, continued to conceive it their duty to persist in their peace-seeking effort. Their decision was supported by many obvious considerations. The American army in Florida preparing for the winter campaign numbered by December 1, 1837 4,437 regulars, 4,028 volunteers, 100 seamen and 178 Indian auxiliaries. The still unapprehended Seminole were estimated to total not more than 2,500 men, women and children. There seemed no possible chance that the Seminole could win the war even in the sense that they might indefinitely evade capture. They could only prolong the unequal struggle. It was therefore with a good conscience that the Cherokee delegates entered the central swamp country to seek and reason with their belligerent cousins. It was a hazardous mission inasmuch as there was every likelihood that the intransigent Seminole might regard them as American agents. After protracted discussion they were able to bring in a group of 12 Seminole chiefs and 20 attendant warriors to a conference at Fort Mellon with Jesup to discuss terms which might lead to an end of hostilities. Jesup smoked a peace pipe with the ambassadors, then had them seized and placed in the St. Augustine prison to be held as hostages for the submission of their families and followers.

The deeply mortified Cherokee delegates were finally discouraged. They abandoned their mediation attempt and returned home. When Ross learned of the advantage that had been taken of his intercession, he wrote an outraged remonstrance to the Secretary of War which closed with:

I do hereby most solemnly protest against this unprecedented violation of that sacred rule which has ever been recognized by every nation, civilized and uncivilized, of treating with all due respect those who had ever presented themselves under a flag of truce before their enemy, for the purpose of proposing the termination of a warfare.[10]

Ross's eleventh hour attempts to rally political support in Washington for a revocation of the removal treaty were encountering frustrations as distressing as had his effort to assist in the pacification of the Seminole. The train of new disappointments had begun with the results of the 1836 presidential election. The opposition political forces gathering to forestall the succession of another Democratic administration adopted a new party name, Whig, signifying anti-royalist, which by their interpretation of the term meant an intention to overthrow the autocratic power of Jackson. They were still insufficiently organized to agree upon a single candidate, however, and resorted to the expedient of nominating three regional candidates, Daniel Webster in New England, William Henry Harrison in the northwest and Hugh White in the south, hoping to deny Van Buren a majority and thus throw the election into the House. Ross naturally yearned for a Whig victory which might bring into office men more favorably disposed to the Cherokee. But for months before the election the margin either party might hope to gain appeared so narrow that the Whigs hesitated to take a stand that might offend any region, as the south would be by any harping on the removal issue, and therefore the Democratic administration's Indian policy this time played little or no part in the campaign. Georgia, for example, could feel so certain that the Indian issue had already been finally determined that the state could feel safe in voting Whig as an expression of its resentment of the selection of a northerner as the Democratic candidate. Van Buren won with a popular vote of 762,000 to 736,000, a majority of 26,000, but with an electoral vote margin of 170 to 124.

When Ross returned to Washington in January of 1838 to make one last appeal to the new 25th Congress he was therefore still confronted by a Democratic administration and obliged to deal with a Congress which was conscious that it had received no popular mandate to heed his solicitations. Van Buren at first declined to recognize him as a spokesman for the Cherokee but presently was reported to be wavering. The critical moment came when Ross's

10 Foreman, *Indian Removal*, p. 355.

petition signed by 15,665 Cherokee repudiating the treaty was presented to the Senate. Frelinghuysen was no longer a member and his post as Cherokee advocate was taken by his New Jersey successor, Samuel Southard. Southard's introduction of the memorial provoked an emotional debate but most senators were wearily reluctant to reopen the invidious controversy. The petition was laid on the table by the overwhelming vote of 37 to 10. The next day Commissioner of Indian Affairs Harris served formal notification upon Ross that:

These proceedings leave no room to doubt that the legislative branch of the govmt. concurs with the executive and will sanction him in the purpose to carry the Treaty into full effect. You will perceive the importance of giving general circulation of these proceedings in forcible language, the unavoidable conclusion that a ready and cheerful acquiescence on their part can alone save them from serious calamities.[11]

The cold finality of the Senate's action stirred a revival of moral excitement among liberal, intellectual and religious circles in the north. Congress was showered with memorials from communities, mass meetings, churches and organizations. But, as Webster decleared in his letter to Ketcham, this renewed manifestation of public opinion had come too late. Moreover, overshadowing this last-minute reawakening of concern for the rights of the Cherokee was the far greater public concern for the daily welfare of every citizen. The year before the terrifying Panic of 1837 had descended upon the country like a modern plague. Prices had plunged. Banks had closed by the hundreds. Bankruptcies had multiplied beyond counting. Congress had been called into special session to cope with the most devastating commercial depression the country had ever experienced.

In the face of this nearer apprehension which was so distracting to the public's attention northern liberals nevertheless persisted in their outcries against what they considered the criminal injustice being inflicted upon the distant Cherokee. This judgment pronounced by many was given representative and impassioned voice by Ralph Waldo Emerson who, for once descending from his

[11] Woodward, *The Cherokees*, p. 200.

loftier habitat into the political arena, addressed an April 23, 1838 open letter to President Van Buren which was widely published:

. . . Sir, my communication respects the sinister rumors that fill this part of the country concerning the Cherokee people. . . . In common with the great body of the American people, we have witnessed with sympathy the painful labors of these red men to redeem their own race from the doom of eternal inferiority, and to borrow and domesticate in the tribe the arts and customs of the Caucasian race. And notwithstanding the unaccountable apathy with which of late years the Indians have been sometimes abandoned to their enemies, it is not to be doubted that it is the good pleasure and the understanding of all humane persons in the Republic, of the men and matrons sitting in the thriving independent families all over the land, that they shall be duly cared for; that they shall taste justice and love from all to whom we have delegated the office of dealing with them. The newspapers now inform us that, in December, 1835, a treaty contracting for the exchange of all the Cherokee territory was pretended to be made by an agent on the part of the United States with some persons appearing on the part of the Cherokees; that the fact afterwards transpired that these deputies did by no means represent the will of the nation; and that . . . the American President and the Cabinet, the Senate and the House of Representatives . . . are contracting to put this active nation into carts and boats, and to drag them over mountains and rivers to a wilderness at a vast distance beyond the Mississippi . . .

In the name of God, sir, we ask you if this be so. . . . Men and women with pale and perplexed faces meet one another in the streets and churches here, and ask if this be so. . . . The piety, the principle that is left in the United States . . . forbid us to entertain it as a fact. Such a dereliction of all faith and virtue, such a denial of justice, and such deafness to screams for mercy were never heard of in times of peace and in the dealing of a nation with its own allies and wards, since the earth was made. Sir, does this government think that the people of the United States are become savage and mad? From their mind are the sentiments of love and a good nature wiped clean out? The soul of man, the justice, the mercy that is the heart's heart in all men, from Maine to Georgia, does abhor this business . . . a crime is projected that confounds our understandings by its magnitude, a crime that really deprives us as well as the Cherokees of a country for how could we call the conspiracy that should crush these poor Indians our government, or the land that was cursed by their parting and dying imprecations our country, any more? You, sir, will bring down that renowned chair in which you sit into infamy if your seal is set to this instrument of perfidy; and the name of this nation, hitherto the sweet omen of religion and liberty, will stink to the world.

You will not do us the injustice of connecting this remonstrance with any sectional and party feeling. It is in our hearts the simplest commandment of brotherly love. We will not have this great and solemn claim upon national and human justice huddled aside under the flimsy plea of its being a party act. Sir, to us the questions upon which the government and the people have been agitated during the past year, touching the prostration of the currency and of trade, seem but motes by comparison. These hard times, it is true, have brought the discussion home to every farmhouse and poor man's house in this town; but it is the chirping of grasshoppers beside the immortal question whether justice shall be done by the race of civilized to the race of savage man, whether all the attributes of reason, of civility, of justice, and even of mercy, shall be put off by the American people . . .

With impressive eloquence Emerson had given expression to the views of very many Americans, including not a few in the south. He went on, however, to a yet more striking admonition. He closed with the somber and prophetic warning that an issue more fateful than that of Indian removal had been raised:

One circumstance lessens the reluctance with which I intrude at this time on your attention my conviction that the government ought to be admonished of a new historical fact, which the discussion of this question has disclosed, namely that there exists in a great part of the Northern people a gloomy diffidence in the *moral* character of the government. On the broaching of this question, a general expression of despondency, of disbelief that any good will accrue from a remonstrance on an act of fraud and robbery, appeared in those men to whom we naturally turn for aid and counsel. Will the American government steal? Will it lie? Will it kill?—We ask triumphantly. Our counsellors and old statesmen here say that ten years ago they would have staked their lives on the affirmation that the proposed Indian measures could not be executed; that the unanimous country would put them down. And now the steps of this crime follow each other so fast, at such fatally quick time, that the millions of virtuous citizens, whose agents the government are, have no place to interpose, and must shut their eyes until the last howl and wailing of these tormented villagers and tribes shall afflict the ear of the world.

I will not hide from you, as an indication of the alarming distrust, that a letter addressed as mine is, and suggesting to the mind of the Executive the plain obligations of man, has a burlesque character in the apprehensions of some of my friends. I, sir, will not beforehand treat you with the contumely of this distrust. I will at least state to you this fact, and show you how plain and humane people, whose love would be honor, regard the policy of the government, and what injurious inferences they draw as to the minds of the governors. A man with your experience in affairs must have seen cause to appreciate the futility of opposition to the moral sentiment. However feeble the sufferer and however great the oppressor, it is in the nature of things that the blow should recoil upon the aggressor.[12]

This formidable letter with its prescient identification of the moral gulf beginning to widen within the nation no doubt added something to Van Buren's already numerous occasions for disquiet. But his necessarily more immediate and practical concern was with the distressing effects of the great panic, even though he had decided as a matter of administration policy that the country's recovery could best be served were the government to refrain from any attempt to interfere with those effects. Whatever doubts he may still have entertained, on the other hand, about his administration's inherited Indian policy were dispelled by the warnings pressed upon him by the governor of Georgia and by Georgia's congressional delegation that any hesitation to execute the Cherokee treaty would inevitably precipitate a war. Van Buren, for his part, most certainly did not want another war along with the panic. On April 10, 1838 he had ordered Major General Scott to proceed to the Cherokee country and there to employ whatever military force was required to compel immediate Cherokee removal.

[12] Emerson, *Works,* Cambridge 1883–87 ed., Vol. IV, p. 697.

18

History records the sufferings of innumerable peoples whose country was overrun and possessed by alien invaders. There have been relatively fewer recorded occasions, as in the instance of the Babylonian Captivity of the Jews, of an entire people being compelled to abandon their country. This has been universally regarded as the ultimate catastrophe that can befall a people inasmuch as it deprives them of the roots which sustain their identity. Upon the exiles has been pronounced a sentence that by its nature denies all hope of reprieve or relief. To Indians, with their inherited conception of the land of their birth as the repository of those spiritual links to their ancestors which were holy and therefore indissoluble, the prospect of expulsion was clothed with added dreads beyond human evaluation.

The threat was in all its aspects so monstrous that in the spring of 1838 the bewildered masses of the Cherokee people, homeless, hungry, destitute, still remained incredulous that so fearful a fate could actually impend. Outrageously as they had been harassed for the past ten years by Georgia and Alabama white men, they still clung to their trust that most white men wished them well. This was a confidence instilled in them by the reports of John Ross who had been made more conversant with the apparent truth by his wide travels across the immense white nation stretching beyond the Cherokee horizon. They had been further prepared to accept his judgment on the inherent goodness of the white race by their own experience with the many white men who had lived among them as teachers, missionaries and counselors, sharing their struggles and tribulations. Their more recent experience with Wool and his officers and with Dunlap and his Tennesseans had strengthened their impression that the white race could not be wholly committed to their destruction.

Ross was still in Washington engaged in a final frantic effort, with some dawning hope of success, to wring from the administration a temporary postponement of removal. His followers were continuing to obey his injunction that they persist in their non-violent resistance. Most continued to refuse even to give their names or a list of their belongings to the agents commissioned to organize the details of the migration. May 23, two years from the date of the President's proclamation of the Senate's ratification of the treaty, was the day, as all had for months been warned, when their residence in the east would become illegal but they still could not believe that a development so frightful could be given reality by that day's sunrise. Even after five regiments of regulars and 4,000 militia and volunteers from adjacent states began pouring into their country they still could not believe.

Major General Scott arrived May 8 to take command of the military operation. His May 10, 1838 address to the Cherokee people proclaimed the terrible reality in terms no Cherokee could longer mistake:

Cherokees—The President of the United States has sent me with a powerful army, to cause you, in obedience to the treaty of 1835, to join that part of your people who are already established in prosperity on the other side of the Mississippi. Unhappily, the two years which were allowed for the purpose, you have suffered to pass away without following, and without making any preparations to follow, and now, or by the time this solemn *address* shall reach your distant settlements, the emigration must be commenced in haste, but, I hope, without disorder. I have no power, by granting a farther delay, to correct the error that you have committed. The full moon of May is already on the wane, and before another shall have passed away, every Cherokee man, woman, and child . . . must be in motion to join their brethren in the far West. . . . My troops already occupy many positions in the country that you are to abandon, and thousands and thousands are approaching from every quarter, to tender resistance and escape alike hopeless . . . Chiefs, head men, and warriors—Will you then, by resistance, compel us to resort to arms? God forbid. Or will you, by flight, seek to hide yourselves in mountains and forests, and thus oblige us to hunt you down? Remember that, in pursuit, it may be impossible to avoid conflicts. The blood of the white man, or the blood of the red man, may be spilt, and if spilt, however accidentally, it may be impossible for the discreet and humane among you, or among us, to prevent a general war and carnage. Think of this, my Cherokee brethren. I am an old warrior, and have been present at many a scene of slaughter; but spare me, I beseech you, the horror of witnessing the destruction of the Cherokees.[1]

Scott sincerely hoped that the enforced removal could be accomplished not only without bloodshed but without undue hardship inflicted upon the unfortunate thousands being ejected at bayonet's point from their homes. He had been impressed by Ross during conferences with him in Washington and like most professional soldiers of his time had developed a genuine regard for Indians. In his May 17 general orders to his troops he sternly admonished them to practice restraint:

Considering the number and temper of the mass to be removed together with the extent and fastnesses of the country occupied, it will readily occur that simple indiscretions, acts of harshness, and cruelty on the part of our troops, may lead, step by step, to delays, to impatience, and exasperation, and, in the end, to a general war and carnage; a result, in the case of these particular Indians, utterly abhorrent to the generous sympathies of the whole American people. Every possible kindness, compatible with the necessity of removal, must, therefore, be shown by the troops; and if, in the ranks, a despicable individual should be found capable of inflicting a wanton injury or insult on any Cherokee man, woman, or child, it is hereby made the special duty of the nearest good officer or man instantly to interpose, and to seize and consign the guilty wretch to the severest penalty of the laws. The major-general is fully persuaded that this injunction will not be neglected by the brave men under his command, who cannot be otherwise than jealous of their honor and that of their country.[2]

Scott's intentions were humane but the larger portion of his army were state levies unaccustomed to discipline and without his professional susceptibilities. The nature of the operation required the army's dispersion in scattered detachments over a wide area.

[1] Mansfield, *Life of General Scott,* p. 306.
[2] *Ibid,* p. 304.

Most of the Cherokee to be removed were inhabitants of Georgia and their apprehension was conducted by Georgia militia who had long as a matter of policy been habituated to dealing harshly with Indians. Prison stockades had been erected at assembly and embarkation points in which the Cherokee were to be herded and confined while awaiting transportation west. There was little or no likelihood of attempted resistance. Most had been disarmed during Wool's regime and the irresistible military power that had been brought to bear was self-evident. The classic account of what next transpired is that recorded by James Mooney. His contribution to the Bureau of American Ethnology, eventually published in the 19th Annual Report in 1900 under the title *Myths of the Cherokee,* included a history of the Cherokee based upon years of field work. His narrative of the 1838 expulsion was drawn from personal interviews with survivors, white officers as well as Cherokee victims, and had therefore much of the vitality of an eyewitness report:

The history of this Cherokee removal of 1838, as gleaned by the author from the lips of actors in the tragedy, may well exceed in weight of grief and pathos any other passage in American history. Even the much-sung exile of the Acadians falls far behind it in its sum of death and misery. Under Scott's orders the troops were disposed at various points throughout the Cherokee country, where stockade forts were erected for gathering in and holding the Indians preparatory to removal. From these, squads of troops were sent to search out with rifle and bayonet every small cabin hidden away in the coves or by the sides of mountain streams, to seize and bring in as prisoners all the occupants, however or wherever they might be found. Families at dinner were startled by the sudden gleam of bayonets in the doorway and rose up to be driven with blows and oaths along the weary miles of trail that led to the stockade. Men were seized in their fields or going along the road, women were taken from their wheels and children from their play. In many cases, on turning for one last look as they crossed the ridge, they saw their homes in flames, fired by the lawless rabble that followed on the heels of the soldiers to loot and pillage. So keen were these outlaws on the scent that in some instances they were driving off the cattle and other stock of the Indians almost before the soldiers had fairly started their owners in the other direction. Systematic hunts were made by the same men for Indian graves, to rob them of the silver pendants and other valuables deposited with the dead. A Georgia volunteer, afterward a colonel in the Confederate service, said: "I fought through the civil war and have seen men shot to pieces and slaughtered by thousands, but the Cherokee removal was the cruelest work I ever knew." To prevent escape the soldiers had been ordered to approach and surround each house, so far as possible, so as to come upon the occupants without warning. One old patriarch, when thus surprised, calmly called his children and grandchildren around him, and, kneeling down, bid them pray with him in their own language, while the astonished onlookers looked on in silence. Then rising he led the way into exile. A woman, on finding the house surrounded, went to the door and called up the chickens to be fed for the last time, after which, taking her infant on her back and her two other children by the hand, she followed her husband with the soldiers.[3]

Within days nearly 17,000 Cherokee had been crowded into the stockades. Sanitation measures were inadequate in those makeshift concentration camps. Indian families, accustomed to a more spacious and isolated existence, were unable to adapt to the necessities of this mass imprisonment. Hundreds of the inmates sickened. The Indian was by his nature peculiarly susceptible to the depressions produced by confinement. Many lost any will to live and, perceiving no glimmer of hope, resigned themselves to death. Those who had become converts found some comfort in the ministrations of their white and native pastors. In every stockade hymn singings and prayer meetings were almost continuous.

All physical preparations had been carefully planned in advance by the federal authorities in charge of the migration so that little time might be lost in getting the movement under way. In the first and second weeks of June two detachments of some 800 exiles were driven aboard the waiting fleets of steamboats, keelboats and flatboats for the descent of the Tennessee. They passed down the storied waterway by the same route taken by the first white settlers of middle Tennessee under John Donelson in 1780. In the shadow of Lookout Mountain they could survey the wilderness vastnesses from which for 20 years bands of their immediate forebears had sallied to devastate the white frontier, some of them commanded by war chiefs who had lived to be condemned to this exile. Then, at Muscle Shoals there came an ironic contrast between the past and the future as Indians being driven from their ancient homeland were committed to transportation by the white man's newest invention. They disembarked from their boats to clamber, mo-

[3] Mooney, *Myths of the Cherokee,* p. 130.

mentarily diverted, aboard the cars drawn by the two puffing little locomotives of the railroad recently constructed to move freight and passengers around the rapids. Returning to other boats, they resumed their seemingly interminable journey in the debilitating heat of an increasingly oppressive summer. The attendant army officers, however sympathetic, were helpless against the waves of illnesses. Scott, moving new contingents toward embarkation, was appalled by the reports he received of the mounting death rate among those who had already been dispatched.

The troops assembled for Cherokee expulsion had been by considered governmental design so numerous as to present a show of military power so overwhelming as to provide no faintest invitation to Indian resistance. By the army's first pounce more than nine tenths of the population had been rounded up and driven into the stockades. There remained only a handful of the wilder and more primitive residents of the higher mountains still at large. This handful, however, represented a problem causing Scott serious concern. Were they provoked to resist they might among their remote and cloud-wreathed peaks prove as difficult to apprehend as were the Seminole in their swamps. From this tactical threat sprang the one heroic action to gleam across the otherwise unrelieved despondency of the removal scene.

Tsali was an hitherto undistinguished mountain Cherokee who suddenly soared to an eminence in Cherokee annals comparable to the homage accorded an Attakullaculla, an Old Tassel, a Sequoyah or a John Ross. The stories of his inspired exploit, drawn from eyewitnesses, survivors and references in contemporary official records, vary in detail and have become encrusted by legend but coincide in most essentials. According to the more generally accepted version, a young Cherokee woman upon being assaulted by two soldiers killed both with a hatchet. Tsali hid the weapon under his shirt and assumed responsibility for his kinswoman's act. Scott could not permit the death of his soldiers to remain unpunished and served notice on the band of mountain Cherokee of which Tsali was a member that a scapegoat must be produced. The band felt that it had a reasonable chance to elude pursuit indefinitely but its councils were impressed by the advice of a white trader, William Thomas, a friend of his native customers in the notable tradition of Ludovic Grant, Alexander Cameron and

John McDonald. Thomas pointed out the advantage that could be taken of Scott's demand. Tsali was prepared to offer his life for his people. His fellow tribesmen thereupon notified Scott that he would be turned over to American justice in return for American permission to remain unmolested in their mountains. Scott, eager to escape the uncertainties of a guerrilla campaign in so difficult a terrain, agreed to recommend this course to Washington. Tsali was brought in, the voluntary prisoner of his compatriots. His Cherokee custodians were required to serve as the firing squad by which he, his brother and his eldest son were executed. The story became one of the few Indian stories with a happy ending. Thomas continued for years to interest himself in the prolonged negotiations with the governments of the United States and North Carolina which eventually resulted in federal and state recognition of Cherokee title to their mountain holdings. Tsali's sacrifice had permitted this fraction of the nation to become the remnant of the East Cherokee to cling to their homeland where they still are colorful inhabitants of the North Carolina mountains.

Aside from the Tsali episode the roundup of the Cherokee proceeded without interruption. By June 18 General Charles Floyd, commanding the Georgia militia engaged in it, was able to report to his governor that no Cherokee remained on the soil of Georgia except as a prisoner in a stockade. Scott was able to discharge his volunteers June 17 and two days later to dispatch three of his five regular regiments to sectors where military needs were more pressing, two to the Canadian border and one to Florida.

Meanwhile so many migrants were dying in the drought and heat to which the initial removal was subjected that Scott was constrained to lighten the inexorable pressures. The Cherokee Council, which though technically illegal still spoke for the Cherokee people, begged for a postponement to the more healthful weather of autumn. Scott agreed. In July Ross returned and in conferences with Scott worked out a further agreement under which the Cherokee would cease passive resistance and under his supervision undertake a voluntary migration as soon as weather permitted. Scott was glad to be relieved of further need to use military force. The administration was glad to be offered some defense against the storm of northern criticism. Even Georgia made no serious protest, inasmuch as the Cherokee had already been removed from their land to stockades and there remained no questioning of the state's sovereignty. The one remonstrance, aside from the complaints of contractors, was voiced by the aging Jackson from his retirement at The Hermitage in a letter of August 23, 1838 to Felix Grundy, Attorney General of the United States:

. . . The contract with Ross must be arrested, or you may rely upon it, the expense and other evils will shake the popularity of the administration to its center. What madness and folly to have anything to do with Ross, when the agent was proceeding well with the removal. . . . The time and circumstances under which Gen'l Scott made this contract shows that he is no economist, or is, *sub rosa,* in league with Clay & Co. to bring disgrace on the administration. The evil is done. It behooves Mr. Van Buren to act with energy to throw it off his shoulders. I enclose a letter to you under cover, unsealed, which you may read, seal, and deliver to him, that you may aid him with your views in getting out of this real difficulty.

> Your friend in haste,
> Andrew Jackson

P.S. I am so feeble I can scarcely wield my pen, but friendship dictates it & the subject excites me. Why is it that the scamp Ross is not banished from the notice of the administration?[4]

Ross, having at last recognized the inevitable, gave to his preparations for the voluntary removal the same driving energy and attention to detail he had until then devoted to resisting removal. All phases of the organization of the national effort were gathered into his hands. All financial arrangements were under his supervision, including the disbursement of the basic federal subsistence allowance of 16 cents a day for each person and 40 cents a day for each horse. For convenience in management en route the 13,000 Cherokee remaining in the stockades were divided into detachments of roughly a thousand to head each of which he appointed a Cherokee commander. At a final meeting of the Cherokee Council it was provided that the constitution and laws of the Nation should be considered equally valid in the west.[5]

The first detachment set out October 1, 1838 on the dreaded journey over the route which in Cherokee memory became known

4 Brown, *Old Frontiers*, p. 512.

5 See p. 17 for excerpt from the Council's last memorial. Many difficulties and much tragic dissension intervened before the Cherokee constitution became operative in the west. Jealousy between the resident West Cherokee, calling themselves the Old

as The Trail of Tears. The last started November 4. The improvement in weather awaited during the tedious summer months in the stockades did not materialize. The spring migration had been cursed by oppressive heat and drought. The fall migration encountered deluges of rain followed by excessive cold. To the hundreds of deaths from heat-induced diseases were now added new hundreds of deaths from prolonged exposure.

The most vivid general account of the 1838 migration is again that of James Mooney, assembled from the recollections of participants:

. . . in October, 1838, the long procession of exiles was set in motion. A very few went by the river route; the rest, nearly all of the 13,000, went overland. Crossing to the north side of the Hiwassee at a ferry above Gunstocker creek, they proceeded down along the river, the sick, the old people, and the smaller children, with the blankets, cooking pots, and other belongings in wagons, the rest on foot or on horses. The number of wagons was 645. It was like the march of an army, regiment after regiment, the wagons in the center, the officers along the line and the horsemen on the flanks and at the rear. Tennessee river was crossed at Tuckers (?) ferry, a short distance above Jollys island, at the mouth of the Hiwassee. Thence the route lay south of Pikeville, through McMinnville and on to Nashville, where the Cumberland was crossed. Then they went on to Hopkinsville, Kentucky, where the noted chief White-path, in charge of a detachment, sickened and died. His people buried him by the roadside, with a box over the grave and poles with streamers around it, that the others coming on behind might note the spot and remember him. Somewhere also along that march of death—for the exiles died by tens and twenties every day of the journey—the devoted wife of John Ross sank down, leaving him to go on with the bitter pain of bereavement added to heartbreak at the ruin of his nation. The Ohio was crossed at a ferry near the mouth of the Cumberland, and the army passed on through southern Illinois until the great Mississippi was reached opposite Cape Girar-

---

Settlers, and the newly arrived East Cherokee long prevented the establishment of a single national government. Major Ridge, John Ridge and Elias Boudinot, the leading signers of the Schermerhorn treaty, were assassinated June 22, 1839 by embittered fellow countrymen as a punishment for their unauthorized sale of Cherokee land. There appeared no direct evidence that Ross was involved in the executions but the federal government withheld all remaining payments due under the removal treaty and declined to recognize Ross's authority to speak for the nation. It was not until August 6, 1846 that a new treaty of unity provided for the payment to the Cherokee of the withheld federal obligations and permitted the reinstitution of self-government under Ross's principal chieftainship.

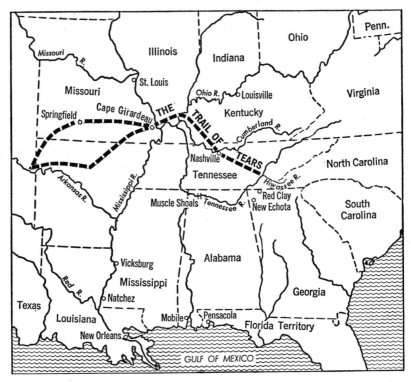

The overland route followed by the Cherokee in their fall migration of 1838, representing a reenactment of the shorter distances covered by the earlier migrations of the Choctaw and Creek in 1832 and 1836, became known as The Trail of Tears. The waterborne spring migration of 1838 descended the Tennessee, the Ohio and the Mississippi to the mouth of the Arkansas and then ascended that river or its valley to the western plains.

deau, Missouri. It was now the middle of winter, with the river running full of ice, so that several detachments were obliged to wait some time on the eastern bank for the channel to become clear. In talking with old men and women at Tahlequah the author found that the lapse of over half a century had not sufficed to wipe out the memory of the miseries of that halt beside the frozen river, with hundreds of sick and dying penned up in wagons or stretched upon the ground, with only a blanket overhead to keep out the January blast. The crossing was made at last in two divisions, at Cape Girardeau and at Green's Ferry, a short distance below, whence the march was made on through Missouri to Indian Territory, the later detachments making a northerly circuit by Springfield, because those who had gone before had killed off all the game along the direct route. At last their destination was reached. They had started in October, 1838, and it was now March, 1839, the journey having occupied barely six months of the hardest part of the year.[6]

President Van Buren in his December 1838 message to Congress announced the administration's view of the event:

. . . It affords me sincere pleasure to apprise the Congress of the entire removal of the Cherokee Nation of Indians to their new homes west of the Mississippi. The measures authorized by Congress at its last session have had the happiest effects. By an agreement concluded with them by the commanding general in that country, their removal has been principally under the conduct of their own chiefs, and they have emigrated without any apparent reluctance.[7]

A traveler who had encountered the Indians en route was moved by the President's words to write his own eyewitness report which was published in the January 26, 1839 *New York Observer* under the heading, "A Native of Maine, traveling in the Western Country":

. . . On Tuesday evening we fell in with a detachment of the poor Cherokee Indians . . . about eleven hundred Indians—sixty wagons —six hundred horses, and perhaps forty pairs of oxen. We found them in the forest camped for the night by the road side . . . under a severe fall of rain accompanied by heavy wind. With their canvas for a shield from the inclemency of the weather, and the cold wet ground for a resting place, after the fatigue of the day, they spent the night . . . many of the aged Indians were suffering extremely from the fatigue of the journey, and the ill health consequent upon it . . . several were then quite ill, and one aged man we were informed was then in the last struggles of death. . . . The last detachment which we passed on the 7th embraced rising two thousand Indians with horses and mules in proportion. The forward part of the train we found just pitching their tents for the night, and notwithstanding some thirty or forty wagons were already stationed, we found the road literally filled with the procession for about three miles in length. The sick and feeble were carried in wagons—about as comfortable for traveling as a New England ox cart with a covering over it—a great many ride on horse-

---

[6] Mooney, *Myths of the Cherokee*, p. 132.
[7] Richardson, *Messages and Papers of the Presidents*, III, p. 497.

back and multitudes go on foot—even aged females, apparently nearly ready to drop into the grave, were traveling with heavy burdens attached to the back—on the sometimes frozen ground, and sometimes muddy streets, with no covering for the feet except what nature had given them. . . . We learned from the inhabitants on the road where the Indians passed, that they buried fourteen or fifteen at every stopping place, and they make a journey of ten miles per day only on an average. One fact which to my own mind seemed a lesson indeed to the American nation is, that they will not travel on the Sabbath. . . . The Indians as a whole carry on their countenances every thing but the appearance of happiness. Some carry a downcast dejected look bordering upon the appearance of despair; others a wild frantic appearance as if about to burst the chains of nature and pounce like a tiger upon their enemies. . . . When I past the last detachment of those suffering exiles and thought that my native countrymen had thus expelled them from their native soil and their muchloved homes, and that too in this inclement season of the year in all their suffering, I turned from the sight with feelings which language cannot express. . . . I felt that I would not encounter the secret silent prayer of one of these sufferers armed with the energy that faith and hope would give it (if there be a God who avenges the wrongs of the injured) for all the lands of Georgia. . . . When I read in the President's Message that he was happy to inform the Senate that the Cherokees were peaceably and without reluctance removed—and remember that it was on the third day of December when not one of the detachments had reached their destination; and that a large majority had not made even half their journey when he made that declaration, I thought I wished the President could have been there that very day in Kentucky with myself, and have seen the comfort and the willingness with which the Cherokees were making their journey.[8]

The first migrants reached their destination on the plains beyond the western border of Arkansas January 4, 1839. Other contingents continued to straggle in until late in March. Examination of all available records by Grant Foreman, outstanding authority on Indian removal, led him to conclude 4,000 Cherokee had died either during confinement in the stockades or on their 800-mile journey west.

While the Cherokee were traversing their Trail of Tears their fellow southern Indians were committed to afflictions as dismal.

[8] Foreman, *Indian Removal*, p. 305.

The processes of removal were grinding out the cumulative calamities that had been visited upon a race by governmental fiat.

The Chickasaw had at length embarked upon their self-governed migration. They were the aristocrats of the Indian world, long noted for the prowess of their warriors, the beauty of their women and the speed of their horses. They had bargained shrewdly until they had wrung every possible advantage from federal authorities, including uninterrupted control over their affairs and a good price for their lands in western Tennessee and northwestern Mississippi. When finally they started west it was a movement under their own leadership undertaken at a time of their own choosing after repeated inspections of their new territory and the route to it by their own representatives. They traveled in comfort, well supplied with equipment, food and money. It might have been expected that were removal ever to be conducted under acceptable conditions it might prove so in their case. But it did not. Their relative prosperity became one of the major causes of their undoing. Sensing unusual profits, contractors gathered stockpiles of supplies along the way in such quantities that the food spoiled before it could be eaten. The travelers were charged exorbitantly for transportation and their every other requirement. They picked up smallpox en route and the disease reached epidemic proportions after their arrival. Most had arrived too late to get in an 1838 crop and they were soon as hungry as their poorer fellow colonists. The move west had made plaintive beggars of the once proud and warlike Chickasaw.

Nearly 2,000 Seminole, rounded up by various devices, pseudo-agreements and military pressures, were also on the way west in 1838. Having suffered so much more than other migrants before their start, they continued to suffer more en route. Many had scarcely emerged from their swampland refuges before they were crowded, naked and undernourished, aboard ship. Others had already endured long periods of imprisonment by which they had been weakened. Most were detained for weeks and months en route in noisome concentration camps in Tampa, Mobile and New Orleans. In addition to all their other privations and afflictions they were continually harassed at every stop and in every new state jurisdiction by the claims of slave dealers to the ownership of Seminole prisoners who showed evidence of Negro blood.

A considerable proportion of Seminole were Negroes who had for generations been considered members of the tribe and even though they were closely guarded prisoners each group of exiles fiercely resisted every attempt to single out any of their number for delivery into slavery. The problem of identification had been complicated by the flight to the Seminole of many actual slaves during the war. Some of the slave traders' claims were thus clothed with a species of legitimacy which made adjudication of every dispute more difficult. As one controversial example, among the Seminole prisoners of war taken by the Creek auxiliaries in 1837 had been 90 black Seminole whom they had sold to traders. In all these disputes federal and state authorities, except for the attendant army officers, in their anxiety to expedite the removal tended to support the traders' claims to an extent that provoked a congressional investigation. Meanwhile, in Florida the war went on, with American troops now under the command of Brigadier General Zachary Taylor, later President of the United States, continuing their attempts to run to earth the some 2,000 Seminole still in hiding.

The year 1838 also witnessed the initiation of a companion Indian removal in an adjoining country. Bowl's band of Cherokee, the first recorded migrants who had fled their homeland in 1794, had eventually settled on the Texas side of the Red River in what was then Mexican territory. Joined by other Cherokee and other Indians, the colony had increased to some 8,000. At the outbreak of the Texas revolution Sam Houston had negotiated a treaty of friendship with Bowl's Cherokee which saved the Americans in Texas from possible attack by Indians at the precarious moment they were being assaulted by Santa Anna in return for a Texan recognition of Cherokee title to the land on which they had settled. But in 1838 Mirabeau Lamar, upon succeeding Houston as President of Texas, immediately proclaimed his intention of expelling all Indians from the republic. In the ensuing 1839 campaign the aged Bowl was killed, still clutching the tin box containing the documents and deeds relating to the 1836 treaty of friendship with Texas. The Texas Cherokee were driven across the Red River to share the fortunes of the West and newly arrived East Cherokee on the upper Arkansas.

Indian removal had now been accomplished. Aside from a few scattered remnants, such as the Seminole fugitives in the Florida swamps, the few mountain Cherokee in North Carolina, the Choctaw residue in Mississippi and an occasional tiny enclave in the north, every Indian nation which had originally occupied the immense expanse of woodland extending across the eastern half of the United States had been compelled to seek new homes on the plains beyond that woodland's western margin. It had required a persisting effort over a period of 15 years, distinguished not only by the sufferings inflicted upon Indians but by the virulent disagreements excited among Americans, to give effect to the outwardly plausible policy announced by Monroe and Calhoun in 1825. Removal had been a contemporary success in the sense that the national government had proved able to impose its will and the states concerned had been rid of unwanted Indian inhabitants. But for the Indians and for the larger interests of the United States it had been a deplorable failure. The opportunity for Indians to become useful and valued members of American society, an achievement many had seemed on the verge of attaining in 1825, had been heedlessly postponed for more than a century.

Most informed Indians had long realized that such an assimilation represented the one lingering hope that Indians might ever regain comfort and security. The mass of Indians, less aware of the economic and political realities, had as long clung despairingly to the more appealing hope that they might yet contrive some escape from the white incubus. Removal dealt crushing blows to both hopes. In the west progressive Indians were compelled to begin again, under far greater handicaps, the painful climb toward citizenship and all Indians were subjected to white exactions more distracting than any they had known in the east. It was only after decades of miraculously patient struggle that Indians were finally to gain recognition of the principle that the rights of the conquered are even more precious than the prerogatives of their conquerors.

During the three centuries Indians had been retreating before the inexorable advance of alien invaders they had been bitterly conscious that they were suffering greater deprivations than the loss of their lands and lives. Their entire way of life, their whole world as they had known it, was in the course of obliteration. They understood, as could nobody else, by how wide a margin their post-invasion opportunities to pursue happiness failed to match the opportunities they had known before invasion. There was little enough comfort in the reflection that these opportunities were being denied them by a force physically too strong for them to resist.

In their despair Indians had sought consolation in resort to the supernatural. Native prophets, such as those who had inspired the followers of Pontiac and Tecumseh, had emerged again and again to preach the doctrine of original blessedness. They had exhorted Indians to eschew every compromise with white influence, especially by forswearing the use of white tools, weapons and alcohol, so that by a return to their ancient purity they might regain the strength to regain their former freedoms. These movements had been frustrated by their adherents' realization that obedience left Indians even more defenseless than before. By the time of the removal Indians were increasingly addicted to more extravagant religious phantasies. A favorite conceit, intermittently erupting for generation after generation until its final resurgence as the Ghost Dance excitement among the Plains Indians in the late 1880's, envisioned the evocation, by appropriate prayers, dances and rites, of the innumerable spirits of all Indian dead who would return to earth as a mighty host capable of expelling the white invaders and thus restoring the land of peace and plenty Indians had once enjoyed.

Even so superior an intellect as Sequoyah's was subject to wishful fancies. He had from his youth believed that the one Indian hope to retain their identity as a people was to withdraw from white contamination. He had himself moved west nearly 20 years before removal and all his life had sought by advice and example to persuade Indians to shun intercourse with whites. In his declining years he became obsessed with the possibility that the Lost Cherokee, reputed by tribal legend to have disappeared into the farthest west in the forgotten past, still lived in innocence, freedom and security in some distant land. In his frail old age, still in pursuit of this relic of the Indian golden age, he set out on a two-year journey in search of a remote Cherokee colony reported to have found sanctuary in the mountains of Mexico. His 1843 death in a Mexican desert, was giving ultimate poignancy to the discovery all Indians were being required to make. For them there was no way back. There was only the way ahead.

19

Removal posed a question of greater concern to humanity than that raised by the immediate sufferings of its victims. No graver charge can be leveled against any government than that it has been proven incapable of dispensing justice. That so serious an indictment could be preferred against the government of the United States clothed the accusation with an added import. Institution of the new American republic upon the principle of devotion to the rights of man had been an event that had encouraged the hopes of mankind everywhere. Its inspired founders had with the most astute forethought fortified democracy by providing balances of power designed to keep government more the servant than the master of the people. Special care had been given to means assuring that the will of the majority must prevail. Yet in the case of Indian removal the application of these carefully instituted processes of democracy had resulted in a flagrant injustice that by flouting their will had bewildered and dismayed the majority of Americans. The miscarriage was made the more startling by the paradoxical circumstance that it sprang not from weaknesses in the American system but from the three primary attributes which were its greatest elements of strength: the division of power between state and national governments, the acceptance of responsibility by political parties and the conception of the country as a haven for refugees from injustice elsewhere.

Of these three elements of strength by far the most dynamic was

the reciprocation of authority between state and national governments. At birth the United States had appeared destined to remain
a loose confederation of maritime states with a place in the hier-
archy of the world's nations on the order of another Holland. It
was presumed that eventually white settlement would penetrate
the continent's little known interior but that the difficulties imposed upon communication by distance would then lead to the
erection of a number of separate nations, a development that did
indeed eventuate under comparable circumstances when the peoples of Latin America gained their independence from Spain. The
American people were saved from so disastrous a dispersion by the
insistence of the first pioneers to cross the mountains that they be
assured in their new homes the political privileges they had formerly enjoyed on the seaboard. Their insistence produced the doctrine of the admission to the union of new states each equal in all
respects to the original thirteen. The consequences of this counter
to the dispersion previously considered inseparable from expansion were prodigious. In 1780 there had been no significant center
of American population farther west than a day's journey from
waterborne access to the Atlantic and a majority of the Continental Congress had voted to consider the Appalachians the
permanent western border of the republic. In 1830, only 50 years
later, the dominion of the United States had already been extended to the Rockies. The doctrine of the admission of new and
equal states had been the engine that had generated such a growth
rate as no other nation had ever experienced. No political device
in the whole history of mankind had ever proved so immediately
and overwhelmingly successful.

By its basic tenet, however, it limited the authority of the national government to interfere with the local predilections of the
inhabitants of each state. These insistences upon local autonomy
tended to be the most urgent in the economic field. The impulse
was not confined to any one region. In 1830 the manufacturers of
New England would have rejected any attempt of the national
government to regulate child labor as vigorously as did the planters of Georgia reject federal attempts to interfere with the expro-
priation of Indian land. The New Englanders would have argued
as strenuously as the southerners that all political power originally

resided in the states and that the Constitution was merely the repository of such powers as the states had chosen to relinquish.

This insistence upon subservience to states' rights, especially in economic affairs, was most strongly evidenced in those states which by reason of geographical situation or a more recent establishment conceived that they had problems not understood in the more populous and developed areas of the north and east. There were very many people in Georgia, Alabama and Mississippi who were appalled by the excesses accompanying Indian removal but there was literally no citizen who did not fiercely deny the right of the United States to interfere. In practice, any state legislature, state governor, militia officer or county official was fully conscious of an inherent license to pursue whatever course without regard for the disapproval of national public opinion, however exercised or however preponderant. General recognition of this fact helped to account for the invariable vigor with which any state authority could take a stand and the timidity with which federal authority invariably recoiled. The national government was, in the actual functioning of the application of political power, precluded from the administration of justice, even in an instance of injustice so flagrant and so widely condemned as that involved in Indian removal.

There could be almost no doubt that a clear majority of the people of the United States disapproved of Indian removal or, at any rate, of the brutal excesses and mortifying breaches of faith that marked the enforcement of the expulsion edict. That local and regional political authority in the south could without serious challenge defy the will of this majority was only in part due to the circumstance that throughout the critical period 1828–36 the President of the United States was the foremost proponent of removal. Congress, presumably more immediately sensitive to the will of the people, grappled again and again with the issue throughout the same period and at every decisive vote evaded giving expression to that will. These equivocal votes in Congress represented responses to the pragmatic functioning of the two party system which in the early 1830's was beginning to coalesce with all the since familiar paraphernalia of national conventions and formulated platforms.

With the emergence of modern democratic governments in the

late 18th century it had not been long becoming apparent that no such government could know stability once its electorate had become splintered into a multiplicity of political parties. In the United States, heir to England's political experience, a two party system evolved, after an extemporaneous sequence of experiments and accidents not even distantly contemplated by the framers of the Constitution. By the 1830's the nation's voters had become aligned into two increasingly organized groups, with names still in the process of change, which gave their allegiance either to the party then in control of the government or to the party seeking to seize control at the next election.

The essence of the two party system had by then been discovered to be the necessary preoccupation of each party with the selection of specific means by which it might hold or regain *national* political power. It had been demonstrated to be insufficient to appeal to local or regional sentiments unless such an appeal could be made to fit into a national pattern. Both parties had learned the central lesson that commitment to the election of some of its candidates was not enough. Each had to be committed to lifting a nationwide majority of its candidates into office. As Jackson's second term neared its end the pressures of these party considerations became intense.

It was under such political clouds that the last chance to save the Cherokee from expulsion came with the submission of the New Echota treaty to the Senate for ratification. Less than at any other moment during the Indian removal controversy could there be much doubt of the will of the country's majority. Yet the Senate voted 31 to 15 for ratification. There could be no question, for example, that the consensus in Maine, New Hampshire, New York, Pennsylvania, Indiana and Illinois was opposed to ratification, either out of sympathy for the Indians or of regard for the nation's honor. Yet both senators from every one of these states voted for the treaty. Senators who voted for it against the sentiments of their constituents, and possibly their own, had a recognized basis upon which to justify their votes. They could argue that victory for their party in the coming election promised to serve the general good of the country far more directly than might any attempt to protect the rights of Indians. The Whig party joined the Democratic party in holding this view, even though there could be no slightest doubt that a vast majority of Whig voters disapproved of removal and even more actively of the treaty.

There was further testimony to the exigencies of party discipline in the voting record in Congress of members who during the next 20 years received that degree of party preferment that enabled them to become President of the United States. Of those seven future Presidents who had had an opportunity to vote on the issue while in Congress, Martin Van Buren, William Henry Harrison, John Tyler, James K. Polk, Millard Fillmore, Franklin Pierce and James Buchanan, each had in every instance voted in support of the removal policy. The eighth future President in that period, Zachary Taylor, had never been a member of Congress but he had commanded an army engaged in the expulsion of the Seminole. Whatever the sentiments of the majority of the American people, advocacy of Indian removal had proved no bar to any man's aspiration to the Presidency.

There had been one direct opportunity for the American people to express its will. In the 1832 presidential election Henry Clay's National Republicans and their allies had made the removal question the central issue upon which they attacked the record of the administration. Their campaign was equipped with the enormous advantage that associated with the Indian question were the apparently unassailable issues of the sanctity of treaties and the authority of the Supreme Court. Their professional pulse-taking of voter sentiment had convinced them that they were attacking Jackson at his most vulnerable point. Of the country's 13 million inhabitants 11 million lived north of the southernmost tier of states in areas in which there was widespread sympathy with Indian sufferings and pained disapproval of the measures taken to deny them their court-defined rights. Clay's hopes proved as unfounded as had been his prognostications. The tabulation of returns indicated that northern voters had been much less influenced by their moral judgments than by what they conceived to be regard for their personal economic welfare.

Clay was learning the hard lesson that more practical politicians were grasping with greater ease. In the privacy of the voting booth the American voter thought first of his own interest. However vocal may have appeared his prior sympathy with an ethical cause, at the moment of stamping his ballot his decision was governed by more immediate, material and egoistic considerations. Of all ethical causes, regard for the threatened rights of a minority was the most likely to engage his outward expressions of sympathy. The more distant the environment in which the minority problem had developed the more ready his indignation. But his mood changed when the problem was one in his own. In his own his primary concern was with an apprehension that his own opportunities might be diminished by a minority's grasp at a share in them. In a national election the whole country became his environment.

The American attitude toward justice in relation to minorities had from the outset been anomalous. Through the earlier colonial years the Indians had not been directly involved in this attitude. Instead of having yet become a tension-producing fraction of the white community they had represented a numerous and powerful foreign enemy. The tolerance problem stemmed from the variances in culture between the later arrivals from Europe and Africa and those already established in the colonies. All Americans had originally been the representatives of minority groups, in flight from religious, political or economic disadvantage. All had realized that it was unthinkable to view this new land in any other light than as a haven which must beckon as appealingly to later comers as it had to the first. All had realized that for those who had already arrived their every hope of security and progress depended upon a continuation of the movement as thousands and then hundreds of thousands of other migrants from the old world sought the wider opportunity offered by the new. Yet the later arrivals had seldom been warmly received by their predecessors. In New England the Pilgrims and Puritans had been harshly critical of their later-arriving fellow dissidents. In the Middle Atlantic states a large proportion of later arrivals had come under indenture contracts committing them to seven years of bond service and thereafter to other years of struggle to outlive the stigma of so humble an origin. The wave of Scotch-Irish beginning to arrive in the early 18th century had been obliged to strain for a precarious subsistence among the perils of the most remote frontier. The impulse to reject had been the more strikingly evident when the newcomers were of another nationality. The first groups of German immigrants were so unfavorably received in New York's

Mohawk Valley that they undertook a second more desperate migration down the wild Susquehanna River to the Pennsylvania frontier where they remained for generations a community distinct from their English neighbors. When the newcomers were of another race the rejection was total. The Negroes from Africa, who came not by choice but compulsion, were committed to slavery.

During the 1830's another 600,000 immigrants were arriving. They tended to huddle into local communities for the sake of mutual comfort. Each such community within the American community was ringed by areas of social and economic friction. By 1830 the pattern had become apparent. It was realized that the extraordinary increase of the United States in population and prosperity was due, in a large part, to the continuing surges of immigration but each immigrant was nevertheless expected to serve an arduous apprenticeship before he could hope for acceptance as a fellow American. Every native born American believed that he believed in democracy and believed that he believed all men were created equal. Most Americans professed tolerance of other stocks and other races and listened with approval to every denunciation of prejudice. But few Americans were ready to welcome as a neighbor a family differing radically from them in appearance or deportment. There was a strange ambivalence in this incessant swing of the American pendulum between tolerance and intolerance. Most was due to the circumstance that Americans had had more actual and intimate acquaintance with distinctions among classes, nationalities and races than had any other people. The fluidity of the American environment and the procession of immigrating foreigners and migrating Americans continually streaming across it accentuated these distinctions. The individual American was a part of this fluidity and this procession and all his life had been conditioned by both. He had become accustomed to changing his environment by moving from one location to another in pursuit of advantage. In his experience this readiness to venture could result in an alteration of his environment so sweeping as to alter his every prospect. But he was necessarily at the same time aware that the exceptional advantages he was seeking were being as actively sought by others. While flatboating down the Ohio he could be glad of the number of his companions, for in numbers there was greater assurance of safety from Indians and of a more rapid rise in property values in his new home. But upon arrival in Kentucky he had to take ruthless care that it was he who got the better land. In a stable old world community the intrusion of a stranger could be accepted as an exotic novelty. In an American community, agitated by the ferment of ever accelerating change, a new neighbor had to be regarded as an immediate and threatening competitor.

When he heard of the afflictions to which the distant Indians were being subjected the average American was moved by his normal goodwill to sympathy and indignation. But he was responding to an idea, not a conviction. Had he been an inhabitant of an Indian border area he would have reacted as the Georgians were reacting. Only in certain religious and intellectual circles did the moral response to removal approach an enduring conviction. It often fell short even there, as was evidenced by the flare of active race prejudice ignited among the God-fearing people of Cornwall by the Boudinot-Gold marriage. The lesson had been well read by practical politicians and party managers. It had been made clear to their shrewd judgment that it was safe for a congressman or senator to vote for removal whenever this seemed a service to the larger aims of his party. His constituents might compose righteous memorials and hold mass meetings of vociferous protest but it was not an issue on which they were very likely ever to turn him out of office.

The irreparable injury that had been inflicted on Indians in the removal period had been through the instrumentality of these three principal forces of American democracy. Personal responsibility for the application of those forces could be apportioned among many. President Jackson could, at the very least, have softened the impact and ameliorated the hardship. Instead, for eight years he devoted the powers of his high office to initiating and expediting removal, proceeding even to the length of asserting his interpretation of the Constitution was invested with a higher authority than that of the Supreme Court. Immediately responsible for the sufferings visited upon the Indians was the aggregation of southern politicians, land speculators, contractors, lawyers and wielders of local police power, acting in concert, who participated personally in the aggressions and oppressions. Their responsibility was shared by all southerners who, though many were troubled, looked the other way and in their zeal to guard the legitimate principles of states' rights continued to reelect the officials who were committing the excesses. A more shameful responsibility pervaded the halls of Congress, many of whose members had again and again voted contrary to their convictions and those of their constituents. A similar responsibility lay upon the partisan councils of party managers who had preferred expediency to principle. But the primary guilt was that of the American people. They had not been revolted by the spectacle of injustice. The failure of the government of the United States to dispense justice had not been due to a breakdown of the processes of American democracy. It had been due to the pharisaical unreadiness of the American people to rise to the demands democracy was making upon them.

For this failure a terrible forfeit was to be exacted. The fight for Indian rights had been lost. What had been generally recognized as a great wrong had as generally been determined to be acceptable. A handful of Indians, numbering less than one two-hundredth of the country's population, had been driven into exile. The uncomfortable episode was already fading into the past and, it was hoped, could be forgotten. And so it seemed to be. When in 1840 the Whigs swept the country their triumphant standard bearer was William Henry Harrison who throughout his long career had been as militantly bent upon Indian dispossession as ever had been Andrew Jackson. But an injustice can never be forgotten. The ten-year-long Indian removal controversy had fanned flames that would not subside until they had become a holocaust.

In 1830 there was no threat that sectional differences of opinion regarding slavery might ever irretrievably divide the nation. Slavery had been gradually eliminated in the northern states. The north had found slavery uneconomic and with some moral concern was moved to restrict its spread but so far felt no slightest inclination to attempt to deprive the south of the right to maintain the institution. When the necessity had arisen to deal with slavery in a national sense the counsels of moderate northerners and southerners had prevailed and moderate compromises had been affected. The north was fully as devoted to the principle of the inviolability of private property as was the south. That still

rare figure, the abolitionist, was in the 1830's still universally regarded as an un-American anarch to be invariably and justly victimized by street mobs. In no national agency of the government,
the Presidency, the Congress, the Supreme Court, or in any northern statehouse, was there in the 1830's any disposition to consider
emancipation in any other light than the south's prerogative. Of
the awful conflict that was to rend the republic there was as yet no
faintest foreshadowing.

It was the eruption of the Indian removal controversy that revealed the latent virulence of sectional antagonism. On this seemingly minor issue the irreconcilability of the two sections' points of
view was unmasked in all its spectral dimensions. The issue became a whipping boy upon which each adversary could vent his
spleen. The greater issue of slavery had been by mutual consent
cloaked in soothing compromise but in the obviously less conse-
quential removal dispute every man could seize the opportunity to
gratify his prejudice. Every renewal of debate in congress, every
expression of opinion by press or pulpit, became progressively
more provocative.

The south might have been content to have successfully defended its stand on states' rights, which it had proved abundantly
able to do and which had at no time during the controversy been
seriously assailed by the north. It had been the assumption of
moral superiority by the north that had aroused the south's full
fury. The damage had been done so far as the south was concerned
even before the essential faintheartedness of the north's impulse to
interfere had been disclosed. It was the north's holier-than-thou
attitude that rankled and left the south imbedded for generations
in its own special posture of resentful belligerency.

The long controversy had been characterized by an incessant
exchange of epithets, threats, aspersions of motive and imputations
of dishonor which neither adversary could ever forget or forgive.
Had the controversy developed areas of agreement, affording even
partial protection for the rights of Indians and some consideration
for the views of the north, had there been the same willingness to
compromise as in former sectional differences, the passions that
had been aroused might have been quieted. But it had burned on
through ten agonizing years to a total victory for the south and a
total defeat for the north. The south was left with a gnawing sense

of secret guilt in having perpetrated so gross an injustice and the north with an equally gnawing and not so secret sense of guilt for having acquiesced in it.

North and south had been maneuvered by the removal issue into the confrontation which they had both previously taken such care to avoid. The heat of the contention had aroused animosities from which there was never to be surcease. The south had been schooled to regard all northerners as sanctimonious hypocrites and the north to regard all southerners as bigoted oppressors of the weak. Each had been provoked to wild threats of subduing the other by arms. North and south had set foot on the road from which there was to be no turning. At the end of that road waited inexorable retribution, the ghastly horrors of the Civil War.

BIBLIOGRAPHY

Among published material available in most larger libraries to the reader disposed to pursue the subject, the following have been found useful in the preparation of this work:

Abridgement of the Debates of Congress. New York, 1857–61.

Adair, James, *History of the North American Indians.* London, 1775. Repr. Kingsport, 1930.

Bartram, William, *Travels.* Philadelphia, 1791. Repr. New York, 1940.

Brown, John P., *Old Frontiers.* Kingsport, 1938.

Cotterill, R. S., *The Southern Indians.* Norman, 1954.

Crockett, David, *A Narrative of the Life of David Crockett, Written by Himself.* Philadelphia, 1834.

Cohen, M. M., *Notices of Florida and the Campaigns.* Charleston, 1836.

Connelley, William Elsey, ed., *The Heckewelder Narrative.* Cleveland, 1908.

Curtis, George Ticknor, *Life of Webster,* 2 vols. New York, 1870.

Davidson, Donald, *The Tennessee.* New York, 1946.

Debo, Angie, *The Rise and Fall of the Choctaw Republic.* Norman, 1934.

Drake, Samuel G., *The Book of the Indians.* Boston, 1841.

Emerson, Ralph Waldo, *Works,* 14 vols. Cambridge, 1883–87.

Filler, Louis and Guttman, Allen, eds., *The Removal of the Cherokee Nation.* Boston, 1962.

Foreman, Grant, *Indian Removal,* rev. ed. Norman, 1953.

———, *Indians and Pioneers.* Norman, 1930.

———, *Sequoyah.* Norman, 1938.

Gabriel, Ralph Henry, *Elias Boudinot*. Norman, 1941.

Govan, Gilbert Eaton and Livingood, James W., *The Chattanooga Country*. New York, 1952.

Harrison, James L., *Biographical Directory of the American Congress*. Washington, 1950.

Heckewelder, John, *Account of the History, Manners, and Customs of the Indian Nations*. Philadelphia, 1819.

Hodge, Frederick Webb, *Handbook of the American Indians*, 2 vols. Washington, 1907–10.

Indian Atrocities: Narration of the Perils and Sufferings of Dr. Knight and John Slover, among the Indians, during the Revolutionary War. Cincinnati, 1867.

James, Marquis, *The Raven, a Biography of Sam Houston*. Indianapolis, 1924. Repr. New York, 1962.

Lewis, Thomas M. N. and Knebers, Madeline, *Hiwassee Island*. Knoxville, 1946.

Lumpkin, Wilson, *Removal of the Cherokee Indians from Georgia*, 2 vols. Savannah, 1907.

McKenney, Thomas L. and Hall, James, *History of the Indian Tribes of North America*, 3 vols. Philadelphia, 1838–44.

Mansfield, Edward D., *Life and Services of General Winfield Scott*. New York, 1852.

Milling, Chapman, *Red Carolinians*. Chapel Hill, 1940.

Mooney, James, *Myths of the Cherokee* (Part I, 19th Annual Report, Bureau of American Ethnology). Washington, 1900.

———, *Sacred Formulas of the Cherokee* (7th Annual Report, Bureau of American Ethnology). Washington, 1891.

———, *Ghost Dance Religion* (14th Annual Report, Bureau of American Ethnology). Washington, 1896.

Mooney, James and Olbrechts, Frans M., *The Swimmer Manuscript* (Bulletin 99, Bureau of American Ethnology). Washington, 1932.

Niles Register, Sept. 1, 1821 (vol. XXI)–Aug. 24, 1839 (vol. LVI).

Nuttall, Thomas, *A Journal of Travels into the Arkansas Territory*. Philadelphia, 1821. Repr. Cleveland, 1906.

Pickett, Albert James, *History of Alabama*, 2 vols. Charleston, 1851. Repr. Birmingham, 1900.

Paullin, Charles O. and Wright, John K., *Atlas of the Historical Geography of the United States*. Washington, 1952.

Paxon, Frederick L., *History of the American Frontier, 1763–1893*. Cambridge, 1924.

Ramsey, J. G. M., *Annals of Tennessee*. Charleston, 1853. Repr. Kingsport, 1926.

Richardson, James D., *Messages and Papers of the President,* 11 vols. Washington, 1897.

Royce, Charles C., *The Cherokee Nation of Indians* (5th Annual Report, American Bureau of Ethnology). Washington, 1887.

————, *Indian Land Cessions* (Extract from 18th Annual Report of the Bureau of American Ethnology). Washington, 1900.

Senate Document 512. 23rd Congress, 1st session, 5 vols. Washington, 1833–34.

Smith, W. W., *Sketches of the Seminole War and Sketches of a Campaign.* Charleston, 1836.

Starr, Emmett, *History of the Cherokee Indians.* Oklahoma City, 1921.

Swanton, John R., *Early History of the Creek Indians and Their Neighbors* (Bulletin 73, Bureau of American Ethnology). Washington, 1922.

Timberlake, Henry, *Memoirs.* London, 1765. Repr. Johnson City, 1927.

Tucker, Glenn, *Tecumseh.* Indianapolis, 1956.

Turner, Frederick Jackson, *Rise of the New West 1819–1829.* New York, 1906. Repr. with foreword by Ray Allen Billington. New York, 1962.

Van Every, Dale, *Ark of Empire.* New York, 1963.

Walker, Robert Sparks, *Torchlights to the Cherokee.* New York, 1931.

Washburn, Wilcomb E., ed., *The Indians and the White Man.* Garden City, 1964.

Williams, Samuel Cole, ed., *Early Travels in the Tennessee Country.* Johnson City, 1928.

Woodward, Grace Steel, *The Cherokees.* Norman, 1963.

INDEX